MASTER POINT PRESS • TORONTO

Master Point Press
331 Douglas Ave.
Toronto, Ontario, Canada
M5M 1H2

(416) 781-0351
www.masterpointpress.com

Distributed in the US by Barricade Books
150 Fifth Avenue, Suite 700
New York, NY 10011

(800) 59-BOOKS

Canadian Cataloguing in Publication Data

Marshall, Miles 1926-
Competitive bidding in the 21st century

ISBN 1-894154-13-4

1. Contract bridge - Bidding. I. Title

GV1282.4.M54 2000 795.41'52 C99-932386-5

Cover and Interior design: Olena S. Sullivan
Editor: Ray Lee

Printed and bound in Canada

1 2 3 4 5 6 7 07 06 05 04 03 02 01 00

Table of Contents

Introduction 7

1. Major-Suit Overcalls 13

The four-card major-suit overcall	13
Standard overcalls	21
Overcalls after a preempt	25

2. Responding to Overcalls 31

Showing support for partner's suit	31
Notrump responses to an overcall	35
Using the cuebid	37
The cuebid double	39
Showing your own suit	40

3. Two-Suited Overcalls 49

General principles	49
Responses to two-suited overcalls	54

4. Bidding the Opponents' Suit 61

Bidding the opponents' suit naturally	61
Useful cuebids	66
Control-showing cuebids	68

5. The Law of Total Tricks 73

How the Law works	73
Using the Law	76
Competitive decisions based on the Law	79
Low-level penalty decisions	80
Bergen Raises — the case against	83

6. Reopening the Bidding 93

Balancing over an opening suit bid	93
Balancing over preempts	96
Reopening when both opponents have bid	97

7. Problems of Opener's Side 109

When not to use a negative double	109
Free bids	110
Higher-level responses	112
Bidding in competition — the Good-Bad 2NT	114

8. Co-operative Doubles 125

The Twilight Zone 125
'Negative' doubles at higher levels 127
Doubling preempts 129
Non-co-operative doubles 130
Telling the difference 132

9. Doubles for Takeout 141

Traditional takeout doubles 141
Negative doubles 153
Responsive doubles 159
Action doubles 160
Doubles of two-suited artificial bids 161

10. Penalty Doubles 171

Typical penalty doubles 171
Inferential doubles 176

11. Conventional Doubles 183

Support doubles 183
'Maximal' doubles 187
Doubling slams 187
Doubling 3NT 190
Other unusual doubles 191

12. Other Doubles 197

Showing extras 197
Doubling artificial bids 198
The 'automatic' reopening double 202
Other doubling situations 203

13. Redoubles 209

The meaning of a redouble 209
To run or not to run 217
Redoubles after an artificial bid is doubled 224

14. All Fifty-Two Cards 231

15. Optional Treatments 241

Auctions after a double 242
Two-way doubles 243
Preempting and bidding again 245
The forcing pass 247
Vasilevsky 250
The useful space principle 251

Conclusion 255

COMPETITIVE BIDDING IN THE 21ST CENTURY

MARSHALL MILES

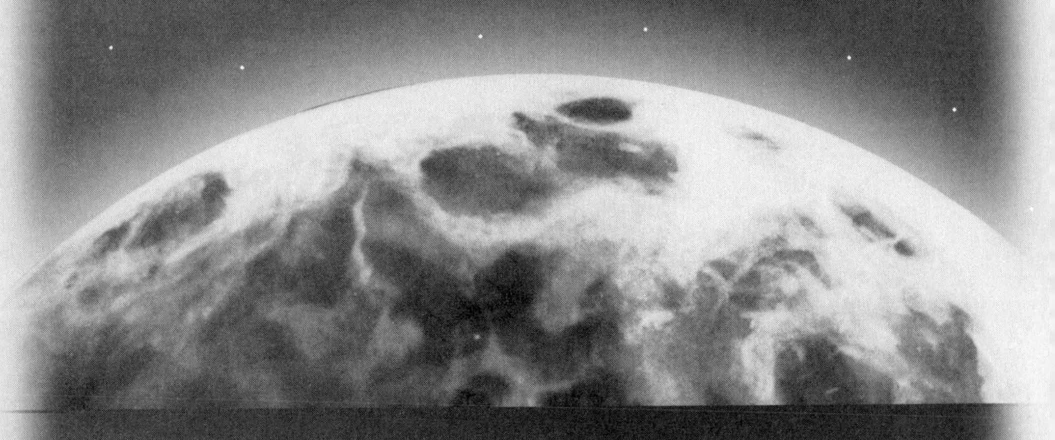

Introduction

When I started to play bridge in the 1940s, the authorities stated that there was little to be gained by competing after the opponents opened the bidding unless your hand was so strong that a game was likely (or, when you had a long suit and a weak hand, you were within two tricks of making your bid when vulnerable and within three tricks not vulnerable). Why risk a sizable penalty just to compete for a mere partscore? And (inconsistently) if your side opened the bidding and the opponents competed, any bid made by responder showed a strong interest in getting to game. No 'free bids' were allowed, even at the one-level, with fewer than nine points, and no 'free' single raises with less than limit raise values. Now the tendency is to compete vigorously for partscores and to enter the bidding whenever it is reasonably safe (and often when it isn't). I estimate that there are at least 50% more competitive auctions than there used to be, and that percentage is still increasing. Consequently, it is important to find ways to compete effectively, yourself, and ways to minimize the advantage the opponents gain by their competitive bidding.

There are three basic principles which should be considered when making competitive decisions:

1) You should compete aggressively at the partscore level.

It is as costly at IMPs (and probably more costly at matchpoints) to let the opponents make a partscore when you can make a partscore as it is to miss a non-vulnerable game. Many players think that at IMP scoring they should not compete as vigorously as at matchpoints because the risks are greater. That's not true! It is safer to compete at IMPs because the opponents are more afraid of doubling you into game. Even if you go down two, it probably won't cost much, if anything. What will cost is letting the opponents make 2♡ when you could make 2♠ or 3♣ your way.

2) The earlier in the auction you make a bid, the safer it is.

Suppose RHO opens 1◇ and you overcall 1♡. LHO holds:

♠ A J 9 5 4 ♡ A 10 8 6 ◇ 8 ♣ J 4 3

He couldn't double you for penalties, even if he wanted to, since it would be a negative double. So, if he wants to try to penalize you, he must pass and hope his partner will reopen with a double, which he may or may not do. But suppose his partner does double (quite likely with a singleton heart). The opponents won't set you badly at the one-level when you and partner have a combined total of eight trumps, and they could almost surely get a better score by bidding and making 4♠. So LHO will bid 1♠ rather than pass and hope for a penalty. But suppose LHO has the same hand, but the bidding goes:

WEST	NORTH	EAST	SOUTH
1◇	pass	1♠	pass
2◇	2♡	?	

Now LHO will be delighted to double. Having already shown his spade suit, he isn't forced to choose between showing spades and trying for a penalty. Or suppose the bidding goes:

WEST	NORTH	EAST	SOUTH
1◇	2♣	2◇	pass
pass	2♡	?	

and LHO holds:

♠ A 7 5 ♡ Q J 8 ◇ 10 6 4 2 ♣ Q 8 5

Having already limited his hand, he can make a cooperative penalty double (and double again if you or partner returns to 3♣). RHO doesn't have to leave the double(s) in, but if he has a somewhat balanced hand, he will be delighted to do so. Once the opponents have partially described their strength and/or distribution, they can make cooperative penalty doubles.

Here is a hand from Al Roth's column in *Bridge Today*.

WEST	NORTH	EAST	SOUTH
		2◇[1]	pass
4♡	pass	pass	?

1. Weak.

♠ K J 5 4 3 ♡ — ◇ 7 6 4 2 ♣ A 10 9 5

What action would you take? Al says you should double. Partner has

♠ AQ102 ♡ 8532 ◇ — ♣ KQ742

and you are cold for a slam in spades (while the opponents are cold for 4♡). Perhaps Al is right about doubling, but I prefer bidding 2♠ right away over 2◇. Admittedly you are rather weak for a two-level overcall, but this hand can make a lot of spades opposite a fit (I was thinking of 4♠, not a slam), and I still think it is safer to bid 2♠ than to pass and have to guess what to do next round at a much higher level.

A corollary to the rule about making your bid early is that when partner bids a suit (especially a major suit) and you have trump support, you should tend to raise whenever you have a close decision. In the old days, you could pass with a minimum or average raise, then give partner a jump raise if he could reopen the bidding. But now, because preemptive raises are so popular, if you don't raise when you safely can, you may have to guess whether to give partner a belated raise at a much higher level.

WEST	NORTH	EAST	SOUTH
	1♡	1♠	?

♠ 86 ♡ Q74 ◇ K8752 ♣ 742

In this auction, regardless of vulnerability, you should bid 2♡. If you pass, West may bid 4♠, and partner will have no idea what to do with

♠ 4 ♡ AK98632 ◇ QJ4 ♣ A5

but if you had raised him, he would have an easy 5♡ bid (making if you had a better hand, a cheap sacrifice opposite your minimum). The same consideration applies to opener's rebid:

WEST	NORTH	EAST	SOUTH
			1♣
1♠	2♡	2♠	?

♠ 987 ♡ A54 ◇ KQ5 ♣ K1096

Do you pass to show a minimum opening? You shouldn't. If you pass, West may bid 3♠, and neither you nor partner will know what to do when partner holds:

♠ J ♡ KJ873 ◇ A10764 ♣ Q3

I am embarrassed to admit that I failed to follow my own advice with the following hand:

♠ K102 ♡ J543 ◇ K107 ♣ 876

We were vulnerable and the opponents were not. LHO opened 2♣, strong and artificial. Partner overcalled 2♠. RHO passed and I passed also, thinking that with a strong hand on my left and at unfavorable vulnerability, it was too risky to raise. LHO, with

♠ J ♡ AKQ1096 ◇ 5 ♣ AKQ105

bid 4♡, which ended the bidding. Partner held:

♠ AQ8753 ♡ — ◇ AJ642 ♣ J4

The opponents were cold for 4♡ and we were cold for 4♠ (actually for 5♠ if partner played double dummy). Partner would have bid 4♠ if I had raised to 3♠. Do you see what my cowardice cost?

3) Since four of a major is the easiest game to bid and make, you should usually plan to show your major if you bid at all.

Approximately two-thirds of the games bid and made are in a major suit. It is obvious why these games are the easiest to make — game in a minor requires eleven tricks while a major suit game requires only ten. With a major-suit fit you need fewer high cards to make game than you would to make three notrump, and you don't need stoppers in every suit. Furthermore, game in a major is the easiest to bid. Once you find a major fit, the bidding is straight-forward. Degree of fit is important, but not nearly as crucial as it is when you are contemplating a slam or a game in a minor. As a consequence, if you are only strong enough to make one bid (without strong encouragement from partner to bid again), or if you have no assurance of another chance to bid, you should usually show your major.

For example, when partner opens 1♣ and you hold

♠ 76 ♡ KJ95 ◇ J8752 ♣ K8

it is better to respond 1♡ than to bid 1◇. If you have a game, it is probably 3NT or 4♡. Either response will get you to 3NT if partner can rebid 2NT (and probably if he can rebid 3♣), but the best chance to get to 4♡ is to respond 1♡. Some players always bid 'up the line' and cannot see any reason to skip over the diamond suit. It usually won't matter which bid you make if the opponents remain quiet, but suppose you do bid 1◇ and LHO bids 2♠. Partner will be stymied if he holds

♠ K43 ♡ AQ103 ◇ 9 ♣ AJ653

while if you had responded 1♡, you would get to a good game. Later, you will discover that partner has a way of showing whether he has a real raise to 3♡ in this kind of auction or a hand worth only a good raise to 2♡ with which he preferred to show his support rather than pass. This time he would show a real raise to 3♡, and you would bid 4♡.

It may seem inconsistent, my always talking about getting to game — after telling you that partscores are important. However, the side that has (and finds) a major-suit fit will probably outbid the opponents when the strength is fairly evenly divided. So it is just a bonus that the same bidding that gets you to the most likely games also allows you to outbid the opponents at the partscore level. If you know (or are reasonably sure) that you will have another chance to bid, it is better to bid something else the first time and your four-card major suit later. That way partner will expect you to hold only four cards in your major, and you will avoid contracts with Q743 of trumps opposite 865. That is the theory behind requiring a five-card suit to open a major. Your minor-suit opening will be kept open by someone, usually partner, at least 95% of the time. However, in competition, things are a little different. When partner makes a takeout double, for example, he doesn't promise another bid, so when you respond to his double by bidding a minor suit, you practically deny a four-card major. The question in almost every bidding sequence, when you hold a four-card major plus another suit, is whether you are likely to be able to show your major later if you don't bid it immediately. If not, you should show it right away.

Nothing I have said so far is new or controversial. What puzzles me is why so many players fail to consider these factors when they overcall.

CHAPTER 1

Major-Suit Overcalls

The Four-Card Major-Suit Overcall

Suppose RHO bids 1♢ and you hold:

♠ AQ52 ♡ 6 ♢ K76 ♣ AJ965

Many players would overcall 2♣, hoping to bid spades later. But in this case, the whole hand is as follows:

West	North	East
	♠ K10873	
	♡ 874	
	♢ 832	
	♣ Q10	
♠ J94	N	♠ 6
♡ AQJ102	W E	♡ K953
♢ Q5	S	♢ AJ1094
♣ 832		♣ K74
	♠ AQ52	
	♡ 6	
	♢ K76	
	♣ AJ965	

If you overcall 2♣ the bidding will go:

WEST	NORTH	EAST	SOUTH
		1♢	2♣
2♡	pass	3♡	all pass

Yes, West will bid 2♡ — in competition this doesn't promise the world (or even a rebid). East, with a minimum opening and a poorly placed ♣K, should only raise to 3♡, and West will probably pass. Perhaps the opponents won't bid so accurately and they will get all the way to 4♡, which is down two — undoubled, of course. Big deal! As the cards lie, you are cold for 5♠ despite the fact that you couldn't safely bid again. But if instead you had overcalled 1♠, partner would have bid 3♠ preemptively whether West bid or passed, and you would have bid 4♠ since you would usually have some sort of play for game opposite four- or five-card spade support.

Your reaction to this example may be skeptical. Of course, you may say, if the cards are laid out this way, a spade overcall would work best. But why should you find such a fine fit? You're right — most of the time you won't, but no harm is done either! The opponents will simply disregard your bid and get to the same contract they were going to get to anyway, since without a good fit, you would be unable to outbid them. Let's look at a deal where things do not flow quite so smoothly. What if partner's and West's hands were interchanged, for instance?

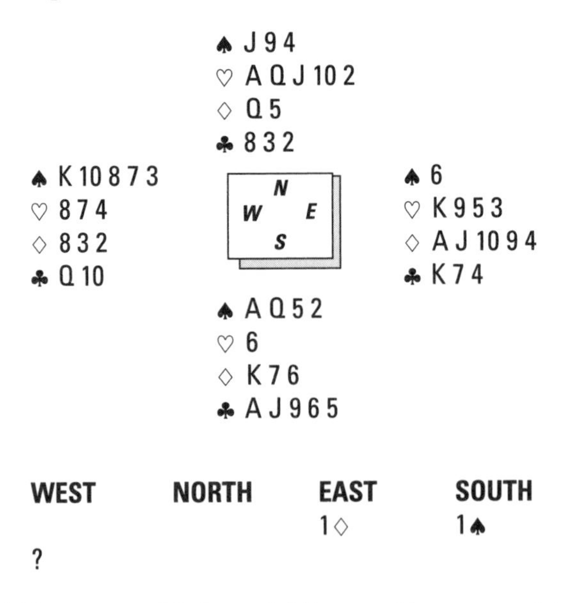

WEST	NORTH	EAST	SOUTH
		1♢	1♠
?			

What would happen on this layout? West would pass your 1♠ overcall, and partner would bid 2♠, which is a reasonable contract despite the bad trump split. Partner wouldn't bid more because he has a poorly placed ♢Q and only three-card trump support. You wouldn't bid more because, as you will see in the next chapter, a single raise is usually made with three-card trump support, and you need a much stronger hand to bid game on a 4-3 fit.

Incidentally, I should at least mention that many experts would choose a third alternative with the South hand; rather than bid either black suit, they would pass, hoping the bidding would go something like

WEST	NORTH	EAST	SOUTH
		1♢	pass
1♡	pass	2♡	?

or

WEST	NORTH	EAST	SOUTH
		1♢	pass
1♡	pass	1NT	?

and in either case they would make a reopening double. I certainly like this sequence better than an immediate club overcall. However, the bidding does not always go the way you hope. If it goes

WEST	NORTH	EAST	SOUTH
		1♢	pass
1NT	pass	pass	?

or

WEST	NORTH	EAST	SOUTH
		1♢	pass
1NT	pass	2♢	?

you will not dare to double since partner would surely bid hearts. Furthermore, even if you avoid that hazard (perhaps by bidding 2♣ instead of doubling in the first case), you won't get to game since partner will play you for a weaker hand, thinking you are just contesting the partscore. My contention is that a 1♠ overcall is quite safe, so why risk a pass? When I say 'safe', I don't mean that you can't go down in 1♠. What I mean is that you will seldom be forced to play it there, either doubled or undoubled. There will usually be more bidding.

There is another good argument in favor of overcalling four-card majors. Once an opponent opens the bidding, showing about fourteen points on average, and leaving twenty-six points to be split among the other three hands, it is unlikely that you can make a game on sheer power or even outbid the opponents at all. If, in fact, you can outbid the opponents in a partscore or make a game, it will usually be when you find a good major-suit fit. In the unlikely event that you can make game on sheer power, you have a better chance of getting there when you bid your four-card major.

Suppose RHO bids 1♢ and you hold:

♠ Q ♡ AK85 ♢ J65 ♣ AKQ104

If you overcall 2♣, partner is likely to pass with:

♠ KJ74 ♡ Q74 ♢ K93 ♣ 863

From his point of view, even 3♣ might be in danger, and he doesn't want to encourage you to bid more with only six useful points, poor club support and no ruffing values. Nor does it pay for him to bid 2NT with less than ten or eleven points, since you don't usually have as good a hand as this for your overcall. However, if you overcall 1♡ he can afford to bid notrump at the one-level, and you will, of course, raise to game.

Most experts overcall four-card majors when there is no reasonable alternative. Over a 1♢ bid they would bid 1♠ with either of these hands:

♠ AQJ7 ♡ 6 ♢ A754 ♣ K752

♠ KQJ5 ♡ 87 ♢ A6 ♣ J7642

The first hand is much too good to pass, while a takeout double is too dangerous with a singleton heart. The second hand is just worth competing on, and certainly both the hand and the suit are too weak for a 2♣ overcall.

However, even when there is a reasonable alternative, I think it is usually better to overcall the major. Nor does the major have to be as strong as in the last two examples.

When you hold a good four-card suit, like AQJx, you can overcall fairly freely. With A1075 or KJ84 you need a very good offensive hand, both in outside high cards and distribution, to overcall. You can get into trouble, in any sequence, if you bid with the worst possible holding and partner raises with the worst possible holding, but the odds are against that combination. Besides, the opponents may misjudge their hands and rescue you if you stay at a low level.

Let's look at three typical situations. Suppose RHO opens 1♢ and you hold one of these hands:

♠ AJ85 ♡ 10 ♢ A8 ♣ AQ10842

♠ A7 ♡ KJ96 ♢ J9 ♣ AKQ103

♠ K9 ♡ KQ86 ♢ J7 ♣ AJ1096

I recommend a major-suit overcall with all three hands.

The first hand is certainly strong enough to overcall 2♣ and risk having to show spades as high as the three-level next time. Yes, that plan will occasionally incur a big penalty, but that's not my real concern: the greater danger is that everyone will pass over 2♣, and you won't get a chance to show your spade suit. If partner has as little as ♠KQ72, you will have a very good play for 4♠, and even ♠K742 plus the ♣J will provide an adequate play. Of course, if partner does pass

2♣, RHO may reopen the bidding, but you can't count on it. You don't need to find much in partner's hand to make 5♣ —

♠ Q 7 4 ♡ 9 7 6 5 ◇ K 6 4 2 ♣ K 7

might be enough if the black suits behave — but even when you can make 5♣, it won't be easy to bid. For example, exchange partner's ♠Q for the ♡Q, and you would have a very poor play for 5♣. How can partner tell that one queen would be valuable and the other queen would be worthless? Or that the ◇K is worth a trick? In reality, if you overcall 2♣ he is unlikely to bid with either hand.

With the second hand the danger of overcalling 2♣ is even greater. When you have so many high cards, there is a very good chance that a two-level overcall will be passed out. Partner would raise a 1♡ overcall with either of these hands:

♠ J 8 5 4 3 ♡ A Q 4 ◇ 8 6 4 ♣ 8 3

♠ Q 5 4 3 ♡ A 7 3 2 ◇ 8 6 ♣ 9 7 4

and he would respond 1NT with

♠ Q J 8 3 ♡ Q 7 ◇ K 10 5 4 ♣ J 5 2

while, with all three hands, he might pass a 2♣ overcall. Sometimes when partner passes, opener keeps the bidding open for you, but with a borderline hand he will compete only when short in clubs. When you have five clubs, rather than six, opener is less likely to be short in clubs and less likely to keep the bidding open.

The third hand is not nearly as good as the first two. If you overcall 2♣ with this hand, even if the bidding is kept open for you, it is not clear that you should risk showing your heart suit. For example, if the bidding goes like this:

WEST	NORTH	EAST	SOUTH
		1◇	2♣
2◇	3♣	pass	?

more often than not, a 3♡ bid now would get you to an unmakable 4♣ contract. Nor will you feel comfortable bidding 2♡ if either opponent bids 2◇ and partner has taken no action. Since the hand is worth only one bid, you might as well show your most important feature, the four-card major. Many players say, 'I will bid 2♣ now, which is fairly safe, and if the bidding develops favorably, I'll show my major.' But they are overlooking the second principle of competitive bidding: the earlier in the auction you make a bid, the safer it is. It is evident that one-level overcalls are not dangerous in themselves. The opponents will seldom be able to defend a doubled contract at the one-level profitably. The real danger is that partner, thinking you have a longer suit, may raise you to the three- or four-level with three-card support. Although this is a concern, it is not as great as you might expect. In the next chapter you will see that partner seldom raises your overcalls to a high level with fewer than four, and you can usually afford to play at the two-level on a 4-3 fit.

Suppose RHO opens 1♢, and you overcall 1♠ with

♠ AJ83 ♡ 6 ♢ A8 ♣ AJ7653

Probably the worst thing that can happen is that everyone passes your 1♠ overcall. You could be set two or three tricks (undoubled). Even when that happens, and even when you are vulnerable, you are sometimes saved from a bad result by the opponents' being cold for 3NT. And what if it does go 'pass-pass-double'? Now RHO is likely to be short in spades for his reopening double; partner didn't raise, and LHO may well have a spade stack with which he would make a penalty pass. So bid 2♣ now — you are in no more danger than if you had overcalled 2♣ in the first place!

Likewise, if the bidding were to continue:

WEST	NORTH	EAST	SOUTH
		1♢	1♠
pass	pass	2♢	?

or

WEST	NORTH	EAST	SOUTH
		1♢	1♠
2♢	pass	pass	?

Now what? Partner's pass doesn't mean he has a Yarborough. Quite likely he has six or seven points without a spade fit. Rather than pass, you ought to bid 3♣ with your six-card suit!

'Isn't that dangerous?' you may ask. 'What if partner takes a preference to spades?' It shouldn't happen! First, if partner had a few high cards (which you assume he has because of the failure of the opponents to bid more strongly) and three or more spades, he would have raised right away. However, with the style of bidding I recommend, partner should know not to take a preference with equal length in the two suits (for example, a doubleton in each). When you actually do have a strong two-suiter, like

♠ KQ10852 ♡ 6 ♢ J ♣ AKJ96

you have to jump rebid — in this case to 4♣ — or take some other action in the first place to show both suits (see Chapter 3). An overcall followed by a jump in a new suit shows a true two-suiter, the suits being equal in length or the first suit being longer. An overcall in a major followed by a new minor at the cheapest level is sort of a canapé, implying that the minor is longer. At first this may seem like a radical suggestion, but it really isn't. You probably do the same thing in many other sequences already. If partner made a takeout double of 1♣ and you held:

♠ KJ53 ♡ 3 ♢ K8754 ♣ 987

you would probably respond 1♠. Then if the opponents bid more and partner passed, you would bid your diamonds.

Returning to the black two-suiter sequences, let's weaken your spades a little

WEST	NORTH	EAST	SOUTH
		1♢	1♠
2♢	pass	pass	?

♠ KJ8752 ♡ 6 ♢ J ♣ AKJ96

and you should simply rebid your spade suit rather than introducing clubs! With either spade holding, game in clubs is remote while game in spades is still probable. With ♠KQ10852 you could rebid 4♣ and gamble on forcing a preference at the four-level since ♠Jx ♣Qx in partner's hand would give you more than an adequate play for game, and partner would hardly move over any invitational sequence with so little. With a suit as poor as ♠KJ8752, game is remote unless partner can raise a 2♠ rebid, which he might do with:

♠ Q4 ♡ K8532 ♢ 985 ♣ Q87

This method of bidding is not perfect, but I believe that by bidding your major at the first opportunity, you will come out ahead in the long run. If you have a major-suit game, you will get to it. If you can outbid the opponents at the partscore level, you will usually do so. When you play in a 4-3 trump fit with a longer unbid side suit, you seldom get the best defense. And if the opponents do catch you for a big penalty on rare occasions, you will more than pick up the difference on the other hands.

The right kind of hand

You may have noticed that in each of my examples, the overcaller had a pretty good hand. Partner can afford to raise on the assumption that you have a five-card suit since you always have extra strength, either in high cards or distribution, to compensate for having a suit that is shorter than normal. If RHO opens 1♢, you can (just barely) overcall 1♠ with these hands:

♠ AQ95 ♡ 86 ♢ 96 ♣ KJ853

♠ KQ104 ♡ 8 ♢ 765 ♣ AJ843

but not with these:

♠ AQ95 ♡ 86 ♢ 962 ♣ KJ85

♠ KQ104 ♡ 84 ♢ 765 ♣ AJ84

The difference is that you have extra playing strength with the first two hands so that, if you find a fit, you will usually take as many tricks as with a typical 5-3-3-2 hand. To overcall with 4-4-3-2 distribution, you need the equivalent of an opening bid plus a good suit.

Another thing you may have noticed in all of my examples of four-card overcalls is that you were short in the other major. With:

♠ AQ74 ♡ J86 ◇ K4 ♣ K876

you would simply double if RHO bid 1◇ or pass if he opened 1♣. It would be presumptuous for you to suggest that the partnership belongs in spades when you have such a mild preference for spades over hearts. Partner can usually tell from the opponents' bidding, or lack of bidding, when you have high cards. An overcall should at least suggest that you want to play the hand rather than defend, and in your suit, rather than partner's suit. It is permissible to overcall with a two-suiter (if you don't have a way to show both suits at once), gambling that you will have a chance to show the other suit, but you need to bear in mind that an overcall does not encourage partner to show a suit of his own.

Above the one-level

Occasionally, overcalling a four-card major is the least of evils even at the two-level! Suppose RHO opens a weak 2◇ bid and you hold one of these hands:

♠ AKQ8 ♡ J ◇ 8753 ♣ AQ87

♠ KQ107 ♡ 6 ◇ AQ7 ♣ QJ1072

Both of these hands have game potential opposite a fit, even when partner is too weak to take action himself. As usual, the best chance for game is four of a major. While you hope to find four- or five-card support, you may even be able to make your game (or partscore) on a 4-3 fit. Partner probably has enough garbage in hearts to keep the opponents from forcing you. In the first case, partner's hand will provide a diamond stopper by ruffing with the short trumps. In the second case, you have a double diamond stopper yourself.

Lest you think this willingness to overcall four-card majors at the two-level is a peculiarity of mine alone, I'll show you a couple of hands from top-level experts. First a hand from the 1997 Spingold, when Mike Passell held:

♠ 7 ♡ AK109 ◇ AQJ8 ♣ A1065

His RHO opened 2♣ (Precision) and he overcalled 2♡. I don't know whether he would have bid with my weaker example hands, but he was willing to overcall an opening bid, as distinguished from a preempt, at the two-level with an appropriate hand.

Even more recently, early in the January 2000 Bermuda Bowl final, Jeff Meckstroth held:

♠ 876 ♡ AKQ5 ◇ A854 ♣ 107

When LHO opened 1♣, and RHO bid 2♣ showing a limit raise or better, Jeff came right in with 2♡!

Finally, the following problem was given recently to the ACBL *Bulletin* bidding panel.

WEST	NORTH	EAST	SOUTH
2♢	pass	3♢	?

♠ A K Q 3 ♡ A 4 ♢ Q 5 ♣ K 9 7 6 5

Eleven (yes, eleven!) panelists chose to bid 3♠. One said, 'I wish Marshall Miles were here on the panel so I wouldn't be all by myself!' Another commented, 'Marshall Miles probably thinks there is no other answer!'

I certainly don't recommend overcalling four-card majors at the two- or three-level as a general rule — in fact, I don't recommend them even at the one-level if there is a safer way (like a takeout double) to find your fit when a fit exists. However, when you have a good hand, and your alternate call risks missing a fit, you should usually overcall your four-card major. This is especially true when you don't expect the opponents to be able to shorten your four-card trump holding by leading opener's suit, which is the most likely opening lead.

I have attempted to persuade you to consider four-card major overcalls in a more favorable light. I have also shown you minimum hands, urging you not to overcall if you have both a poor suit and a poor hand (or a hand that is primarily defensive). Four-card overcalls at the one-level are becoming more and more popular, but they are dangerous unless you adopt a disciplined approach.

'Standard' Overcalls

Suit quality issues

Now let's consider overcalls with longer suits. Directing the lead and interfering with the opponents' bidding are two reasons for overcalling, but trying to buy the contract should be your main objective. With

♠ 8 7 5 ♡ A K 10 9 6 ♢ 8 7 ♣ 9 5 4

not vulnerable, you might scrape up a 1♡ overcall since if the opponents play the hand, you almost surely want a heart lead. With

♠ 8 7 5 ♡ K Q 10 7 3 ♢ A 8 7 ♣ 9 5

you would overcall 1♡ whether vulnerable or not, both in the hope of buying the contract and to prevent the opponents from stealing a game in 3NT when partner makes the wrong lead. But when the bidding goes:

WEST	NORTH	EAST	SOUTH
1♢	pass	1♡	?

I think it is wrong to overcall 1♠ with

♠ A9854 ♡ A107 ◊ J8 ♣ 1094

especially when vulnerable. It is unlikely that you can outbid the opponents when both of them have bid and partner has passed. It is very unlikely that a spade lead will be crucial to the defense or that (if it is) partner won't find a spade lead without your help. Yes, the opponents probably won't be able to double you for penalties at the one-level, but the real danger is that partner, thinking you have a better playing hand, will compete too vigorously.

However, suit quality is not the only factor. I remember overcalling 1♠ after an opening 1♣ bid with

♠ 87654 ♡ A6 ◊ AK ♣ 10874

and a teammate was aghast. 'How can you bid such a bad suit?' he asked. 'Because I had a good hand and, with the spade suit, we might easily outbid the opponents,' was my reply. Note that 5-4-2-2 distribution is much better than 5-3-3-2 distribution. When partner has four spades and a doubleton club, we may successfully outbid the opponents when they have twenty-two points to our eighteen. Yet partner, with his seven points, would not be able to take action if I passed. My teammate's approach was to pass and bid later if the auction developed favorably, but no matter how the bidding might go, it is safer to bid immediately than to bid later (or not at all).

When you hold secondary values in the opponents' suit, you need more, not fewer, high cards on the side. The reason is that when you overcall either a four-card suit or a weak five-card suit, your hand should be primarily offensive rather than defensive. Suppose RHO opens 1♡ and you hold one of these two hands:

♠ KQ87 ♡ AQJ8 ◊ Q7 ♣ 1094

♠ J8764 ♡ KQ107 ◊ A7 ♣ Q6

It is a mistake to overcall 1♠ with either hand. If the opponents bid 4♡ (or if partner expects them to bid 4♡), partner might well bid 4♠ with

♠ A1053 ♡ — ◊ 98542 ♣ J543

and it will be a phantom sacrifice since you would easily defeat 4♡.

Hand strength considerations

How strong can an overcall be? It depends upon many factors, including the level of the bidding. The best rule, although it is not always easy to apply, is that you shouldn't be so strong that you are likely to miss game if partner fails to take action. If RHO opens 1♣ and you hold

♠ AJ5 ♡ AJ10763 ◊ AQ ♣ K7

you are much too strong for a simple overcall. You can't expect partner to keep the bidding open over a 1♡ overcall with:

♠ K874 ♡ Q9 ◇ 9865 ♣ 1054

So you double and bid hearts later. In fact, it is close as to whether, after making a takeout double, you should rebid the cheapest number of hearts or jump rebid in hearts. With the same high-card strength, but one fewer heart and one more minor-suit card, you would still double, but clearly bid only a minimum number of hearts next time. You need a very good hand and a very good suit to double and then jump in your suit, which asks partner to raise with almost any excuse. On the other hand, with

♠ 87 ♡ AJ542 ◇ AKJ ♣ KJ6

your hearts are too weak to allow you to bid them safely at a high level over a possible spade preempt, so it is better just to overcall 1♡ over an opening bid of one of a minor. However, if the opening bid were 1♠ you would double with this hand and, if possible, bid 2♡ on the next round. In a way, this is even safer than bidding 2♡ immediately since, if partner has a long minor and a singleton heart, he will rescue you from 2♡ because your double implies support for other suits.

Suppose RHO bids 1♣ and you hold:

♠ AJ75 ♡ KQJ83 ◇ A96 ♣ 7

Despite totaling only 15 HCP, this is a good playing hand; as well, your hearts are good enough to rebid over a 2◇ response, and you don't want to miss a possible spade fit. So you should double rather than overcall, since partner would pass 1♡ holding either of these hands:

♠ 1086432 ♡ 7 ◇ K8 ♣ J652

♠ Q862 ♡ 73 ◇ KQ2 ♣ 9643

In both cases, after doubling you would raise partner's spade response, and he has enough to bid again.

Weaken your hand further to:

♠ K106 ♡ AQ874 ◇ AQ8 ♣ 72

Now you should just overcall 1♣ with 1♡; if you have a game, partner will bid over your overcall. A double followed by 2♡ shows a much better hand, and usually (as we have seen) a better suit. However, if you bid 1♡ and the bidding continues 'pass-pass-2♣' (or '2♣-pass-pass'), you can now double to show a good overcall with support for the remaining suits. Although game is no longer likely, you don't want to let the opponents make a partscore when your side can make a partscore.

Jump overcalls

Suppose RHO opens one of a minor and you hold:

♠ AQ10765 ♡ K9 ◇ AJ6 ♣ 94

Most players would overcall 1♠ and, if partner passed and RHO reopened (or LHO raised and opener passed) they would rebid 2♠ to show their extra values and playing strength. That is the way I would bid also — if we were not vulnerable. But remember, the principle that the sooner you make your bid, the safer it is (also the more effective it is). I'll admit the danger of bidding 1♠ followed by 2♠ is slight, but if your system allows you to bid 2♠ right away, the danger would be even less. One other advantage of bidding 2♠ immediately is that if LHO preempts, partner can support you at a high level with less than normal trump support.

Another point in favor of bidding 2♠ immediately is that LHO may have enough to bid over 1♠ but not over 2♠, and as a consequence, the opponents may not find their fit when it is their hand. Or, when they can make exactly 3♡, they may not be able to stop there since a new suit by responder over your overcall is forcing. Most people play preemptive jump overcalls regardless of vulnerability, but I almost never get hands where I want to make them when I am vulnerable, especially against non-vulnerable opponents. Rather than have a bid that I seldom use, I prefer to play intermediate jump overcalls when vulnerable.

The following hands are typical intermediate jump overcalls over a minor opening:

♠ K Q 10 9 7 4 ♡ 9 ◇ A Q 10 5 ♣ J 6

♠ K 8 5 ♡ A Q J 10 7 6 ◇ K 7 ♣ Q 9

♠ A 7 ♡ A Q J 8 5 4 ◇ A 7 5 ♣ J 8

'Intermediate' means neither too weak nor too strong. Add the ◇Q or even the ◇J10 to the last hand, and you should make a takeout double, followed by a heart bid.

An extra advantage of playing intermediate jump overcalls is that partner can draw inferences when you do bid 1♠ followed by 2♠. If you had a very strong, semi-balanced hand, you would have made a takeout double, followed by a spade bid. With an intermediate hand you would have bid 2♠ immediately. So for this sequence, you must have lots of distribution and too many playing tricks for an intermediate jump overcall. (When you have lots of distribution, your one-level overcall is not likely to be passed out.) You might hold one of these hands, for example:

♠ K J 8 6 5 3 ♡ 8 ◇ A ♣ K J 9 7 5

♠ Q J 8 7 6 5 3 ♡ A Q ◇ — ♣ Q J 10 6

Although the topic of this chapter is major-suit overcalls, I might mention that a vulnerable jump overcall in a minor should be slightly stronger (since it is usually at the three-level) and should show a hand suitable for play at notrump. Over 1♡ you should bid 3◇ with:

♠ A8 ♡ J6 ◊ AKQ1085 ♣ Q108

but only 2◊ with

♠ K9 ♡ 8 ◊ AJ98754 ♣ AQ6

You don't want to encourage partner to bid 3NT opposite the latter hand unless he has both a heart stopper *and* a good diamond fit.

Overcalls After a Preempt

Regardless of your system agreements, some jump overcalls have to be intermediate or strong based upon the logic of the situation. A basic rule is that you never preempt over a preempt — the partner of the preemptor knows fairly accurately what his partner has, so a competing preempt would not be effective. Besides, you need all of the remaining bidding levels to describe your own hand. So if RHO opened 2♡ (weak), you should jump to 3♠ with

♠ AQJ965 ♡ 9 ◊ KQ105 ♣ K7

since partner would not move over a 2♠ overcall with two small spades and two bare aces. Also (although we will discuss this at greater length in a later chapter), when a bid of one of a suit is passed around to fourth hand, a jump is intermediate rather than weak regardless of vulnerability. There is no need to make a preemptive bid in this situation since you can simply pass with a weak hand.

So what do you need to overcall a preemptive bid? At the one-level, you can compete with a mediocre hand since you are not likely to be penalized severely, but when you have to enter the bidding at a higher level, you need game prospects to justify the risk. The general rule is that you need opening-bid values to compete, although good distribution may compensate for lack of extra high cards. Remember, games can be made on distributional hands just as easily as on high cards. If RHO opens 2♡ (weak), you should overcall 2♠ with

♠ KQ8752 ♡ 6 ◊ A85 ♣ 942

since it is easy to visualize hands where you can make 4♠ while the opponents can make 4♡. If you pass, and LHO bids 4♡, what could poor partner do with:

♠ A106 ♡ 1083 ◊ KQ973 ♣ J6

Actually, I think you should overcall in spades on this hand whether RHO opens 2♡, 3♡ or 4♡! Yes, you risk a 1400-point set if you overcall at the four-level, but there are more good things than bad things that can happen:

1) you may make 4♠
2) the opponents may bid 5♡, down one
3) the opponents may fail to double
4) 4♠, doubled, may turn out to be a cheap sacrifice.

You and RHO have less than half the high cards — why shouldn't partner have his share of the remaining honors?

Beware of exciting partner too much, however. For this reason, if the opponents open 3♡, you should bid 3♠, not 4♠, with:

♠ KQJ108764 ♡ 87 ◇ QJ ♣ 4

There is much more danger that 4♠ would entice partner to bid a losing slam than that he would pass 3♠ when you were cold for game.

When you have a fairly strong hand, it pays to think ahead a little before deciding what to bid over the preempt. Suppose RHO opens 3♠ at IMPs; what would you bid with each of these hands?

♠ A6 ♡ AKQ10854 ◇ KJ5 ♣ 9

♠ A6 ♡ AKQ10854 ◇ QJ5 ♣ 9

♠ A6 ♡ AKQ10854 ◇ 75 ♣ 92

With the first hand, you should double and bid hearts over partner's response. It is too good for a simple 4♡ overcall. With the second hand, you should just bid 4♡. You don't need much from partner to make it; the ◇K may be enough. With the third hand you should bid 3NT! All you need to find with partner is an ace, while to make 4♡ you need to find two tricks in his hand. Even if LHO does have AQxxx of a minor (opposite his partner's king), he is not likely to lead the suit. Also, even if partner is aceless, there will still be a chance to make the hand by ducking the first spade trick and playing LHO for both missing aces when dummy has the minor suit kings. So the worse your hand is, the more inclined you should be to bid notrump with a solid suit of your own and a stopper in theirs!

Similarly, if you hold:

♠ 10 ♡ AQ7 ◇ AKQJ54 ♣ K87

and the bidding goes 3♠ on your left, passed around to you, you should double. Perhaps partner can bid 3NT. If he passes the double, you should do well on defense. If he bids 4♡, he will probably make it. If he bids 4♣, you can bid 4◇, and perhaps he will be able to raise. But suppose you hold this hand on the same auction:

♠ 10 ♡ A7 ◇ AKQJ543 ♣ J87

Now (especially if you are vulnerable and the opponents are not), you should bid 3NT yourself! LHO probably doesn't have solid spades (he would likely open 1♠ or even 4♠ with ♠AKQxxxx, even with little or nothing on the side, and RHO didn't raise, so that means partner probably has a spade stopper. There is a better chance of finding partner with one trick in spades than three tricks elsewhere (to make 5◇).

SUMMARY

1. Compete aggressively for partscores.
2. The earlier in the auction you make a bid, the safer it is.
3. Four of a major is the most likely game once the opponents have opened the bidding.
4. Overcall a four-card major at the one-level rather than a five-card minor at the two-level. You have more chance of safely introducing your minor suit later in the auction than your major, and you have more chance of winning the partscore auction if you are bidding a major suit. *Partner should not give preference to your major with equal length*.
5. Overcall a four-card major only with a good hand and shortness in the other major.
6. Do not overcall with a poor suit and a poor hand.
7. Competing for the partscore is a more important objective than directing the lead or interfering with the opponents.
8. If you are so strong that you might miss a game opposite a hand on which partner would pass an overcall, start with a double.
9. Play jump overcalls as intermediate when vulnerable — this comes up much more often than the opportunity to make a preemptive bid.
10. You need opening-bid values (or the equivalent in distribution) to overcall a preempt. Don't preempt the preemptor.

What is your next bid with each of the following hands?

1. *Both vul.*

WEST	NORTH	EAST	SOUTH
		1♢	?

a) ♠ A Q 8 6 ♡ K 8 ♢ 6 ♣ A J 10 7 4 2
b) ♠ Q 7 5 2 ♡ 9 ♢ A 6 ♣ K Q J 10 6 4
c) ♠ 6 ♡ K J 10 8 ♢ A 6 5 4 3 ♣ A J 9
d) ♠ A 8 3 ♡ K Q J 8 ♢ A 8 7 5 4 2 ♣ —
e) ♠ K 10 7 6 ♡ 8 ♢ K Q 10 6 ♣ A 7 5 2
f) ♠ Q 8 7 5 2 ♡ K 7 ♢ A Q J 7 ♣ Q 8
g) ♠ Q 8 7 4 ♡ K J 9 8 4 2 ♢ A K ♣ 8

2. *Neither vul.*

WEST	NORTH	EAST	SOUTH
		2♢[1]	?

1. Weak.

♠ 6 ♡ A Q 8 7 5 ♢ — ♣ 9 8 7 6 5 3 2

3. *Both vul.*

WEST	NORTH	EAST	SOUTH
1♡	pass	2♡	?

♠ K Q 10 6 ♡ 7 6 ♢ 9 ♣ A K 10 7 6 4

SOLUTIONS

1. a) 1♠. If you could count on West to pass, your best call would be a double, intending to rebid 2♣ over a 1♡ response. The trouble with doubling is that West may bid something like 2♢ or 3♢. Then, if partner bids hearts at a minimum level, you will have no idea what to do since he might well have only a four-card suit.

   b) 2♣. There has to be a limit to four-card major overcalls, and this is it. Because your suit is so weak, a spade overcall gambles everything on finding a spade fit. If you don't, this hand will take very few tricks in spades while it will take several tricks in clubs. Furthermore, with this weak a hand and this weak a spade suit, game is very unlikely unless partner can either bid 2NT or cuebid over 2♣, in which case you will show your spades. Surprise — I am not quite as crazy as you thought!

   c) 1♡ — before the opponents bid spades. You have good defense against a diamond contract, but the opponents are not likely to play in diamonds.

   d) 1♡. It is a disadvantage that you have good support for spades, but it is vital to get into the bidding before somebody (possibly your partner) bids clubs. This hand will make a lot of tricks if you find a heart fit, and it is still possible for partner to bid spades at the one-level with a fair five-card suit. Again, it is wishful thinking for you to pass, hoping to defend a diamond contract. This is an example of my bidding philosophy in another respect. I stated a 'rule' that you shouldn't overcall a four-card major with three cards in the other major; it is a very good general rule, but hardly any rule should be followed blindly. Good bidding means choosing the best bid available, no matter how many 'rules' you have to break.

   e) Pass. This is clear-cut. The combination of a weak four-card suit and a lot of your strength in the opponent's suit (where partner is probably short) should discourage you from bidding. Even if the opening bid had been 1♣, you should pass. The disadvantage of bidding 1♠ is that you will not enjoy playing 1♠, even undoubled, if everyone passes and partner has only one or two spades; nor will 2♠ be a bargain opposite three-card support. There are not many hands where it pays to pass and plan to reopen the bidding later, but this is one of the few. If LHO bids 1♡ and opener raises or bids 1NT, you can double to show the other two suits and a hand unsuitable for an immediate overcall. If the bidding goes some other way, you will pass throughout without fear of missing a game.

   f) 1♠. You have good diamonds, too good to make it likely that the opponents will bid 5♢ and partner sacrifice over it. If partner has a spade fit, the hand should play well in spades, especially if you get an opening diamond lead.

g) 1♡. This hand has the right strength for an intermediate jump overcall, but a 2♡ bid might easily preempt partner out of bidding spades. If your spades and clubs were interchanged, you would have an ideal 2♡ bid. With the actual hand it is better to bid 1♡ and see what happens. Besides, with your spade holding, you are not particularly worried about being outbid.

2. I think you should bid 2♡, even at IMPs! That is what I did when I held this hand. Several players thought I was crazy, but it worked like a charm. West bid 6◇ and partner bid 6♡ with:

♠ A9854 ♡ K9642 ◇ 86 ♣ J

Just based on our two hands, this actually isn't a bad slam. It was no surprise that West had a void in hearts for his 6◇ bid, and with the clubs 4-1, down two was the best we could do, but the cost of sacrificing against the opponents' cold slam was less than the value of their game. Of course, I was lucky to find such a good fit, but the best chance to get to game or to find a cheap sacrifice against 5◇ (not to mention 6◇) was to find partner with length in hearts and shortness in clubs. The risk of overcalling was negligible — since I was missing twelve spades and thirteen diamonds, no one was going to let me play this hand at the two-level in hearts, and in the very unlikely event that someone had doubled 2♡, I would have run to 3♣. The greater risk was that partner might double the opponents' final contract, but when it is obvious that everyone is bidding on distribution, you should tend not to double without aces or trump tricks. This is a prime example of how much safer it is to bid right away rather than wait until later, and also of how much there is to gain compared to how little there is to lose.

3. 2♠. Obviously there is some danger, and you will have to guess what to do if partner raises (possibly with three-card support). But the prospects for game are good enough to justify the risk. If partner has ♠Axxx, you will have a play for game even if he has nothing else. Ironically, with:

♠ KQ10x ♡ x ◇ xx ♣ AK10xxx

(a singleton heart rather than a singleton diamond) there is more reason for bidding 3♣. With the latter hand, there is a greater chance that one of the opponents will bid 3♡, allowing you to bid 3♠. After that, partner will return you to clubs if he lacks four-card spade support.

CHAPTER 2

Responding to Overcalls

Showing Support for Partner's Suit

If your partner takes the first chapter seriously and is willing to overcall four-card majors more frequently than he used to, probably the first question that comes to mind is how that should change your responses. The simple answer is that it has very little effect. Occasionally you will take a pessimistic view with bad three-card support, but you should assume that partner has a five-card suit. (He usually does, and when he has a four-card suit, he has extra values in either high cards or distribution.) However, it is even more important than before to show whether you have three- or four-card support whenever it is possible to do so. In addition, when partner overcalls a major and later bids a minor (without your having supported him), be reluctant to return to the major, even with three small of the major (and a hopelessly weak hand, which is why you didn't support him earlier).

When partner overcalls, you have five choices:

1) pass
2) show some degree of support for his suit
3) bid notrump
4) cuebid
5) bid a suit of your own.

I strongly recommend passing with a weak hand and no fit. If partner overcalls 1♡, you should pass rather than rescue to 1♠ with:

♠ J10965 ♡ 6 ◇ Q875 ♣ Q94

If you bid anything , partner will play you for a better hand and will probably bid too much. Of course, if opener reopens with a double, and RHO passes it, you can (and should) bid 1♠.

With a balanced hand you should give partner a single raise of his one-level overcall with just about the same hands as you would raise his opening bid, with the following exception: with four-card (or longer) support, you should usually bid immediately to the three-level, or higher. I say 'bid' rather than 'raise' to the three level because with a hand worth a limit raise I like to make a jump cuebid:

WEST	NORTH	EAST	SOUTH
1♣	1♡	pass	3♣

With a weaker hand along with four-card support, raise to three of partner's suit preemptively.

Some players use the following structure: a double raise is preemptive and shows a very weak hand defensively, probably not a single defensive trick (the main advantage in playing that way is that partner can tell when to sacrifice). With a little defensive strength and a distributional raise, they make a jump cuebid, and with a limit raise (no matter how many trumps they have) they make the cheapest cuebid. Playing that way, when the bidding goes

WEST	NORTH	EAST	SOUTH
1◇	1♡	pass	?

they would bid as follows:

a)	♠ J763 ♡ Q9852 ◇ 87 ♣ 85	3♡
b)	♠ A763 ♡ Q985 ◇ 8 ♣ 9874	3◇
c)	♠ A8 ♡ Q985 ◇ 987 ♣ QJ52	2♡
d)	♠ AJ8 ♡ Q9852 ◇ 86 ♣ KJ6	2◇
e)	♠ AJ8 ♡ Q98 ◇ J86 ♣ KJ74	2◇

Incidentally, the jump cuebid with hand (b) is called a "mixed raise."

I played that way for a while, but I now think it is better always to bid to the three-level with four or five trumps and to use only two gradations: a limit raise or a preemptive raise. My recommendation is to bid 3♡ with (a) — although a pass is tempting at unfavorable vulnerability — and 3♡ also with (b) despite the fact that it is a considerably stronger hand than (a). With both (c) and (d) I would bid 3◇, a limit raise with four or more trumps. With (e) I would bid 2◇, a limit raise with three-card support. Rather than strive for super-accuracy, it is more important to hike the bidding up when you have lots of trumps because, as you will see in Chapter 5 when we discuss the Law of Total Tricks, the more trumps your side has, the better you are positioned for offense and the worse for defense. In other words, when your three-level contract is set despite a combined holding of nine or more trumps, the opponents can usually make something at the three-level themselves. Moreover, you are forcing your opponents to make difficult decisions when they have to compete at the three- or four-level.

Actually, I recommend three minor exceptions to the rule that you raise to the three-level with four trumps. First, with a completely balanced hand (4-3-3-3 distribution) you may treat your four-card support as three-card support. When your hand is balanced, the other hands tend to be balanced too, and neither side can take as many tricks as usual. Nor will the opponents compete as vigorously with balanced hands, so a preempt may not be necessary since the opponents weren't going to try to outbid you anyway. Why incur a set at the three-level when you could have bought the hand for 2♡ or 2♠ and made it?

The second exception is when you have a semi-balanced hand with lots of secondary honors — more defense than offense. Here are a couple of examples:

WEST	NORTH	EAST	SOUTH
1♣	1♡	pass	?

♠ J9865 ♡ 10875 ♢ Q8 ♣ K8

♠ KJ87 ♡ J1076 ♢ QJ8 ♣ QJ

With both these example hands I recommend a simple raise to 2♡. You are not as worried as usual about being outbid with the first hand since you have the spade suit. With a similar hand, but with the diamond and spade holdings reversed, you should preempt because of the increased likelihood that the opponents could outbid you in spades if you failed to preempt. The second hand, despite its 11 HCP, is weak offensively while the club holding may be worth something defensively (if partner has ♣Kxx or ♣10xx). Even when it is worth nothing, either on offense or defense, your club holding may slow down the opponents' bidding. West will be nervous about bidding 3♣ opposite a passing partner with ♣AK10542, not knowing your doubleton queen-jack are onside for him — with ♣AKQJ52, he would be more inclined to compete; and with your spade holding, the opponents are again unlikely to outbid you (successfully) in spades.

The third exception is when you have a fairly balanced hand (like 4-4-3-2) with most of your strength outside the trump suit. If LHO opens 1♢ and partner overcalls 1♡, I think a raise to 2♡ is sufficient with:

♠ K984 ♡ 9832 ♢ QJ8 ♣ K7

You have reasonable defensive values despite your heart length, and you have enough high-card strength to expect to buy the hand for 2♡. Neither a preemptive 3♡ bid nor an invitational 3♢ bid looks right with this hand.

With very few exceptions, you should not raise and later raise again. The following sequence should almost never occur:

WEST	NORTH	EAST	SOUTH
1♡	1♠	2♡	2♠
3♡	pass	pass	3♠

If South had enough offense to go to 3♠, he should have done it right away. When the strength is equally balanced, it is seldom right to compete to the three-level with eight trumps (as you will discover in a later chapter), and if you have four-card support (and presumably nine trumps together), you should (usually) have bid to the three-level immediately, which gives the opponents many more problems. The only time the above sequence is possible is if you hold something like:

♠ Q 10 9 6 ♡ J 7 4 ◇ K 7 3 ♣ Q J 6

You didn't jump the first time because you had 4-3-3-3 distribution and reasonable defense. However, LHO failed to make a game try and with partner likely to have a singleton heart, the hands should fit well. Partner however, couldn't justify competing to the three-level on his own with a mediocre five-card spade suit. It is quite possible that both sides can make three of a major and, if partner doesn't make 3♠ (probably because trumps split 3-1 and he misguesses), it is a cinch that the opponents could make at least nine tricks in hearts. Nevertheless, you should normally avoid raising and raising again. Even in this sequence, there is a danger that the opponents will realize what a good fit they have (when spades are 3-1 and clubs are 4-2) and bid and make 4♡.

If raising partner's overcall to the two-level followed by a raise to the three-level is usually a bad idea, a single raise (or pass) followed by a game bid is worse. The bidding, with neither side vulnerable, goes:

WEST	NORTH	EAST	SOUTH
1♡	1♠	3♡	?

♠ K 9 8 6 ♡ J 6 ◇ Q 8 7 5 4 ♣ 9 7

There are two reasonable choices. You could bid 4♠ on the theory that the opponents are probably going to bid 4♡, in which case 4♠ will probably be a good sacrifice. An immediate 4♠ bid, even when it is wrong on a double-dummy basis, certainly gives the opponents a problem. Opener's pass wouldn't be forcing, so he has to guess right away whether to pass, double, or bid 5♡, while responder, having limited his hand, is almost forced to pass whatever opener does.

However, a 4♠ bid is pretty wild since you don't know whether opener was going to bid again and you don't know how good a hand partner has. He might have enough defense to defeat 4♡ and/or he might be down three in 4♠ doubled. Your better choice is to bid 3♠, intending to accept partner's decision if the opponents bid again. But bidding 3♠ and later 4♠, or passing 3♡ 'because the opponents were not in game' followed by bidding 4♠ over 4♡ is terribly wrong. Even if you don't get a bad result from a 'slow' 4♠ bid, it will cost you in the future. Partner will double 4♡ when he shouldn't, just to keep you from taking a unilateral sacrifice. Instead, why not bid 3♠ now to suggest a save and let partner decide whether to take it or not? As will be explained in a few pages, there is a way to show a good raise to 3♠, so if you're using it, just bidding 3♠ directly shows this type of hand.

Notrump Responses to an Overcall

Your notrump responses to an overcall should be different from those made after an opening bid. Especially when playing a forcing notrump, you often have to respond 1NT to an opening bid with hands quite unsuitable for notrump, just to give partner another chance in case he has 19 or 20 HCP or another suit that fits your hand better. In contrast, when partner overcalls, you need a little extra high-card strength to bid notrump. While there is a big overlap, both his minimum and maximum high-card strength are lower than when he opens the bidding. Also a notrump response to an overcall is non-forcing, and strongly suggests actually playing notrump. If partner opened 1♠, you would respond 1NT with

♠ 3 ♡ Q 9 8 7 5 ◇ A 8 7 5 4 ♣ 6 2

to give him another chance (hoping for him to rebid 2♡), but if partner overcalls 1♠, you should never consider bidding 1NT, no matter what the opening bid was. A 1NT response to an overcall shows roughly 8-12 HCP with at least one stopper in the opponent's suit, and probably two stoppers if you are at the lower end of the range. So, if the bidding goes

WEST	NORTH	EAST	SOUTH
1◇	1♠	pass	?

you should bid 1NT with hands like these:

♠ J 6 ♡ Q 10 8 ◇ K 10 7 5 ♣ Q J 4 2

♠ 8 ♡ K J 8 7 ◇ Q 9 7 4 ♣ A Q 7 5

You would respond 2NT (non-forcing) with 13-14 HCP and bid 3NT directly with 15 HCP and poor spade support. With fair spade support you would cuebid first and plan to bid 2NT or 3NT next round, to give partner a choice of contracts.

What about this kind of problem:

WEST	NORTH	EAST	SOUTH
1♢	1♠	pass	?

♠ Q8 ♡ A765 ♢ 96 ♣ A9543

Partner could easily be strong enough for game, so you want to keep the bidding open. However, neither of your suits is worth bidding since you wouldn't want to play 2♡ or 2♣ opposite a singleton or a worthless doubleton, and you don't have a stopper for notrump. What do you do? The answer is that you should simply raise to 2♠, even playing with me! On average, partner will have at least five spades for his overcall (and six more often than four); this hand should actually play well in spades, even on a 4-2 fit. In other words, even though I recommend four-card overcalls, they are only made with certain kinds of hands, and you shouldn't pervert your responsive bidding to guard against the possibility. On the other hand, if you hold

♠ AJ8 ♡ K85 ♢ QJ87 ♣ 985

you should bid 1NT in this auction instead of showing spade support. Your hand is ideal for notrump, while your diamond strength may be wasted in a suit contract. Give partner one of these hands

♠ KQ974 ♡ QJ3 ♢ 93 ♣ AK6

♠ KQ9742 ♡ A10 ♢ 642 ♣ AJ

with either of which he would raise you to 2NT, and you would get to your best game. The moral: *raise on hands that will play better in a suit and bid notrump on hands that will play better in notrump*. Partner should realize that your 1NT response does not deny spade support. If you bid 1NT with:

♠ AJ8 ♡ K85 ♢ QJ87 ♣ 985

and partner rebids 2♡, now you can bid 3♠ since your hand looks very good opposite partner's major two-suiter, and he should bid 4♠ with

♠ K10964 ♡ AJ103 ♢ 4 ♣ AQ7

However, if he rebids 2♣ instead of 2♡, you should merely take a preference to 2♠ despite your good spade support. Your six points in the red suits are all dubious values.

Using the Cuebid

With few exceptions, when the opening side cuebids, it promises another bid, but this is usually not true for the defenders. Indeed, a cuebid by an overcaller's partner definitely does not guarantee that he will bid again; most of the time, he just has a good raise of his partner's suit, and if overcaller rebids his suit at a minimum level, the cuebidder can, and usually will, pass.

What does this cuebid promise then? First, you should realize that on this auction:

WEST	NORTH	EAST	SOUTH
1♠	2♢	pass	?

you should bid 3♢ with as little as:

♠ 9754 ♡ A7 ♢ Q87 ♣ Q865

Partner's two-level overcall covers a wide range, these hands being about the minimum and maximum possible:

♠ Q6 ♡ K82 ♢ AKJ105 ♣ 975

♠ AJ6 ♡ K9 ♢ AJ109543 ♣ A

As a result, you want to keep the bidding open in case he is very strong. Note that if he has the weaker hand, 3♢ is probably down one, but this is no catastrophe since the opponents can surely make 3♡, if not 4♡, and the raise may well prevent them from finding their fit.

However, if a hand as poor as

♠ 9754 ♡ A7 ♢ Q87 ♣ Q865

is worth a raise to 3♢, you have to take stronger action with:

♠ 87 ♡ A987 ♢ Q87 ♣ A1085

You don't want to go past 3NT, which may well be the best spot if partner has a spade stopper, so you cuebid 2♠ (or the equivalent if you are playing transfer responses, as explained in the next few pages).

How weak a hand can you have to cuebid? On this auction:

WEST	NORTH	EAST	SOUTH
1♢	1♠	pass	?

♠ K65 ♡ A754 ♢ 96 ♣ K1054

would be worth a cuebid to show a good raise to 2♠. To cuebid with as few as 10 HCP, you need your points to be all working (in other words, ignore kings, queens and jacks of the opponents' suit). With only three-card support for partner and this strong a hand, you are not particularly worried about being outbid by the opponents. You will sell out if the opponents bid at the three-level and partner passes, since you probably have only an eight-card fit. And, of course, you will also pass if partner simply rebids 2♠. Strengthen your hand to

♠ K 6 5 ♡ A 7 5 4 ◇ 9 6 ♣ A J 10 4

and you are slightly too strong to cuebid and pass, so if partner rebids 2♠ over 2◇ you will raise him to 3♠ anyway. This shows a stronger raise, but still three-card support. With one of these hands

♠ K 6 5 4 ♡ A 7 4 ◇ 9 4 ♣ A J 10 4

♠ Q J 7 6 ♡ A Q 7 3 ◇ Q 8 ♣ A 10 9

you would make a cuebid without jumping (despite your four-card support) and cuebid again to show a very invitational hand with four-card support. When you have so strong a hand, it is unlikely that the opponents will compete vigorously, but if they do, you will show your support at the four-level, if necessary; if your next chance to bid is at the three-level, you should gamble by raising partner to game rather than test him with an ambiguous 3♠ bid that would often be made competitively on a weaker hand.

With a singleton you don't try to cut things so closely. A hand like

♠ K 8 7 4 ♡ 7 ◇ 8 7 5 ♣ A Q 10 9 6

will make game opposite a fitting minimum overcall — for example

♠ A Q 6 5 2 ♡ J 5 4 ◇ 9 2 ♣ K 8 3

but it may also offer only a poor play for game opposite a much stronger hand. When you can't tell whether it will make or not, and you have strong support and a singleton, it pays simply to jump to game (unless you play a single jump as a splinter bid). Also note that, while you can make 4♠ opposite this fitting hand, the opponents can probably make 4♡ and they certainly have a cheap sacrifice in either hearts or diamonds. An immediate jump to game may shut them out (while a splinter bid may allow them to compete more safely, perhaps by doubling).

How do you cuebid when the opponents haven't shown a suit?

WEST	NORTH	EAST	SOUTH
1NT[1]	2♠	pass	?

1. 15-17.

♠ Q 9 5 4 ♡ 8 4 ◇ A K J 8 ♣ 7 5 4

You would surely raise to 3♠ in this sequence with

♠ Q J 2 ♡ 9 5 4 3 ◇ A Q 9 ♣ 8 7 6

and you actually have a much stronger hand. You would like to cuebid to show a good raise, but you don't know what the opponents' suit is. The solution? Bid

2NT. After an opponent's strong notrump, it is very unlikely that you would want to play 3NT. If you can make a game, it will be in a suit contract, based upon a distributional fit, so 2NT takes the place of a cuebid. Likewise, when the opponents open a strong 2♣ and partner overcalls a suit (natural), it is unlikely that you belong in 3NT, so 2NT again becomes a cuebid, showing a strong raise of partner's suit.

The Cuebid Double

What call would you make here?

WEST	NORTH	EAST	SOUTH
1♡	1♠	2♡	?

♠ Q98 ♡ J6 ◇ A872 ♣ A942

Without the raise on your right, you would have cuebid 2♡ since you have a good three-card raise to 2♠. A 3♠ bid would be preemptive. So what do you do? You could bid 2♠, the same bid you would make with

♠ Q98 ♡ J6 ◇ K872 ♣ 9842

or you could bid 3♡ and give up on distinguishing between three- and four-card raises. However, on this hand there is some danger that you will go down in 3♠ when no one can make anything at the three-level. Then there's this situation:

WEST	NORTH	EAST	SOUTH
2♡	2♠	3♡	?

a) ♠ Q754 ♡ 74 ◇ KJ93 ♣ J72

b) ♠ Q754 ♡ 74 ◇ AK93 ♣ J72

c) ♠ Q74 ♡ 74 ◇ AK93 ♣ Q1083

Do you bid 3♠ with all three hands and force partner to guess whether your raise is invitational or competitive?

When partner has overcalled a major and RHO has raised opener's suit, I think a double should be used to show a good raise to the same level. I call this a 'cuebid double' because the double takes the place of a cuebid. At the two-level it should show three-card support since with four-card support you can cuebid at the three level, and if that is one trick too high, the opponents can probably make a contract of their own. At the three-level, the double merely shows a good raise as distinguished from a normal raise or a skimpy raise. You can no longer differentiate between three- and four-card support. Showing whether you have a good, rather than a bad or mediocre, raise of partner's major is a better use of this double (and the hands for it occur much more frequently) than playing it as responsive (showing the other two suits). When the bidding goes:

WEST	NORTH	EAST	SOUTH
1♡	1♠	3♡	?

for example, how often will you hold 5-5 in the minors and enough strength that you want to compete to the four-level, as compared to the times you will have some kind of raise of partner's suit?

WEST	NORTH	EAST	SOUTH
1♠	2♡	2♠	dbl

The double has the same meaning here. It shows a good raise to 3♡, but since a 3♠ cuebid would force you to game, the double does not distinguish between three- or four-card support. In fact, you might even have two-card support since a two-level overcall of a one bid guarantees a good five-card suit or longer. Only when the opponents open at the two-level, usually as a preempt, will you even be tempted to overcall with a four-card major above the one-level. Consequently, after

WEST	NORTH	EAST	SOUTH
1♠	2♡	2♠	?

you should make a cuebid double with:

♠ 87 ♡ Q10 ◇ AQ754 ♣ K876

Partner, with

♠ 92 ♡ AK8754 ◇ KJ6 ♣ Q5

would definitely pass a simple raise to 3♡ but would bid a game over your double. Incidentally, I understand that cuebid doubles are popular in England.

Showing Your Own Suit

As has been mentioned several times already, when partner overcalls, he is not inviting you to introduce a suit of your own, but sometimes you do have a suit worth showing. Should a new suit bid by the partner of the overcaller be forcing? Experts disagree, but a majority play it as merely invitational, which is the treatment adopted in 'Bridge World Standard'. However you play it, you need a good suit to suggest playing your suit rather than partner's (or to imply a source of tricks in case partner wants to try 3NT). But wouldn't it be nice if you could show your good suit, even with a bad hand, without misleading partner? And wouldn't it be even nicer if, after showing your suit, you could stop on a dime with a bad hand — yet have the opportunity to show additional features if your hand called for it? There is a solution that works part of the time, depending on how much bidding room there is — and it never costs! This solution is to play transfer responses, as recommended by *Bridge World* editor Jeff Rubens. In fact, Jeff also plays them at high levels, but to avoid complica-

tions, I merely recommend that they be used after simple overcalls of one-bids.
This is the way they work:

WEST	NORTH	EAST	SOUTH
1♣	1♠	pass	?

1NT	natural
2♣	transfer to diamonds
2♢	transfer to hearts
2♡	cuebid (takes the place of a 2♣ cuebid)
2♠	natural

Now when you hold:

♠ 5 ♡ 985 ♢ KQJ865 ♣ J43

you can bid 2♣, transferring partner to diamonds, and pass, while with

♠ 5 ♡ Q87 ♢ AQJ854 ♣ QJ6

you can transfer to diamonds and then bid 2NT. If partner has no interest in playing notrump, for example holding

♠ AJ7642 ♡ K104 ♢ 732 ♣ 8

he can remove 2NT to 3♢.
If you have some tolerance for partner, for example with

♠ K8 ♡ K94 ♢ AJ9854 ♣ J6

you can transfer to diamonds and then bid 2♠ to show diamonds and (mediocre) spade support. If partner has something like

♠ A10742 ♡ AJ6 ♢ Q10 ♣ 973

he should take you back to diamonds, but with strong spades and a diamond fit, say

♠ AQJ754 ♡ Q7 ♢ K62 ♣ 94

you will get to a good game in spades.
Even more valuable is the ability to transfer to hearts. With

♠ 5 ♡ AQJ943 ♢ J87 ♣ 954

you would bid 2♢ to transfer to hearts and then pass; with

♠ 5 ♡ AQJ943 ♢ A87 ♣ 973

you would transfer to hearts and then raise to 3♡. With

♠ 5 ♡ AKQJ75 ♢ A87 ♣ 973

you would transfer to hearts and then cuebid 3♣ in an effort to get to 3NT if partner has a club stopper. With

♠ J7 ♡ AQJ105 ♢ QJ6 ♣ A106

you would transfer to hearts and bid 3NT yourself to give partner a choice of contracts.

Normally, when you transfer partner to a suit, he should bid it, but if you transfer him to hearts and he has

♠ KQJ9754 ♡ 5 ♢ KJ7 ♣ 92

he should refuse the transfer and rebid 2♠. Improve his diamonds to ♢AQ7 and he should jump to 3♠. Likewise, when you bid 2♢ to transfer to hearts, he should 'super-accept' by jumping to 3♡ with:

♠ AK876 ♡ J95 ♢ A7 ♣ Q102

since, if you had bid a natural 2♡, he would have raised.

You don't need more examples to visualize the many possibilities that transfer responses open up. This is how they work in general:

1) All responses below a cuebid of the opponent's suit are natural.
2) The cuebid is a transfer to the next-higher suit (unless that is the suit partner overcalled); the next bid is a transfer to the next suit, and the bid just below partner's suit is the cuebid.

Here are some more example auctions:

WEST	NORTH	EAST	SOUTH
1♠	2♡	pass	?

2♠	transfer to clubs
2NT	natural
3♣	transfer to diamonds
3♢	cuebid

WEST	NORTH	EAST	SOUTH
1♣	1♡	pass	?

1♠	natural
1NT	natural
2♣	transfer to diamonds
2♢	cuebid

WEST	NORTH	EAST	SOUTH
1♢	1♠	pass	?

1NT	natural
2♣	natural
2♢	transfer to hearts
2♡	cuebid

The closer partner's overcall is to the opening bid, the fewer transfers there are. After a touching suit overcall (1♡- 1♠, for example) there are no transfer bids. The transfers only apply when the overcall is of a one-level opening and when there is no intervening bid other than a negative double.

I mentioned that Jeff Rubens plays transfer responses at higher levels. However, the standard method, which I play, is as follows: when partner overcalls at such a level that your new suit response is below the game level, but at the three-level or higher, your bid is forcing.

WEST	NORTH	EAST	SOUTH
3♢	3♡	pass	?

Consequently in this auction, 3♠ would be forcing, perhaps with

♠ K J 8 7 4 3 ♡ J 6 ♢ 9 4 ♣ A J 8

You are not sure that any game will make, but you have a good enough hand to bid something, and you might as well give partner an alternative.

SUMMARY

1. Do not alter your system of responses to cater for the possibility of overcalls on four-card suits.
2. Give priority to raising partner with any kind of fit. Bid to the three-level immediately with four or five trumps, using a jump cuebid to show a limit raise. Use a simple cuebid to show a three-card limit raise.
3. Bid to the limit of your hand as quickly as possible; it's more effective and safer.
4. Notrump responses to an overcall are natural, and suggest playing in notrump, except where no real suit has been bid by the opponents, in which case a notrump bid can be used as a cuebid.
5. 'Cuebid doubles' come up much more often than responsive doubles, and, in my view, perform a more useful function. Use them to distinguish between competitive raises and hands with serious game interest when RHO raises opener's suit.
6. Transfer responses to overcalls of an opening bid at the one-level offer a flexible structure for showing your own suit, as well as the strength of your hand and any delayed support for partner that you may have.

What is your next bid in each of these auctions?

1. *Both vul.*

WEST	NORTH	EAST	SOUTH
1♡	2♣	pass	?

♠ A J 9 7 6 ♡ A 8 3 ◇ 7 6 ♣ J 9 2

2. *Neither vul.*

WEST	NORTH	EAST	SOUTH
1◇	1♠	dbl	?

♠ K Q ♡ 8 7 6 5 2 ◇ A 8 6 4 ♣ A 10

3. *Neither vul.*

WEST	NORTH	EAST	SOUTH
1◇	1♠	2◇	?

♠ J 8 7 5 4 ♡ 9 3 ◇ Q 8 2 ♣ 9 7 6

4. *Vulnerability immaterial*

WEST	NORTH	EAST	SOUTH
1◇	1♠	pass	?

♠ K 10 6 ♡ A J 6 ◇ K Q 7 ♣ J 8 5 2

5. *North-South vul.*

WEST	NORTH	EAST	SOUTH
1◇	2♠	pass	?

♠ Q 9 8 6 ♡ A K 7 ◇ 3 ♣ K 10 8 6 3

6. *East-West vul.*

WEST	NORTH	EAST	SOUTH
1♢	1♠	3♢	?

♠ QJ5 ♡ AQ74 ♢ 8 ♣ 98732

7. *East-West vul.*

WEST	NORTH	EAST	SOUTH
1♢	1♠	pass	?

♠ QJ5 ♡ AQ74 ♢ 8 ♣ 98732

8. *Vulnerability immaterial*

WEST	NORTH	EAST	SOUTH
		pass	pass
1♣	1♡	pass	?

♠ A865 ♡ J1093 ♢ A973 ♣ 2

9. *Neither vul.*

WEST	NORTH	EAST	SOUTH
1NT[1]	2♠[2]	pass	?

1. 15-17.
2. Spades and a minor.

♠ J984 ♡ 8752 ♢ A8 ♣ AJ6

SOLUTIONS

1. Bid 2♡. You don't need a better spade suit to transfer to because you are not going to pass partner's 2♠ response. You intend to bid 3♣ next, and if partner has honor-third of spades he will return to spades, bidding either 3♠ or 4♠ depending upon the overall strength of his hand. Isn't it nice that you can suggest playing in spades without being stuck there when partner has only one or two small spades?

2. Your hand is worth a cuebid in support of spades despite having only a doubleton, but I hope you remembered that your cuebid was 2♡ not 2◇ (which is a transfer to hearts!). You bid the same way over a negative double as over a pass. Some players use a redouble here to show exactly two-card support with a good hand, and if you play that way, you should redouble.

3. Pass. If you are going to make a preemptive raise with

   ♠ Q 8 7 6 5 ♡ 8 ◇ 8 7 4 ♣ Q J 8 2

   you can't make the same bid with such a hopeless hand — you don't want to suggest a sacrifice that may easily be down four. Even a 2♠ bid would lead partner astray. My philosophy with weak balanced hands is to stay out of the bidding and save my attempts at brilliancy for when I have a distributional hand.

4. A 2NT bid would describe your strength, and it would be my choice with one fewer spade. But you could easily belong in spades, so you should cuebid (by bidding 2♡, of course), followed by bidding 2NT if partner shows a near-minimum by rebidding 2♠. Change your king of spades to the jack, and I would bid 1NT right away, despite the three-card spade support.

5. Did you remember that a vulnerable 2♠ is an intermediate jump overcall, showing a good six-card suit and better than a minimum opening bid? So you should bid 4◇, an obvious splinter bid. A slam is likely if partner has no wasted strength in diamonds.

6. Double. This hand with nine points, none of which are likely to be wasted, plus a useful singleton, easily justifies a cuebid double.

7. Bid 2♡ to show a good raise to 2♠. If the opponents pass and partner just bids 2♠ you will pass, but if the opponents compete to the three-level, you will bid 3♠ rather than sell out (while with only three-card support and a balanced hand, you would tend to give up after having described your strength). The singleton is worth much more than a stray queen or

jack when your side plays the hand. And when you have a singleton, the opponents probably have extra length in the suit, making it easier for them to make more their way. This is the sort of hand where both sides can probably make nine tricks in their best contract.

8. Bid 4♡. You may or may not make it, but partner wouldn't know when to accept an invitation. If partner has as little as

♠ K7 ♡ KQ8752 ◇ 62 ♣ 976

game is cold (and the opponents will make ten tricks in clubs unless you find a spade ruff). With unbalanced hands and strong trump support it pays to take an aggressive view.

9. You have a very good hand opposite spades and a minor. If partner has 5-5-2-1 distribution, say

♠ AQ762 ♡ 10 ◇ KJ732 ♣ 95

you belong in game. Depending upon how light partner's overcall can be, perhaps it is right to jump to game now — but if he has

♠ KQ1076 ♡ J4 ◇ KJ104 ♣ 95

you would have no play for game. The solution? Normally when partner bids a major, showing that major and a minor, a 2NT bid asks partner to bid his minor (and is slightly more forward-going than 3♣, which says 'pass or correct'). But what does it mean if you bid 2NT and correct to 3♠ over his minor? I recommend playing that it shows a stronger raise than just bidding 3♠ immediately — highly invitational.

CHAPTER 3

Two-Suited Overcalls

General Principles

There are many conventional bids which show two-suiters, the two most popular being the Unusual Notrump and Michaels. However, all bids showing two suits have certain characteristics in common.

1) *When you show two suits, you make it very hard to play in a suit not shown by you.*

For example, over RHO's 1♡ opening, if you bid 2NT with

♠ AJ6 ♡ — ◇ KQ984 ♣ AJ1075

you almost eliminate any chances of playing a spade contract. Consequently, I think you should make a takeout double instead. Change your hand to

♠ 954 ♡ — ◇ AQJ96 ♣ KQJ84

and it is less likely that you belong in spades, so a 2NT bid is acceptable.

2) *When you show a two-suiter and the opponents play the hand, they can often play it double-dummy by finessing against your partner's queens and jacks in the other two suits.*

You should not reveal your shape unless there is a likelihood that your side will play the hand, either to make what you bid or as a sacrifice. It is foolish, in my opinion, to bid 2NT over 1♡ or 1♠ with

♠ Q 8 ♡ J ◇ Q J 8 7 5 ♣ K J 8 5 4

First, there is a good chance that you could be severely penalized at the three-level. If disaster doesn't strike immediately, what do you have to gain to compensate for the risk (including the risk that partner will take you seriously and bid too much)? It is very unlikely that you can outbid the opponents to a making contract or have a successful sacrifice at the five-level.

3) Most of your high cards should be in your two suits.

With a marginal hand you would pass with KJ643 of a suit, but bid with KJ1085. Also, you want partner to make the right decisions in competitive auctions. Suppose the bidding goes

WEST	NORTH	EAST	SOUTH
1♠	2NT	3♠	?

and you hold:

♠ 8 4 ♡ J 10 5 ◇ K 8 5 ♣ Q 10 8 5 3

At equal vulnerability you should bid 5♣ since you are almost sure the opponents can make 4♠, and quite possibly 5♠. The opponents will have to guess whether to double or bid 5♠. You can hardly go wrong if partner has one of these hands

♠ 9 ♡ 8 6 ◇ A Q J 7 4 ♣ K J 9 6 2

♠ 9 ♡ 8 ◇ Q J 9 6 4 3 ♣ A J 9 7 2

or even if he has:

♠ 9 ♡ K 6 ◇ A Q 9 7 4 ♣ A K J 7 6

But if he holds

♠ A ♡ K 7 ◇ Q 10 7 6 3 ♣ A 9 7 4 2

your bid will be a phantom sacrifice. With the latter hand, therefore, he should just overcall 2◇ and give up on showing clubs unless the auction takes an unusual turn.

Hand strength

The major issue is whether or not to play two-suited overcalls like simple overcalls, with a continuous range for the strength of the hand. Some players say you should bid the Unusual Notrump with these hands:

♠ 7 ♡ 5 ◇ KQ985 ♣ QJ7653

♠ 7 ♡ A8 ◇ AQJ98 ♣ AKJ105

but not with

♠ 75 ♡ 8 ◇ AKJ87 ♣ KQ1093

Likewise, they would bid a Michaels 2◇ over 1◇ with one of these hands:

♠ AJ975 ♡ Q10986 ◇ 87 ♣ J

♠ AQJ10 2 ♡ KQJ96 ◇ AQ ♣ 5

but not with either of these:

♠ AKJ54 ♡ KQ962 ◇ J5 ♣ 8

♠ AKJ54 ♡ AQJ82 ◇ J5 ♣ 8

This approach is known as 'mini-maxi' — to make a two-suited overcall, you either have a very weak hand or a very strong hand, but not something in the middle. Obviously, with the very strong hand, after showing their hand pattern and coaxing their partner to bid one of their suits, people who play this way either bid game or strongly invite it. Their contention is that partner won't know what to do opposite what could be a medium-strength hand. There is something to be said for this approach, but I prefer continuous ranges for several reasons. The main one is that you almost always play in the right suit, even though you occasionally have to guess about the level. Over an opponent's diamond opening I hate to overcall 1♠ with

♠ AKJ54 ♡ KQ962 ◇ J5 ♣ 8

and have everyone pass when partner holds either of these example hands:

♠ 8 ♡ A1075 ◇ 985 ♣ A9643

♠ 3 ♡ A1075 ◇ 985 ♣ J9643

Whether we get to game or play a partscore, I much prefer to play in hearts.

Over the Michaels bid partner should invite game when he has a fit and a few useful cards, like aces and major-suit honors. The first hand above is easily worth a game try. Getting back to the Michaels bidder's problems, with

♠ AKJ54 ♡ KQ962 ◇ J5 ♣ 8

he would pass a minimum response, but would raise partner's major-suit response with

♠ AKJ54 ♡ AQ1082 ◇ J5 ♣ 8

and would raise all the way to game with the king-jack of hearts in place of the queen. Occasionally partner will have two small in both majors and some useless queens and jacks in the minors, in which case you will get a bad result, but I think playing continuous ranges and assuming partner has at least three-card support for one of your suits gains in the long run. Also partner can draw a negative inference when you overcall spades and bid hearts next time — you have at least one more spade than hearts and you may be 6-4. If you had equal length in the majors and were strong enough to bid again without encouragement, you would have used Michaels.

The right shape

Ideally, Michaels over a minor shows at least 5-5 in the majors. However, as always it doesn't pay to follow rigid rules which prevent you from trusting your judgment. Suppose RHO bids 1♢ and you hold

♠ A K J 8 ♡ Q 9 7 5 4 ♢ K 8 7 ♣ 3

If you overcall 1♡, there is a very good chance that you will miss a spade fit. Even if the bidding is kept open by somebody, you aren't strong enough to rebid spades and force the partnership to the three-level if partner has a preference for hearts. Meanwhile, a takeout double is extremely risky with a singleton club, so I think a 2♢ bid is the least of evils. Since there is more reason to bid Michaels with four good spades and five hearts than when your spades are longer, many people play that Michaels practically guarantees five hearts, but not necessarily five spades.

Then you are dealt a hand like this:

♠ A K J 8 ♡ A Q 10 6 ♢ K 9 8 5 ♣ 6

What would you do if your RHO opened 1♢? I think you should bid 2♢ and give partner a single raise when he bids a major. Partner will have a hand like one of these

♠ Q 6 4 2 ♡ K 8 ♢ 7 4 ♣ J 8 7 5 4

♠ 10 7 6 4 3 ♡ K 8 ♢ Q 7 ♣ Q 8 7 4

more often than this:

♠ 6 4 2 ♡ 7 3 ♢ J 4 2 ♣ Q 5 4 3 2

Partner may even bid and make game on a 4-3 major suit fit!

Michaels over majors

While almost everyone plays Michaels over the minors, there is a difference of opinion as to whether it should be played over a major-suit opening (if you do, 1♠-2♠ shows hearts and a minor and 1♡-2♡ shows spades and a minor). Some players prefer to play 'top and bottom', where the cuebid always shows clubs plus the other major. The advantage of 'top and bottom' is that you know immediately what partner's minor suit is, and you can tell how well the hands fit. The advantage of Michaels is that it should come up approximately twice as often as 'top and bottom'. Incidentally, can you guess why 'top and bottom' is chosen in preference to 'top and middle' or the 'two higher suits'? Suppose RHO opens 1♠ and you hold

♠ 4 ♡ KQ97 ◇ AQJ743 ♣ Q6

You make a takeout double because, if partner responds 2♣, you can bid 2◇. This is called an 'equal-level conversion' and it does not guarantee more high-card strength than a minimum takeout double when you convert to diamonds. You still need extra values to bid a major or raise the level of bidding after doubling. But now think about this hand after a 1♠ opening:

♠ 4 ♡ KQ97 ◇ Q6 ♣ AQJ743

A double followed by conversion of a 2◇ response to 3♣ conventionally shows at least something like

♠ 42 ♡ K98 ◇ AQ ♣ AKJ973

opposite which partner doesn't need much to bid 3NT with a spade stopper and a club fit. So there is no satisfactory way to show your heart suit with

♠ 4 ♡ KQ97 ◇ Q6 ♣ AQJ743

unless you are playing either 'top and bottom' or Michaels. And you will notice that you only require four hearts to make this bid. (Warning! You had better discuss this with your partner. Some misguided players — probably 90% of the population — think you need five hearts.)

You are allowed to have five mediocre hearts — with a *good* five-card heart suit you should simply overcall hearts. (Warning: remember, this is my recommendation, but most players play differently.) And you should never make a two-suited bid showing a major and a minor below the 3NT level when your major is six long. I once kibitzed a player who bid 2♡ over 1♡ with

♠ AK10954 ♡ 7 ◇ J ♣ KJ643

and his partner had:

♠ J6 ♡ Q1053 ◇ A987 ♣ AQ9

How could she possibly guess the best game was 4♠, not 3NT (let alone that 6♣ or even 6♠ are not the worst contracts the world has ever seen)? If he had one more club and fewer spades, 3NT would be the spot.

However, whether you play Michaels or 'top and bottom', the minor suit should be good enough and the hand should be good enough so that you can reasonably expect to take nine tricks in the minor.

♠ AJ96 ♡ K8 ◇ 7 ♣ K87642

Here the club suit is far too weak to bid 2♡ over 1♡, so you should simply overcall 1♠. You don't have quite the same luxury when the opening bid is 1♠ and you have four hearts.

Bidding over weak twos

Leaping Michaels is a popular way to show a strong two-suiter over a weak two in a major. Suppose RHO bids 2♠ (weak) and you hold one of these hands:

♠ K6 ♡ AQJ95 ◇ KQJ83 ♣ J

♠ 7 ♡ KJ965 ◇ 8 ♣ AKJ1064

If you are playing Leaping Michaels, you bid 4◇ with the first hand and 4♣ with the second, showing the suit bid plus at least five of the unbid major. I have no strong feelings either for or against these bids. They give up invitational bids with a one-suited minor, and it is hard for partner to tell when to return to the major suit with two-card support. If partner shows diamonds and hearts, and you have

♠ KQ6 ♡ Q7 ◇ J65 ♣ K8753

4♡ might be easier to make than 5◇ since there could be three tricks off the top, and your strength in the side suits may prevent the opponents from shortening partner's trump suit. With

♠ 8754 ♡ Q7 ◇ K65 ♣ A754

you may prefer to play five of the minor since you are unlikely to have three top losers and don't want to lose control if your trump suit breaks badly. You often have a difficult decision since the Leaping Michaels bidder's strength may vary considerably — either of these hands qualify:

♠ 8 ♡ K9875 ◇ A ♣ A109852

♠ — ♡ AKJ98 ◇ K7 ♣ AKJ754

On the other hand, if you are not playing Leaping Michaels, what do you do with these hands? One possibility is to use the cuebid to show a two-suiter, but this gets complicated. After 2♠- 3♠, showing a two-suiter, does partner bid his cheapest three-card suit or his longest suit? After

WEST	NORTH	EAST	SOUTH
2♠	3♠	pass	?

should four of a minor be forcing if it hits the cuebidder's suit? And how can you afford to jump to show extra values when you don't know what your partner's suits are? Those who play Leaping Michaels treat the cuebid as asking partner to bid notrump with a stopper — presumably the cuebidder has a long, solid minor.

Responses to Two-Suited Overcalls

Mark Bartusek, a frequent partner of mine, has developed a method of responding to Michaels over a minor (which also works well in response to an overcall of 1NT that promises the majors). These responses are very good, and fairly easy to remember, since they follow the same pattern in both situations. For simplicity, assume in each case the overcall to show both majors is 2♣. If so, the responses go as follows:

2♢	natural, showing, diamonds
2♡ or 2♠	weak and natural
2NT	invitational in both majors (usually with three of each), and asking partner to describe his hand further
3♣	invitational in hearts with at least two spades
3♢	invitational in spades with at least two hearts
3♡ or 3♠	invitational with a singleton in the other major

Over the 2NT bid, partner bids:

3♣	bad hand
3♢	medium hand with equal length in the majors
3♡ or 3♠	medium hand with greater length in the major bid
4♣ or 4♢	strong hand with shortness in the minor bid and an interest in slam if partner has no wasted values

Playing this system of responses, suppose you bid Michaels with

♠ Q 10 8 7 5 ♡ A K J 8 7 ♢ K 3 ♣ 5

and partner bids 3♡. Now you like your hand because partner is short in spades. If he bids 3♠, however, you won't like your hand because he is short in hearts, and you have too much wasted strength. If he bids 3♣ or 3♢, you have a close decision, but would probably jump to game.

If the opponents compete, this is Mark's recommendation:

WEST	**NORTH**	**EAST**	**SOUTH**
1♣	2♣	3♣	?

Here, 3♢ is invitational in one of the majors; if East had bid 3♢ instead of 3♣, double would be invitational in one of the majors:

WEST	**NORTH**	**EAST**	**SOUTH**
1♢	2♢	3♣	?

Again, 3♢ is invitational in one of the majors.

WEST	**NORTH**	**EAST**	**SOUTH**
1♢	2♢	3♢	?

In this auction, double is invitational in one of the majors.

How does the Michaels bidder know what to do in these sequences when he doesn't know which major you have? Suppose he has:

♠ AKQ74 ♡ J7543 ◇ J ♣ Q8

He would like to accept the invitation if your suit is spades or reject it if your suit is hearts. So he bids 3♡, saying, 'If your suit is hearts, I'm too weak to accept.' But if you now return to spades, he raises to game. With

♠ J7543 ♡ AKQ74 ◇ J ♣ Q8

partner bids 3♠, saying, 'If your suit is spades, I reject the invitation, but if it is hearts, we belong in game.' With a hand worth acceptance in either major, he bids 3NT (which has an added advantage of making the hand which has shown its distribution the dummy, creating greater problems for the defenders).

This idea of showing an invitation in either of two suits, when there has been no chance to agree upon the suit below the invitational level, can be applied in many other situations.

WEST	NORTH	EAST	SOUTH
1♠	2♠	pass	?

♠ J76 ♡ Q974 ◇ K873 ♣ Q7

Playing 'top and bottom', what would you bid here? The king of diamonds is a dubious value since partner has at least ten cards in hearts and clubs but your four-card heart suit and two key queens might be enough if partner holds one of these hands:

♠ 98 ♡ AKJ2 ◇ J ♣ AJ10953

♠ A ♡ J8653 ◇ J ♣ AK9842

Besides, the king of diamonds might be worth a trick. So do you bid 3♡ or 4♡? There ought to be some middle ground, allowing you to invite game without actually bidding it. Since, when partner shows at least ten cards in two suits, it is very unlikely that you would want to play in the fourth suit, it makes sense to treat 3◇ as an invitational bid in hearts. With an invitational hand in clubs, you can bid 4♣.

Another possibility, if you don't mind complications, is to treat 3◇ here as a game try in either suit. Partner can then bid 3♡ to reject a game try in hearts; 4♣ would accept a game try in hearts but reject a game try in clubs; 4◇ would accept a game try in either suit, as would 4♡, but the latter bid would also show a five-card heart suit (in case you have three of both suits and, without some indication from him, intended to play the hand in clubs). Playing this way, an immediate jump to 4♣ over 2♠ would show a singleton or void in hearts, while the slow way would show two or more — similar to the Bartusek method after a 2♣ bid showing the majors.

SUMMARY

1. Don't make a two-suited overcall without good prospects of playing the hand, either to make or as a sacrifice. These bids give away too much information to the opponents about the distribution for you to want to defend the hand.
2. Play a continuous range for hand strength for two-suited overcalls.
3. Ideally, you show 5-5 distribution, but there are exceptions. If you play Michaels over majors, for example, you should only promise four of the other major.
4. Leaping Michaels is a reasonable way to show two-suited hands over the opponents' weak two-bids.
5. Bartusek's system of responses to an overcall showing both majors allows you to make invitational bids despite having little bidding room.

What is your next bid on each of the following hands?

1. *Neither vul., IMPs*

WEST	NORTH	EAST	SOUTH
	pass	1♡	?

♠ J 10 7 6 3 ♡ 9 ◇ A 10 7 4 3 ♣ Q 6

2. *Both vul., IMPs*

WEST	NORTH	EAST	SOUTH
1♡	pass	2♡	?

♠ A 9 7 4 3 ♡ — ◇ Q J 10 7 6 3 ♣ 7 6

3. *Both vul., IMPs*

WEST	NORTH	EAST	SOUTH
1♡	pass	3♡	?

♠ A K 7 4 2 ♡ 8 ◇ A K 4 8 3 ♣ 8 5

4. *Both vul., IMPs*

WEST	NORTH	EAST	SOUTH
		1◇	2◇
3◇	dbl	pass	?

♠ A J 9 8 5 ♡ A J 10 4 3 ◇ 6 ♣ Q 4

5. *Both vul., IMPs*

WEST	NORTH	EAST	SOUTH
		1◇	2◇
3♣	3◇	pass	?

♠ 9 7 6 5 2 ♡ A Q 10 5 3 ◇ J 5 ♣ A

SOLUTIONS

1. Just overcall 1♠. When this hand came up on OKbridge, South bid 2♡ (Michaels), and North, with

   ♠ Q 5 4 ♡ J 6 5 4 2 ◇ Q 5 ♣ A K 8

   bid 4♠, which would require a miracle to make (and there was no miracle). Perhaps North should just have invited, but he thought he had a super-maximum for a passed hand, with an exceptionally good fit no matter which minor his partner had. The problem is that there is less room to invite over a bid showing a two-suiter — plus the fact that partner will expect not only distribution, but more high cards in the two suits. After a 1♠ overcall, South can just cuebid and probably will pass a 2♠ rebid — even if he does raise to 3♠, that would be better than getting to 4♠.

2. There is a wide diversity of opinion among the experts regarding this hand. Some would bid 3♡ to show the two-suiter. Some would bid 3◇ and plan, if possible, to bid spades later, even at the four-level. I think either action is too dangerous, and I would just bid 2♠. If you find a spade fit, you might belong in 4♠, either as a sacrifice or because it could make. It is very unlikely that you belong in 5◇.

3. Again your future, if any, is in spades, and I would bid 3♠. Admittedly, partner is going to have to do some guessing, since you would make the same bid without the king of diamonds. As the problem was originally presented in *Australian Bridge* magazine, East bid 3◇, a Bergen Raise showing four hearts and 7-9 HCP. Over that bid, 3♡ looks best since if partner has 2-3-4-4 distribution, for example, you will get to 4◇ rather than 3♠.

4. This was just a memory-tester. Partner shows an invitational hand in one of the majors, and no matter which major he has, you want to accept. So you should bid 3NT (not 4◇, which would be both a splinter and a slam try).

5. Some players who make a Michaels bid on extremely weak hands would consider this enough to accept, whichever major partner has. Despite the point count, I don't like the singleton ace, two quick losers in the opponents' suit and bad spades. So I don't think the hand is quite strong enough to force to game in both spades and hearts. I would bid 3♠, accepting partner's invitation if he has hearts, and rejecting it if he has spades. Notice that the fact that you would accept a game try in hearts means that you don't have a hopelessly weak hand, so if partner has good spades, he can still raise to 4♠.

CHAPTER 4

Bidding the Opponents' Suit

Bidding the Opponents' Suit Naturally

Not every bid of an opponent's suit is a cuebid. The modern tendency is to open very short minor suits and to bid very weak four-card majors as responder, so sometimes your best trump suit may be a suit the opponents have bid. How can you tell whether a bid of an opponent's suit is natural or a cuebid? Common sense will often give you the answer, but it doesn't hurt to have a few rules and agreements.

So far as common sense is concerned, a bid is probably natural, rather than a cuebid, when the bidder is known to be so weak that he wouldn't be likely to want to make a forcing bid. Similarly, if an opponent has opened a major suit (and therefore probably has at least five), it is unlikely you will want to play in that suit yourself. On the other hand, if they have opened a minor and only *responded* in a major, it is much more likely that you would choose to make a natural bid in that suit. As an example, if RHO opens a major and you jump to three of that major, this is not a natural bid — in fact, conventionally you show a long, solid minor and enough outside strength that you want partner to bid 3NT with a stopper in the opponent's suit. However, if your RHO opens a minor, a jump by you in that minor should be natural and preemptive. Let's consider several specific auctions:

WEST	NORTH	EAST	SOUTH
1♣	pass	1♡	?

What should it mean if you bid 2♣? What should it mean if you bid 2♡? A few players treat both as cuebids — 2♣ might be weaker than 2♡ and would not promise a rebid. But is this really the right way to play it? Surely one cuebid should be enough, perhaps more than enough, and the other bid should be natural. That is the way many players play — a bid of opener's suit is a cuebid, while a bid of responder's suit is natural. But the consensus among the experts is that neither should be a cuebid. A takeout double will suffice with most hands, and with a very distributional hand you can bid a 'sandwich notrump' (a 1NT overcall for takeout when both opponents have bid). This would differentiate

♠ KQ87 ♡ A5 ◇ KJ863 ♣ Q5

(on which you would double) from

♠ KJ875 ♡ 5 ◇ KJ7542 ♣ 8

(on which you would bid 1NT). Of course, with the latter hand, you could just overcall 1♠ in this auction, so the sandwich notrump is more valuable when responder has bid 1♠ and you have hearts and the unbid minor. But the hand you are more likely to hold, and that you wouldn't have a bid for if every bid were a cuebid, is

♠ A85 ♡ KQ10873 ◇ K8 ♣ J9

If you don't bid your hearts now, when will you bid them? If you pass and opener bids 1NT and responder raises to 3NT, do you double for a heart lead? Quite likely, if the contract can be set it will require a heart lead, but there is no assurance that it can be set with any lead. It would have been much better to overcall 2♡, get your heart lead, and enable partner to compete to the three- or four-level with an appropriate hand.

Then again, what if the bidding goes:

WEST	NORTH	EAST	SOUTH
1♣	pass	1♡	pass
2♣	pass	3♣	?

Now do you bid your hearts at the three-level? Or pass and risk being stolen blind when partner holds

♠ K63 ♡ A4 ◇ Q7632 ♣ 752

with which he would have competed to 3♡ if you had bid 2♡ over 1♡? Needless to say, you need a good suit, almost always six long, to bid RHO's suit, since you know it is going to break badly. Consequently, partner can raise safely with a doubleton.

WEST	NORTH	EAST	SOUTH
1♣	1◇	1♡	?

What if partner has overcalled? I think any heart bid by you should still be natural, whether it is 2♡, 3♡, or 4♡ (of course, 3♡ and 4♡ would show stronger hands than 2♡). If you want to cuebid after partner has overcalled, you can bid opener's minor, since once partner has overcalled, it is unlikely that you would want to play in opener's minor, but you might like to play in responder's major. For example:

WEST	NORTH	EAST	SOUTH
1♣	1♡	1♠	?

Here, 2♣ would show a good raise to 2♡ while 3♣ would show a limit raise with at least four hearts, and 2♠ would show spades. Notice the difference between this auction and

WEST	NORTH	EAST	SOUTH
1♣	pass	1♡	2♣

which shows clubs. Only when partner overcalls should a club bid be a cuebid.

Now think about this sequence :

WEST	NORTH	EAST	SOUTH
		1♣	pass
1♠	dbl	pass	2♣

Is 2♣ a cuebid or a natural bid? When both opponents have bid and partner has made a takeout double, you will often have a very weak hand, and therefore you are unlikely to want to cuebid. Pass would be for penalties, so what choice would you have with something like:

♠ 974 ♡ 72 ◇ 97 ♣ Q109752

You have invitational 3◇ or 3♡ bids available (with far different hands, of course), and if you feel that you must cuebid you could bid 2♠. Partner would recognize this as a cuebid since if you thought you could take eight tricks in spades, you would simply pass the double.

How about this auction?

WEST	NORTH	EAST	SOUTH
		1♣	pass
1♠	pass	2♠	pass
pass	dbl	pass	3♣

Partner made a reopening double because he hated to sell out to 2♠; he cannot be especially strong or he would have doubled one round earlier, while you couldn't bid over 1♣. Is it likely that you would be trying for game now? No, you probably have a hand similar to the last one, but with a few more high cards to account for the opponents' failure to bid game. Perhaps you hold:

♠ Q84 ♡ J7 ◇ 85 ♣ K109643

and you are happy that your clubs are as good as they are (you might have had to bid clubs with ♣J76432).

This next auction is perhaps a bit more controversial than the previous ones:

WEST	NORTH	EAST	SOUTH
		1♢	1♡
pass	1♠	pass	2♢

Is your 2♢ bid natural or a cuebid? Probably a majority of players treat it as a cuebid, but I don't think that treatment is logical. Your hand is somewhat limited by the overcall (not strong enough to double and bid your major later). What makes your hand so great when partner merely bids 1♠? The explanation could be that you have a good spade fit, perhaps:

♠ A J 8 ♡ K Q 10 9 4 ♢ A J 5 4 ♣ 8

But you know partner has a good spade suit, so what are you waiting for? Simply raise to 4♠ on this hand, or if you have no courage, raise to 3♠. On the other hand, what would you bid with:

♠ — ♡ A J 8 7 5 ♢ A Q J 8 4 ♣ J 6 5

Would you pass partner in 1♠? Or perhaps bid 1NT? Surely neither alternative is appealing. Some players would have anticipated the problem and passed 1♢ to avoid it, but that appeals to me least of all. You didn't know whether West or partner would have the longer spade suit and you wanted to show your heart suit while you could still do so safely. Consequently, 2♢ here should be natural and it should show a good suit given East's opening bid.

There was a long discussion of this type of sequence in the November, 1998 issue of *The Bridge World*. Problem G in the Master Solvers' Club was:

WEST	NORTH	EAST	SOUTH
		1♣	1♢
pass	1♠	pass	?

♠ — ♡ A 10 9 ♢ K 10 6 5 3 ♣ A J 8 6 3

Twenty panelists voted for 1NT, compared to six who bid 2♣ (although some of the panelists said they preferred 2♣ in their own methods but thought it wasn't part of Bridge World Standard).

Eric Kokish said, 'If two clubs were deemed natural, might you find yourself hamstrung over one spade with a good hand? No, you would not. You could make a value bid in notrump or spades, with a splinter raise as an option. You could reverse to two hearts, showing a strong, but limited hand, or jump in diamonds. You'd like to have a cuebid available with exactly two spades and about an ace more than a minimum but, in a pinch, you can raise with that. When you have clubs, you're simply out of Schlitz if you can't bid them naturally.'

Kit Woolsey expressed the majority view: 'One notrump. Whether we like it or not, two clubs is a cuebid, not natural...' But why should it be a cuebid? The problem brought out strong feelings on the subject. Ira Rubin said, 'Two clubs. There's nothing in my book that says two clubs is a cuebid. However, if two clubs is a cuebid in your book, then I'll make book that you're a loser . . .'

What do you think this next sequence means?

WEST	NORTH	EAST	SOUTH
		1♠	pass
pass	dbl	2♢	2♠

Should 2♠ be natural or a cuebid? You may be trying to show a spade stopper and a good hand for failing to overcall, but with weakness in diamonds — possibly

♠ KJ84 ♡ J82 ♢ 6 ♣ AJ983

with which you are hoping partner can jump to 3NT (since you will pass 2NT). The general rule when the opponents bid two suits is that you cuebid the one you have strength in to suggest weakness in the other. If partner can't bid notrump, he will bid the cheaper unbid suit with equal length. Alternatively, you might hold

♠ KQ3 ♡ 9853 ♢ K7 ♣ AQ63

and want to find a heart fit if there is one, and otherwise play in 3NT. (You will eventually discover that my reopening doubles have a higher minimum than many people's.) Anyway, there is a legitimate use for a cuebid, and you don't often try to play in opener's five-card major. (Against Bob Hamman and Paul Soloway, who open major suits with four small, you might want to change your system.) In the absence of discussion, partner will assume that bids of opener's majors are cuebids while bids of opener's minor may or may not be natural, depending upon the sequence.

Here's one last auction:

WEST	NORTH	EAST	SOUTH
		1♢	dbl
1♠	dbl	2♢	2♠

Here, partner's double of 1♠ showed spades. It was a penalty double, not a responsive double (see the discussion of responsive doubles in Chapter 9). So if partner showed spades and you implied at least three spades by your takeout double, is there any reason why your spade bid shouldn't be natural? None that I can think of; bidding 3♠ or 4♠ should also be natural (but stronger).

Useful Cuebids

WEST	NORTH	EAST	SOUTH
	1♠	2♢	?

Most experts play that a jump raise by responder in competition (a bid of 3♠ here, for instance) is preemptive. How then do you show a limit raise? The standard method is to cuebid 3♢, which shows a limit raise in spades (or better). Consequently, when opener would accept a limit raise, he should rebid 4♠. If he has a borderline hand, and there is room, he should bid a new suit, which is artificial, asking responder to bid 3♠ with a skimpy limit raise or 4♠ with a good limit raise or a forcing raise. Any new suit bid beyond the 3♠ level is a slam try.

Playing five-card majors, responder does not need four-card support to cuebid. However, the cuebid makes it difficult to play in any contract except spades, and with

♠ J94 ♡ AQ7 ♢ A87 ♣ 10972

I prefer to make a negative double, intending to take a jump preference to spades if partner rebids 2♡, or to raise a 2NT rebid to 3NT, which will be your best game if, for example, partner has:

♠ KQ863 ♡ K83 ♢ Q54 ♣ A6

When opener's side hasn't found a major-suit fit (and frequently, even if it has), and the bidding is below the 3NT level, a cuebid of the opponents' suit (called a Western cuebid) asks partner to bid notrump with a stopper. The logic is obvious: if you had the suit stopped yourself, you would bid notrump trusting partner to produce tricks and stoppers elsewhere. Occasionally, even when you have a stopper, you will cuebid either because you think you may need a double stopper or because, if partner has a stopper, 3NT will play better from his side. For example:

WEST	NORTH	EAST	SOUTH
	1♣	1♠	2♢
pass	3♢	pass	?

♠ A5 ♡ AJ8 ♢ Q108742 ♣ 94

It is unlikely that the diamonds will run without loss, but partner may have a spade stopper (even Qx will be a second stopper if he plays the hand). So you cuebid 3♠ instead of bidding 3NT. Partner should bid 3NT with ♠Qx and an otherwise suitable hand since it may provide a second stopper opposite your actual holding or a combined stopper opposite other holdings (such as Jxx or even 10xx when the jack is with the short spade holding). Even when partner has nothing but small spades, the overcaller may lead small from the ace-king if he has no outside entries, or may cash a high spade from AKJxx(x) then shift to another suit, waiting for his partner to gain the lead and lead through what he believes to be declarer's guarded queen. Also, if partner has something like:

♠ 43 ♡ K65 ◇ AK6 ♣ A7532

he will bid 3♡, giving you another chance to bid 3NT after having expressed doubt by not bidding it immediately.

Whatever the exceptions may be, the general rule is that a cuebid below 3NT asks partner to bid notrump with a stopper — provided the opponents have only bid one suit. If the opponents have bid two suits, you bid the one you have stopped. In the simplest situation

WEST	NORTH	EAST	SOUTH
			1♣
1♠	2♣	2♡	?

♠ KQ8 ♡ 97 ◇ AK7 ♣ AQJ86

♠ 52 ♡ AQ7 ◇ A4 ♣ AK8753

you would bid 2♠ with the first hand and 3♡ with the second.

Suppose an opponent shows two suits without actually bidding them — for example:

WEST	NORTH	EAST	SOUTH
	1◇	2◇[1]	?

1. Michaels.

When responder has a strong enough hand to invite 3NT, he should cuebid the major he has stopped. If opener rebids 2NT, he shows a stopper in the other major with a minimum hand. Now if responder has only eleven points he can pass.

Should you bid in similar fashion here?

WEST	NORTH	EAST	SOUTH
	1♠	2NT	?

No, because 3NT is no longer the most likely game. Game in either major is a strong possibility. Most experts play a convention called 'Unusual over Unusual', where bidding three of a minor promises limit raise values or better in one of the majors. Bidding three of partner's major over 2NT is just competitive, while three of the unbid major shows a good suit, but is non-forcing. There are two ways to play this convention, but the simpler is that 3♣ always shows hearts and 3◇ shows spades. The way I prefer is to play that 3♣ always shows the unbid major and 3◇ always shows a limit raise of partner's major. That gives you more bidding room when you most need it. For example, if you hold

♠ AJ9542 ♡ K4 ◇ KJ7 ♣ 102

you are too strong for a non-forcing 3♠ bid after:

WEST	NORTH	EAST	SOUTH
	1♡	2NT	?

so you bid 3♣. Now, with:

♠ 6 ♡ AJ753 ◇ 863 ♣ AK94

partner should bid 3◇ to deny spade support, a good heart suit, or stoppers in both minors, and you would bid 3♡ to offer a choice of contracts. No game looks very good with this misfit, but hearts are better than spades. Partner (opener) could still bid 3♠ over 3♡ with

♠ 108 ♡ A10763 ◇ AQ8 ♣ Q94

and you would choose a spade contract. With

♠ 6 ♡ AQ10875 ◇ A54 ♣ Q87

partner would rebid 3♡ over 3♣, and you would definitely arrive in the superior contract. So you can see the advantage of having extra bidding room.

Control-Showing Cuebids

Beyond the 3NT level, a cuebid implies slam interest. The first cuebid (not necessarily in the opponents' suit) should show length so that partner can evaluate his hand. Consequently, when there is sufficient bidding room to show control of the opponents' suit later, failure to cuebid does not deny a control. But if you are at such a high level that partner has to bid a slam or not bid a slam, failure to cuebid the opponents' suit does deny a control, even a second-round control.

How would you bid the following hand?

WEST	NORTH	EAST	SOUTH
			1♠
pass	3♠	4♡	?

♠ KQ875 ♡ 6 ◇ AQ104 ♣ AQ8

If you cuebid 5♣ or 5◇, partner will be worried about losing the first two heart tricks. Meanwhile Blackwood is no help — you could be missing an ace and still be cold for slam, but you need to know that partner has the right stuff. You should bid 5♡, which says, 'I have a control in hearts, so look at the rest of your hand to see whether it is a good hand for slam.' (You wouldn't risk bidding at the five-level with no control in either minor suit.) Surely partner will now bid on with:

♠ A932 ♡ 83 ◇ K62 ♣ K643

and perhaps even with

♠ A9432 ♡ 3 ◇ J62 ♣ KJ43

but definitely not with

♠ AJ932 ♡ K83 ◇ 2 ♣ 7643

since he now knows the ♡K is worthless.

Perhaps this is the time and place to state what should be an obvious exception to my comment that failure to cuebid the opponents' suit at a high level denies a control. The following hand was in the August 1999 *ACBL Bulletin.* You are vulnerable and the opponents are not. The bidding commences:

WEST	NORTH	EAST	SOUTH
	1♢	3♠	?

♠ AJ52 ♡ AKJ7632 ♢ K ♣ J

I think you should bid 5♡ here. I don't contend that I have the only right answer, since the experts' votes were almost evenly distributed among five choices: 4♡, 4NT, 5♡, 6♡, and double. However, some of the comments bothered me. One panelist said, '5♡ asks for spade control and I have one...' (meaning he didn't need one from partner), so he eliminated 5♡ from consideration. If a suit were agreed upon, that would be true. But in a crowded auction like this you can't afford to cuebid (in this case, by bidding 4♠) when you plan to play the hand in a suit that has never been bid (partner might jump to 6♢).

When there is no room, 5♡ simply invites 6♡, and partner must look at his whole hand, including his heart holding. Suppose you bid 5♡. It is quite likely that partner does have a spade control, either a singleton or void. But if he had one of these hands:

♠ 6 ♡ 4 ♢ AQ8732 ♣ KQ943

♠ KQ ♡ — ♢ QJ7532 ♣ KQ643

do you really think he should bid 6♡, simply because he has second-round spade control? (On the first hand, of course, he would happily bid 6♢ if you cuebid 4♠, promising diamond support.) Similarly, with

♠ 64 ♡ Q4 ♢ AQ732 ♣ AQ43

should he pass, playing you for two losers in spades and no losers elsewhere? That would give you

♠ 52 ♡ AKJ109876532 ♢ — ♣ —

— a rather unusual hand.

Likewise, if the bidding has gone:

WEST	NORTH	EAST	SOUTH
	1♣	4♡	?

♠ AQ987542 ♡ A7 ♢ K4 ♣ 9

I can't imagine bidding anything other than 5♠. A 5♡ cuebid here would show club support.

SUMMARY

1. You often want to bid an opponent's suit naturally, especially a major in which they have responded, not opened.
2. The logic of the auction will tell when a bid of the opponent's suit is natural rather than a cuebid.
3. Low-level cuebids are often 'Western', asking for a notrump stopper. If two suits have been bid by the opponents, then bidding one of them shows a stopper there.
4. When there is sufficient room to show control of the opponents' suit later, failure to cuebid does not deny a control. But if you are at such a high level that partner has to bid a slam or not bid a slam, failure to cuebid the opponents' suit does deny a control.

What is your next bid with each of the following hands?

1.

WEST	NORTH	EAST	SOUTH
1♣	pass	1♡	?

♠ 5 ♡ K Q 10 9 7 4 ♢ A J 10 6 ♣ A 5

2.

WEST	NORTH	EAST	SOUTH
1♢	1♡	pass	1♠
pass	2♢	pass	?

♠ A Q 10 8 4 ♡ 9 5 ♢ 7 5 ♣ Q 10 7 6

3.

WEST	NORTH	EAST	SOUTH
			1♠
pass	3♠	3NT	?

♠ A Q 7 6 5 4 ♡ A 7 ♢ Q J 10 7 3 ♣ —

4.

WEST	NORTH	EAST	SOUTH
			1♣
1♡	2♣	2♢	?

♠ A J ♡ K 8 ♢ J 7 ♣ A K J 10 6 5 2

SOLUTIONS

1. Bid 3♡. Partner doesn't need much for you to make game — just ♡Jx and ◇KQ should be enough, and you would be on a finesse for game opposite even less. Besides, the opponents probably have an eight-card spade fit, and you are unlikely to buy the hand for 2♡.

2. Pass. Since partner bid only two diamonds it is unlikely that you have game, so you should resist the temptation to bid notrump. Just as I urged you in the first chapter to avoid taking a preference to partner's major when he overcalls two suits, I think you should do the same here. Partner's diamonds should be at least as long and as good as his hearts. He might hold, for example:

   ♠ 5 ♡ A Q J 7 ◇ A Q 10 9 7 3 ♣ J 4

3. I suppose you should ask West what he thinks 3NT means, but my guess is that East has clubs and hearts. Surely, 3NT isn't natural. Rather than waste your time with a double, I think you should bid 4◇. That way, if partner has a close decision later in the auction, he will evaluate diamond honors highly and tend to discount honors in hearts and clubs.

4. You could bid 2♡ to show a heart stopper so that partner could bid notrump with a diamond stopper. But East would probably lead a heart through your king. My inclination would be to bid 3NT, hoping either that West will make the wrong lead or that partner has a little help in diamonds. This is not the type of hand that figures to make exactly eight tricks in notrump. Either you will make 3NT or you will go down several tricks. To account for the bidding, including partner's failure to make a negative double, the opponents probably have a 4-4 spade fit. Perhaps, after a confident 3NT bid by you, they will try the surprise lead of a spade!

The Law of Total Tricks

How the Law Works

Every serious bridge player should read Larry Cohen's *To Bid Or Not To Bid* and its sequel, *Following The Law*. I cannot cover in a few pages all of the material contained in those books, but since so many decisions in competitive bidding are affected by the Law of Total Tricks, I'll give you a brief synopsis.

According to the Law, the total number of tricks available to the two sides on any deal is equal to the total number of trumps, assuming each side plays in its best fit. However, that does not mean that each side can take the same number of tricks as it has trumps or that the side with the greater number of trumps can take the greater number of tricks. Let us look at an exaggerated example:

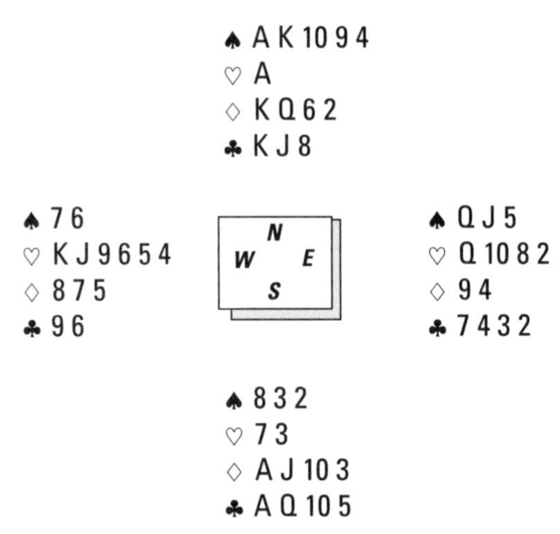

Your East-West partnership holds ten hearts and the opponents hold eight spades (as well as eight diamonds). If the Law is accurate, there should be a total of eighteen tricks. It turns out that there are, but despite your having more trumps than the opponents, they can take twelve tricks if they play the hand in either spades or diamonds, and you can take only six tricks in hearts.

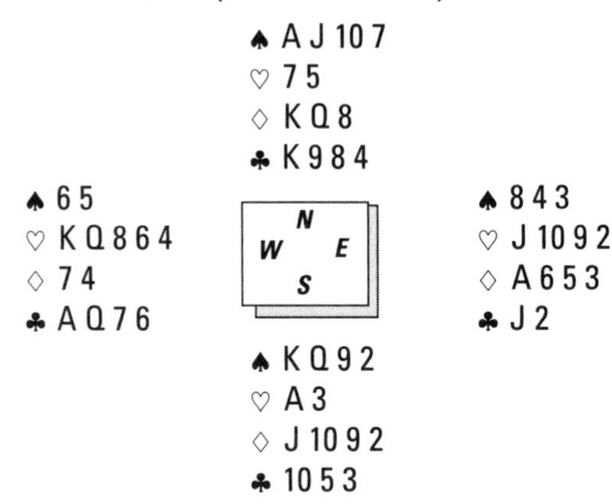

On this deal, North-South have eight of their longest suit, spades, and East-West have nine of their longest suit, hearts. The total number of tricks each side can make in its best contract should be 8+9=17. Let's see whether that is true. North-South can take nine tricks in spades, losing a heart, a diamond, and two clubs; meanwhile East-West can take eight tricks in hearts, so the Law is quite accurate this time. Now switch North-South's minor-suit holdings, so the hand looks like this:

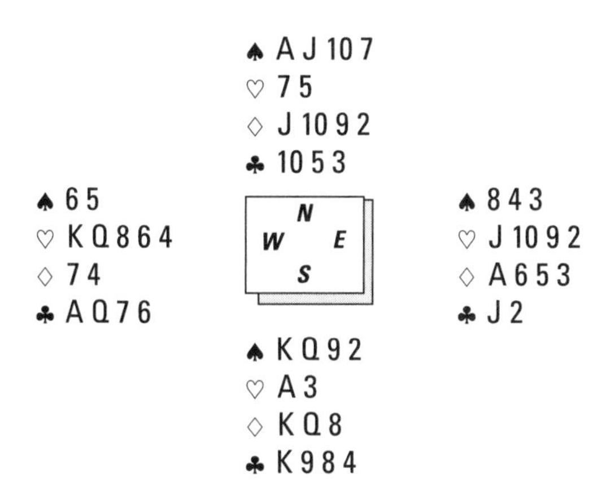

With the club finesse working, East-West can take nine tricks in hearts, so North-South should only be able to take eight tricks in spades; but that is not quite true. North-South can still hold their club losers to two unless the defenders get a club ruff. If West leads a diamond to the ace to get a club lead through, East will get his ruff, but the defenders will lose their heart trick. So you can see that the Law does not always attain the predicted result (just as twenty-six points do not guarantee making a game). However, when the hands are fairly balanced, the Law frequently gives you an answer right on the button, and if it is off one trick occasionally because of entry problems or timing, it is still a very good guide.

When one or more hands contain a singleton or void, however, the Law is less accurate:

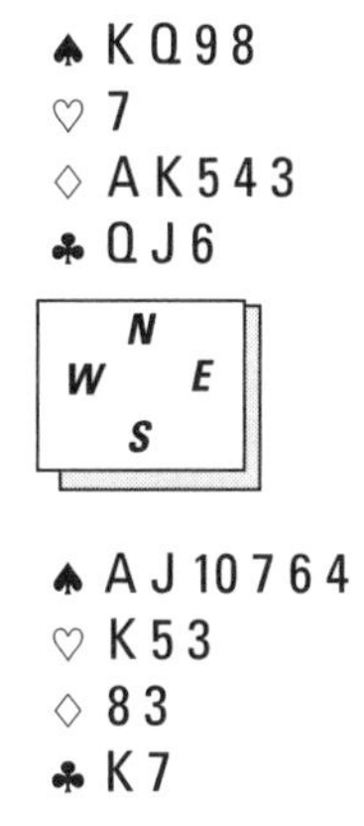

Here you have ten spades, while the opponents have nine hearts, and so according to the Law there will be nineteen total tricks. Since you have eleven tricks in spades, the opponents should therefore have eight tricks in hearts. But their actual trick total will vary depending upon whether spades split 2-1 or 3-0, and also on whether their diamonds are 3-3 or 4-2 (in the former case you can get a ruff). And who has the ace of hearts? If West has it, the opponents have no heart losers (other than a possible ruff); if East has it, you are entitled to a trump trick. If you had a doubleton heart in each hand, then finding the ace favorably located would mean one more trick for you, one fewer for them. However, with a singleton heart and no worthwhile discard, the location of the ace of hearts is immaterial to you in the play of a spade contract, but very important to the opponents if they play the hand. As you can see from this example, you shouldn't place undue reliance on the Law when the hands are unbalanced.

Larry Cohen also talks about various adjustment factors — the presence of double fits, 'pure' hands (with no wasted strength in the opponents' suits) and very long suits all require you to make upward adjustments to the trick total. This hand is an extreme example:

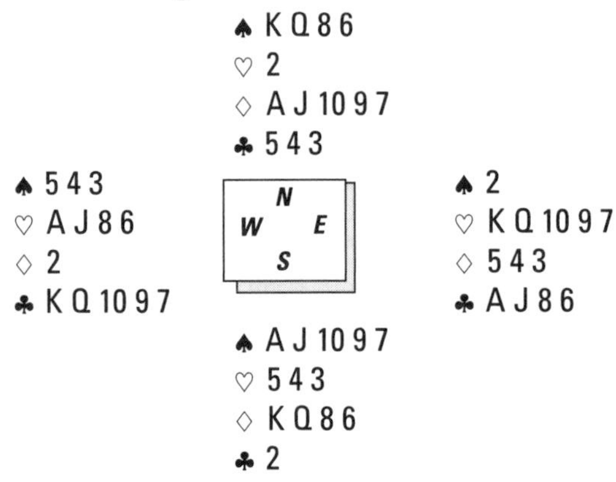

The Law (without adjustments) says there should be a total of eighteen tricks. Actually there are twenty-two tricks since both sides can make eleven tricks in either of two suits!

Weak suits and secondary honors in the opponents' suits require downward, or negative, adjustments to the trick total. If the opponents are bidding hearts vigorously and you hold ♡QJ98, you probably have two heart tricks on defense, but if partner plays the hand in spades, your heart holding will be completely useless opposite his singleton or void. Larry would make a negative adjustment of two tricks with that holding. (Of course, the lower the total number of tricks available on a hand, the more you should favor deciding to defend.)

Using the Law

The Law, while still an empirical tool, is nevertheless at least as reliable as point count. Holdings of K85 of partner's suit and QJ8 of the opponents' suit both count three points. If partner were to play the hand, you would much prefer the former holding; if you end up defending, you prefer the latter holding. Just as experience has taught you to make this kind of adjustment in evaluating any hand based on point count, experience will tell you when to make adjustments in applying the Law.

You have probably spotted one difficulty, though: how can you tell how many trumps each side has? You have to make certain assumptions and approximations. Assume that an overcall at the one-level shows a five-card suit (usually it does, even with me), and that a weak two-bid shows a six-card suit. A weak jump overcall at the two-level shows a six-card suit; at the three-level it shows a seven-card suit (against a very frisky pair of bidders, you may revise these estimates downward by half a card.) Partner's opening bid in a major shows five (with a longer suit, he will often rebid it, whatever action you take). His club opening shows four; his diamond opening shows 4½.

This last number brings us to another point: when either of two possible distributions seems equally probable, you can use fractions, intending to round off the final result. Suppose partner, playing five-card majors, opens 1♡ and RHO overcalls 2♢. You first assume partner has five hearts and RHO has 5½ diamonds. If you have four diamonds, the total number of diamonds between you and RHO is 9½. Of the remaining 3½ diamonds, give LHO two and partner 1½ (partner's length in hearts leaves less room for other cards in his hand). Now, if you have two of partner's suit, you assume your side has seven hearts to the opponents' 7½ diamonds. The total on the hand, then, is 14½ tricks. Roughly half the time there will be fourteen total tricks, and half the time there will be fifteen tricks, usually when RHO has six diamonds rather than five. If you have ♢Axxx or ♢xxxx with a doubleton honor is spades, all of your points are 'working', and you can make an upward adjustment to at least fifteen, and perhaps sixteen total tricks. If you hold ♢QJ97, you should make a substantial downward adjustment to thirteen tricks. Remember that the lower the trick total, the more you want to defend.

Larry mentions one more formula in applying the Law. Suppose the opponents have overcalled and you are trying to decide whether to penalize them or bid notrump. The total number of tricks available is supposed to be seven plus the opponents' combined trump length. This formula works out rather well when neither you nor partner has a long, running suit:

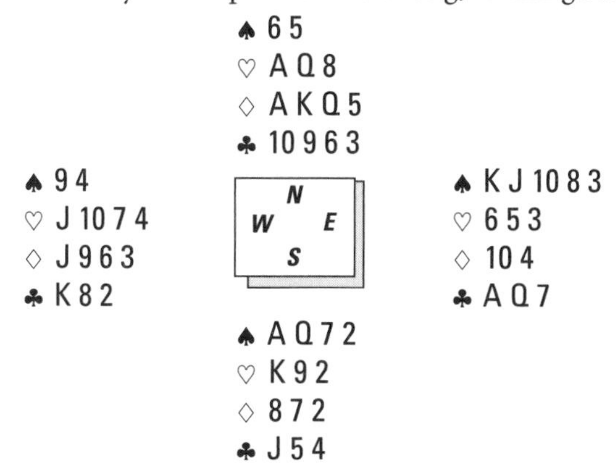

Here the total number of tricks should be fourteen (7 + 7 spades), and it is.

East-West can take six tricks in spades and North-South can take eight tricks in notrump. This formula, however, is not as reliable as other aspects of the Law. If the spades were 6-1 or if North's diamonds were ♢AKQ653, the total tricks would be considerably different, one reason being that the formula does not take into consideration the suit lengths of the notrump bidders. Even so, the formula still helps in close situations:

WEST	NORTH	EAST	SOUTH
3♢	dbl	pass	?

♠ Q 8 7 ♡ K 7 5 ♢ J 10 6 4 ♣ K 4 2

There is no reason to believe that partner has a long suit; in fact, his most typical distributions are 4-4-1-4 and 4-4-2-3. Let's be slightly pessimistic and figure partner for a singleton diamond, giving the opponents eight diamonds: the total tricks will be fifteen. The fact that the diamonds are probably 7-1 rather than 5-3 or 6-2 calls for a positive adjustment; the fact that you have ♢J1064 rather than ♢A764 or ♢7642 requires a negative adjustment, and the two adjustments cancel each other out. So if you can take nine tricks at notrump, the opponents can only take six tricks in diamonds.

If you *knew* you could take nine tricks in notrump, you might or might not bid 3NT, depending upon vulnerability; but suppose you could take only eight tricks at notrump and they could take seven tricks in diamonds? Now you would definitely do better to defend. If you could take ten tricks at notrump and they could take only five tricks in diamonds, you would still get a better result by defending. Remember, sometimes partner has a doubleton diamond or a singleton honor. What if partner has a diamond void? That will throw your calculations off, perhaps reducing your anticipated two- or three-trick set to one trick, and occasionally even allowing the opponents to make it. But voids occur less frequently than singletons and doubletons, and you have to play the percentages.

Let's keep the same bidding but change your hand:

WEST	NORTH	EAST	SOUTH
3♢	dbl	pass	?

♠ 6 4 ♡ K 6 3 ♢ Q 9 8 5 ♣ A 7 6 2

Now another alternative is to bid 4♣ or 5♣. However, there is no assurance that partner has four clubs. Even if he does, that means you only have a total of eight clubs and the opponents probably have a total of eight diamonds. If so, the trick total is sixteen, which means that if you can score 130 in clubs, the opponents are going down three in 3♢. A more likely result is down one in clubs your way and down two in diamonds their way. I think this hand is a clear-cut pass, although I still prefer trying 3NT to bidding any number of clubs. Although the last formula gives you the same answer whether you have 2-3-4-4 or 2-2-4-5 distribution, I think a 3NT bid is reasonable with:

♠ 6 4 ♡ J 7 ◇ Q 9 8 5 ♣ A J 10 8 6

Now you have a source of tricks. Give partner a typical double

♠ A K 8 3 ♡ A 10 4 2 ◇ 6 ♣ K 9 8 5

and you will see what I mean.

Competitive Decisions Based on the Law

The Law is helpful in deciding what to do over an opponent's advance sacrifice.

♠ A 6 5 ♡ K 9 8 6 2 ◇ 8 7 ♣ K J 4

WEST	NORTH	EAST	SOUTH
3◇	dbl	5◇	?

What call should you make? It is tempting to place partner with perfect cards

♠ K Q 8 4 ♡ A Q 7 3 ◇ 6 ♣ A 10 7 5

in which case you are cold for 5♡ and might make six. But partner doesn't always hold four hearts. He might easily hold one of these hands for his double:

♠ K Q J 5 ♡ Q 5 4 ◇ 6 ♣ A Q 7 6 3

♠ K Q 8 7 ♡ A 7 5 ◇ 5 3 ♣ A Q 8 6

Also, when an opponent has a long suit as indicated by his preempt, your suits may break very badly. While you might make 5♡, it is unlikely the opponents can win anything but their trump tricks if they play the hand. Applying the Law, you have 8¾ hearts and the opponents have 9¾ diamonds, for a total of 18½ tricks. Therefore, if you can take eleven tricks in hearts, the opponents can take only 7½ tricks in diamonds. At matchpoints, vulnerable against not, it might be right to bid 5♡. At any other vulnerability, or with IMP scoring, you should double.

If you 'follow the Law', you will tend to defend more often than you have been doing in the past, but occasionally the Law will persuade you to bid more. For example, with both sides vulnerable here:

WEST	NORTH	EAST	SOUTH
3◇	dbl	4◇	?

♠ J 9 8 6 5 3 ♡ Q 8 5 ◇ 8 7 5 ♣ 6

What action do you take? Your natural reaction is probably to pass. A game seems unlikely when your hand is so weak, and you don't want to sacrifice against a mere partscore. Before making the 'instinctive' bid, though, give partner a typical 4-4-1-4 hand and see what the Law tells you. The opponents have nine diamonds and you have ten spades, for a total of nineteen tricks. Since all of your points are working, with nothing wasted in diamonds, the total tricks may well be as high as twenty. If the opponents can take ten tricks in diamonds, you should be able to take ten tricks in spades. Not convinced yet? Then give partner a typical hand — not an exceptionally good fit, but just a normal fit:

♠ AK72 ♡ A1064 ◇ 9 ♣ K985

You are cold for 4♠ if you have no trump loser and can hold your heart losers to one. On defense, however, you probably have one spade trick and either a club and a heart or two heart tricks. A typical result would be 4◇, making four, or 4♠, making four. Exchange partner's king of spades for the king of hearts, and you still belong in 4♠. If you knew for sure that partner had only three spades, you would pass, but a three-card holding is not necessarily fatal

♠ A72 ♡ AK64 ◇ 9 ♣ K9854

gives you an adequate play for 4♠, with still no assurance that you could defeat 4◇.

There is a shortcut in applying the Law. When your side has nine trumps you can usually bid to the three-level. When you have ten trumps, you can usually bid to the four-level. When you have a six-card suit, partner's fair share of the remaining cards is 2⅓, giving you a total of 8+, so the two-level should be safe. When you have a seven-card suit and partner has his fair share of two trumps, the total is nine, and the three-level should be safe. Remember, this is just a shortcut — it assumes that partner will have his share of the remaining cards, and it doesn't take into account adjustment factors. Using this shortcut, you might bid the same way with J765432 as with QJ109832, which intuition tells you must be wrong.

Low-Level Penalty Decisions

If you apply the Law only to competitive decisions on individual hands, you are not obtaining the full benefit of the Law. You should use it to determine when it is likely that you can penalize the opponents and when it is not, then build your system around your conclusions. For example, suppose the bidding goes

WEST	NORTH	EAST	SOUTH
	1♡	1♠	?

and you are wondering whether to try to defend 1♠ doubled. Since an immediate double would be negative, if you want to defend you have to pass and hope partner will reopen with a double, which you will leave in. Sometimes he won't double when you want him to, but let's assume for the moment that he will always double with a singleton in the opponent's suit. When should you pass the overcall, hoping to pass partner's reopening double? Obviously, you need good spades. With ♠J8653 you can't hope to draw declarer's trumps, even with one lead through declarer's hand from partner, so the overcaller will usually score five trump tricks and another trick or two (if he has nothing on the side, you can surely make a game or even a slam your way).

Now suppose you have good spades but you also have three hearts. There is a general rule that you don't want to defend doubled contracts unless you expect a two-trick set. Sometimes the double enables declarer to play double dummy and endplay you in trumps. Sometimes your opening lead costs a trick, or all the opponents' finesses work, or, heaven forbid, partner misdefends. So you want a margin of safety. If you don't double unless you expect to set the contract two tricks, you will probably always set it one, even with bad luck. However, when you have five spades, and partner makes a reopening double with a singleton, that gives the opponents seven spades to your side's eight hearts, and there should be a total of fifteen tricks. If you can set the contract two tricks by holding the opponents to five tricks in their spade contract, you can make ten tricks in hearts! To put it another way, even if the double is 'successful', you could lose out by obtaining an insufficient penalty. It almost never pays to defend a doubled contract at the one-level, and seldom at the two-level, when you hold three of partner's major.

It is easy to demonstrate the futility of trying for a penalty when you have a fit for partner's major, but suppose he has opened a minor? When the opponents have eight trumps between them, the least combined length in one of your suits will be seven, and frequently eight, so there should be fifteen or sixteen total tricks. If you can hold the opponents to five tricks in their suit, you should have ten or eleven tricks in your best suit. When you have strength in the opponents' suit, you might also consider playing the hand in notrump. The notrump formula says that the total tricks will be seven plus the opponent's length, which in this case is eight. If you can hold their one-level contract to five tricks, you should have ten tricks in notrump! It looks as though it can almost never pay to try to penalize the opponents at the one-level when you have a fit for partner or when the opponents have eight trumps.

Of course, we know that it is possible to defeat one-level contracts for more than the value of game (or defeat one-level contracts when we can't make game), but that is only true when there are several negative adjustment factors. One hand has to have very good trumps, at least five, with secondary honors and good spot cards, and the other has to have at least one trump to go with his partner's five so that the opponents can't have a combined total of eight. All of these factors lead me to conclusions that differ greatly from those commonly held.

1) *A reopening double should seldom be made with a void. (I'm not the first player to suggest this — Larry Cohen feels the same way.)*

The common belief is that your void is good for the defense because partner probably has more trumps. This is a fallacy because the defense suffers when you can't lead a trump through declarer, and when you have a void, it makes it more likely that the opponents have eight trumps between them. This reluctance to make a reopening double with a void should apply at all levels of bidding. If LHO bids 3♡, which is passed around to you, the percentage bid with

♠ A Q 10 9 7 ♡ — ◇ K Q 7 6 ♣ A 9 3 2

is 3♠ (rather than double). Likewise, if LHO opens 4♡, you should bid 4♠. Yes, I know that partner might hold ♡KJ987, but he is more likely to hold a balanced hand with ♡K975, in which case the penalty will be inadequate to compensate you for your missed game in spades. Partner will make his 'Law' decision based on the assumption that you have at least one heart, and he can't bid spades with a three-card suit (and he may not bid them at the four-level even with a four-card suit).

2) *Opener shouldn't strain to make a reopening double at the one-level with a poor defensive hand or an off-shape hand, just because responder might want to make a penalty pass.*

The odds are about ten to one that responder passed because he was too weak to bid, and not because he wanted to penalize the opponents. Remember, he needs five of the opponent's suit with secondary honors, plus a misfit, to be tempted to try for a penalty, and what are the odds on his having that? When the bidding goes

WEST	NORTH	EAST	SOUTH
			1◇
1♠	pass	pass	?

it is foolish, in my opinion, to double with

♠ 8 7 ♡ J 3 ◇ K Q 9 7 4 ♣ A Q 5 2

(hoping partner will pass rather than bid 2♡) or

♠ 5 ♡ Q J 7 ◇ Q J 7 6 5 4 ♣ K Q J

(hoping that partner won't pass unless he can take five or six tricks by himself).

However, if you have the right distribution as opener (5-4-3-1), you don't need much extra to double because you have two ways to gain. Perhaps partner can pass for penalties, but even if he can't, you might make something your way:

WEST	NORTH	EAST	SOUTH
			1◇
1♠	pass	pass	?

Here it is logical to double with

♠ 6 ♡ A J 5 ◇ A K 8 6 5 ♣ Q 8 5 4

If partner passes, you can contribute some defensive tricks. If he can't pass, it may still be your hand (when he holds:

♠ 9842 ♡ Q7 ◇ 72 ♣ AJ962

for example). Even with the right distribution but a poor defensive hand like

♠ 6 ♡ QJ8 ◇ KQ965 ♣ KJ82

I think it pays to sell out. And with a doubleton spade and a minimum opening such as

♠ 98 ♡ QJ6 ◇ KQ653 ♣ KJ2

I think a reopening double in sickening. You know you can't make anything your way, and the only way your double could gain is if partner has a penalty pass; I don't think you should bet when the odds are 10 to 1 against you.

It seldom pays to defend a doubled contract at the one-level when the opponents have at least eight trumps between them, especially when the bidder is on your left so that your trump holding can be finessed. Consequently, a one-level negative double will almost never be left in. You should be somewhat careful about making negative doubles with no defense at the two-level or higher (because when the opponents have bid partner's second suit, he will usually leave in the double). In the following sequence:

WEST	NORTH	EAST	SOUTH
	1♣	1♡	?

it is all right to double with

♠ Q1085 ♡ 3 ◇ K876543 ♣ J

while if the overcall had been 2♡, a double would be too dangerous — partner would pass with:

♠ 73 ♡ KJ106 ◇ A98 ♣ KQ96

Bergen Raises — The Case Against

Many followers of the Law adopt Bergen Raises of major-suit openings. A 3♣ response to a major shows 7-10 points with four trumps while a 3◇ response shows a limit raise (and a double raise in the major is preemptive). The theory is that when your side has nine trumps, the opponents usually have eight or nine trumps, making a trick total of 17 or 18. So if you are down one at the three-level, the opponents can probably make a three-level contract themselves. Bergen Raises must work well some of the time, or they wouldn't be so popular. However, I don't like them for three reasons.

First, I like strong jump shifts and believe that used properly (which they seldom are, but that's not a subject that belongs here), they help your slam bidding considerably. Second, the opponents can safely double for a lead, knowing that it is almost impossible for you to play there (rather than in your nine-card major fit). They can also draw an inference from their partner's failure to double the artificial response. Third (the main reason) is that I believe they jeopardize your plus with little to gain. Suppose partner opens 1♠ and you hold:

♠ J 7 5 4 ♡ Q 8 7 ◇ A 10 5 4 ♣ J 5

Now suppose you know somehow that partner can take eight tricks in spades and the opponents could take nine tricks in clubs. Does that mean you should bid to the three-level immediately? I don't think so. If the bidding goes

WEST	NORTH	EAST	SOUTH
	1♠	pass	2♠

the opponents will enter the bidding only some of the time. The potential reopener may have a balanced hand or a very weak hand or a hand with which he is afraid to double for fear his partner will bid the wrong suit (perhaps with 4-2-2-5 or 3-2-3-5 distribution, the clubs being queen-fifth). Why risk down one when the opponents may let you play at the two-level? If they reopen, you can always bid 3♠ at that time.

There are, of course, two dangers to passing and then bidding 3♠ in competition. One, it is easier for the opponents to double for penalties when you run into a bad break. Two, they may find a miraculous fit and compete to the four-level, while bidding to the three-level immediately would have shut them out. But I think those two dangers, combined, are remote as compared to the danger of going one down at the three-level when the opponents were going to let partner play at the two-level. After an overcall you were advised to bid to the three-level immediately (most of the time) on the theory that if you couldn't make it, the opponents could make something at the three-level. But that's a very different situation — once the opponents have entered the auction there is a much greater chance of their competing at the three-level than when you and your partner have been the only bidders.

SUMMARY

1. The Law of Total Tricks gives fairly accurate estimates on balanced hands. On unbalanced hands, it is less reliable, even after accounting for 'adjustment factors'.
2. You can make reasonable assumptions from the bidding to estimate the likely number of total tricks available.
3. You can use the Law to help you make 'bid on or defend' decisions in competitive auctions.
4. The Law can also be useful in deciding whether it is going to be worthwhile to try to penalize the opponents at a low level.
5. A reopening double should seldom be made with a void.
6. Opener shouldn't strain to make a reopening double at the one-level with a poor defensive hand or an off-shape hand, just because responder might want to make a penalty pass.
7. Despite the Law, I do not recommend Bergen Raises because a) I prefer strong jump shifts, b) they allow lead-directing doubles, c) they often get you too high unnecessarily.

What is your next bid on each of the following hands?

1. *Both vul., matchpoints*

WEST	NORTH	EAST	SOUTH
		1♠	pass
pass	dbl	pass	?

♠ K J 10 8 ♡ Q 5 4 ♢ J 7 6 ♣ J 9 8

2. *Neither vul., IMPs*

WEST	NORTH	EAST	SOUTH
	1♠	pass	3♠
4♢	4NT	5♢	?

♠ J 10 7 5 ♡ Q J 3 ♢ Q 6 4 ♣ A J 7

3. *Neither vul., IMPs*

WEST	NORTH	EAST	SOUTH
	2NT[1]	3♡	?

1. 20-21 HCP

♠ Q 8 7 ♡ 7 5 2 ♢ A 8 5 3 ♣ 8 7 6

4. *Both vul., IMPs*

WEST	NORTH	EAST	SOUTH
	1♠	pass	2♠
3♣	dbl	pass	?

♠ Q 10 8 5 4 ♡ J 8 3 ♢ Q 9 7 5 ♣ 6

5. *Neither vul., IMPs*

WEST	NORTH	EAST	SOUTH
			1♠
2♢	pass	pass	?

♠ K Q J 8 5 ♡ K Q 10 6 ♢ — ♣ A J 9 8

6. *Neither vul., IMPs*

WEST	NORTH	EAST	SOUTH
		pass	pass
1♡	1NT	3♡	?

♠ K J 8 4 2 ♡ 7 6 3 ♢ A 3 ♣ J 8 4

7. *Both vul., IMPs*

WEST	NORTH	EAST	SOUTH
			1♢
3♡	dbl	pass	?

♠ A Q 4 3 ♡ A 10 9 2 ♢ Q J 8 ♣ 7 6

8. *Both vul., IMPs*

WEST	NORTH	EAST	SOUTH
	1♢	dbl	2♢
2♠	3♣	4♠	?

♠ 8 5 ♡ 9 7 2 ♢ Q 8 7 6 ♣ Q J 10 5

SOLUTIONS

1. Bid 1NT. Since it is matchpoints, it could be right to pass and try for +200, but you cannot be confident of setting the hand, and if you can set it, you might have a game your way. For example, partner might hold

   ♠ 5 ♡ K J 8 3 ◇ K Q 5 3 ♣ Q 7 5 4

   in which case East would surely make his contract, or partner might hold

   ♠ 5 ♡ K J 3 ◇ A K Q 5 3 ♣ A 10 5 4

   in which case declarer is probably down only one while you are cold for 3NT. The opponents hold 7½ spades and your side has at least a seven-card fit. Even if you round down to fourteen total tricks, it is too much of a gamble to assume that you will take seven on defense. Generally you need five good trumps behind the bidder to try for a penalty at the one-level. In the long run, you will do better to bid 1NT.

2. Double! Despite your 11HCP, you don't have a good hand for a slam: no ruffing value, three dubious jacks and a wasted ◇Q. If you give partner 5½ spades and a singleton diamond (to justify his 4NT bid, since he would be unlikely to bid Blackwood with a void), there are 18½ total tricks. For this sequence partner is more likely to have six spades than five, but even so, if you can take twelve tricks, the opponents probably can take seven. If you double, the most likely result is an 800-point set, which could lose 5 IMPs, but will gain 8 IMPs if your opponents fail to bid a slam, or 13-14 IMPs if they bid a slam and don't make it. The four hands might be:

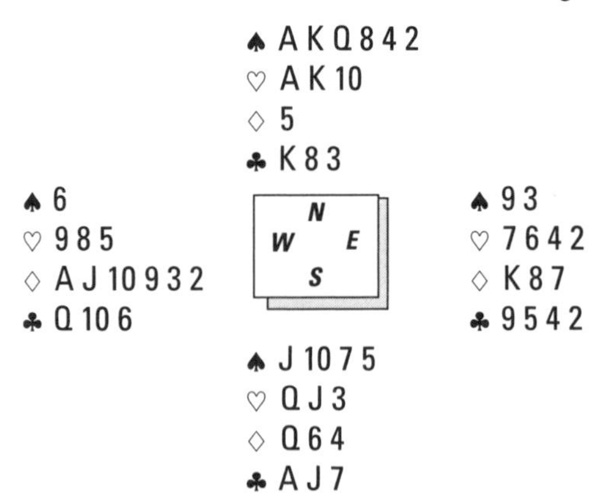

   You may believe that the opponents would not bid so much with these hands, but the evidence is before your eyes. They can't have much more shape than this because they don't have enough diamonds. You may argue that, if East had passed, you would have shown your ace, and partner would have bid a slam which depended upon a finesse, so why should you do something different? The answer is that you hope to gain by East's indiscretion, not merely come out even. Also note that if the club finesse worked because East had the queen, so that partner could make the slam for +980, you could score +1100 on defense! Oh, do you play that a double shows how many aces you have? And that there is no way to penalize the opponents unless your double shows too many aces are missing? If so, I suggest you change your system so that pass is your first ace-showing step.

3. Double. Again you could get the normal result by bidding 3NT, as you would have done if East had passed. Partner should have two or three hearts, so the opponents have 7½ hearts between them. Since East probably has a seven-card suit, you round up to fifteen tricks, which means the opponents can take only six tricks if you can take nine. More important, if they can take seven tricks, you may only take eight! The Law is just a shortcut to visualizing the hands. Give partner a typical hand:

   ♠ A 6 2 ♡ K 9 4 ◇ K J 6 ♣ A K Q 4

   and East, as declarer, has to lose a heart trick since dummy will probably have no hearts or, at most, a singleton. He may never get a spade trick since he can't get to dummy to lead toward his king. And, of course, you are not a cinch to make 3NT. Partner should pull the double if he holds

   ♠ A 6 2 ♡ K 9 ◇ K 7 6 ♣ A K Q J 4

   since his hand is better than normal for offense and worse than normal for defense.

4. Bid 3♠. Your side has ten spades; the opponents probably have eight clubs. There should therefore be a total of eighteen tricks, so you should pull the double. If partner holds

   ♠ A K 9 3 2 ♡ A 6 ◇ K 8 ♣ Q 10 7 2

   he will bid 4♠, expecting you to have at least four spades and shortness in clubs.

5. Bid 3◇! Many players would double because they require a better hand to reopen with a cuebid, but partner needs very little to make game. Hands with a void are great for offense, terrible for defense. If partner holds

   ♠ 9 6 ♡ J 9 8 5 3 ◇ A Q 10 5 ♣ 7 5

he will bid and make 4♡ if you cuebid, or pass for a one-trick set if you double. The cuebid should be made with a void and hands of varying strength — perhaps as few as 13 HCP — and responder's non-jump responses are not forcing. The Law tells you not to defend at the two-level when the opponents have nine diamonds and you have an eight- or nine-card fit somewhere.

6. Double. For the bidding to make sense, West must have opened a four-card heart suit in third position. Partner would be unlikely to overcall 1NT (instead of doubling) with ♡Ax or ♡Kx and three or four spades. Maybe West even psyched with a three-card suit. Anyway, the opponents have, at most, eight hearts (more likely seven) and you have, at most, eight spades. If you can take ten tricks in spades or nine tricks in notrump, the opponents should have only six tricks in hearts. The Law says you should double, and that is what a majority of experts did in a bidding panel for *International Popular Bridge Monthly.*

7. Pass. What amazes me is that in a bidding panel of international experts, nineteen panelists bid 3♠ while only twelve passed. I think the 3♠ bidders were out of their minds! Considering the adjustment factors (♡A1092 is worth two tricks on defense and is much better than ♡A652), the total tricks should not exceed fifteen, even when partner has four spades. So if you can take nine tricks in spades, the opponents should take no more than six tricks in hearts. More likely you have eight tricks in spades to the opponents' seven tricks in hearts. And if partner happened to double with

   ♠ K98 ♡ 62 ♢ A642 ♣ KQ42

   (hoping you would bid 3NT) and corrects your 3♠ bid to 4♢, how will you like that?

8. Bid 5♣ (or 5♢). Partner has

   ♠ 6 ♡ 63 ♢ AK10942 ♣ AK84

   You have no defense against 4♠ and are down one in five of either minor for a cheap sacrifice. (In fact, if the opponents don't cash out, you can make 5♣!) You have ten diamonds between you and the opponents have nine or ten spades. Furthermore, you have a double fit with all your cards in partner's suits and none in the opponents' suits, which means that you should make an upward adjustment in applying the Law. It is more logical for you (with your admittedly weak hand) to bid than for partner to do so. After all, you could hold something like

   ♠ 632 ♡ QJ4 ♢ QJ63 ♣ J52

   in which case 4♠ is probably down one while a phantom sacrifice would cost 500.

CHAPTER 6

Reopening the Bidding

Balancing Over an Opening Suit Bid

When LHO opens one of a suit and the next two players pass, you can bid or double with fewer values than you would require in second position. Everybody knows that, of course; the question is how much lighter your bids and doubles can be. The general guide I follow is that I can be a queen lighter for my suit bids and doubles and slightly lighter than that to balance with a one notrump bid. I play that a 1NT bid in fourth position shows 12-16 HCP over a major and 12-14 points over a minor. The reason for the distinction is that if you make a balancing double after a minor-suit opening, partner's response will usually be at the one-level, and you can then rebid 1NT with 15-17. Over a major, partner's response to your double will usually be at the two-level; you don't want to double and then bid 2NT with only 15-16 points opposite what could be a Yarborough.

Some players adopt a slightly lower range like 10-14 for the balancing 1NT over a major. The theoretical problem is how to describe all of the hands of various strengths where you wish to compete without having impossibly wide ranges. With 10-11 points, game is improbable, and if you do choose to reopen with a balanced hand, you can double, intending to pass partner's response. A balancing double followed by a 2NT bid over a two-level response shows 17-19 points, while an immediate 2NT bid is not Unusual Notrump — it shows 20-21 points, or perhaps less with a good minor suit.

WEST	NORTH	EAST	SOUTH
1♡	pass	pass	?

Here you should bid 1NT with:

♠ A 7 6 ♡ Q 10 8 ◇ K J 9 5 ♣ A J 6

Double with this hand

♠ A 7 6 ♡ Q 10 8 ◇ K J 9 5 ♣ A K 7

intending to bid 1NT over a 1♠ response or 2NT over a minor-suit response. Obviously, rebidding 2NT with 17 HCP opposite a possible Yarborough is dangerous, but the risk is worthwhile. With either of these hands

♠ A Q 7 ♡ K J 8 ◇ K J 9 5 ♣ A Q 7

♠ A 7 ♡ K J 8 ◇ A K J 10 7 6 ♣ Q 8

you should bid 2NT immediately.

Of course, a 12-16 HCP range is very wide and presents problems to a responder with about ten useful points. Often partner must either risk getting to 2NT with inadequate values or risk missing 3NT when you have the top of your range. As a theoretical matter, it is better to have a wide range for 1NT than a wide range for 2NT (or a 2NT rebid). Over 1NT you at least have room for invitations, while over 2NT you simply have to guess whether to bid game or not. In *Bridge Today* Kit Woolsey suggested a way to cope with the very wide range. Say the bidding starts:

WEST	NORTH	EAST	SOUTH
		1♠	pass
pass	1NT	pass	?

With the weakest holding (let's say 10 HCP if the 1NT bid shows 12-16), you bid 2♣, Stayman, and if partner bids 2◇ or 2♡, you use the cuebid as the weaker step. 2♠ is presumably a raise to 2NT, but weaker than bidding 2NT which shows 11-12. Or 2♠ could be a weak raise of hearts if partner bids hearts (if partner bids 2NT over 2♠, you will bid 3♡; if he bids 3NT over 2♠, you will bid 4♡).

Some players treat an overcall in fourth position as weak since they double whenever they have opening bid values. To me, this seems like an unplayable system. If RHO opened 1◇, you would overcall 1♡ with

♠ A 8 ♡ K 10 8 7 6 ◇ A 7 6 ♣ K 5 2

It wouldn't (or shouldn't) occur to you to double since you don't want partner to bid spades on a four-card suit, and you aren't strong enough either in high cards or suit quality to correct to hearts, especially at a high level. Suppose LHO opens 1♢ and the next two players pass; this is still a 1♡ bid for the very same reasons. A double merely asks for trouble on a hand like

♠ 6 ♡ K 10 8 7 6 ♢ A K 5 ♣ A 9 7 3

You should be aware that 2NT isn't the only bid that has a different meaning in fourth position than in second. There is no need for a jump overcall to be preemptive since, with a weak hand, you could just pass the opponent's bid. So a single jump is intermediate rather than weak, even when not vulnerable. Second-seat cuebids show two-suiters (Michaels or 'top and bottom'), but in fourth chair, a cuebid merely shows a hand with much more offense than defense. In second seat you don't worry about making takeout doubles with voids since partner seldom has the right hand to pass, but in fourth position the risk is much greater.

WEST	**NORTH**	**EAST**	**SOUTH**
1♢	pass	pass	?

On this auction you should bid 2♢ holding any of the following hands:

a) ♠ K Q 7 ♡ A K Q 10 9 7 5 4 ♢ 6 ♣ A

b) ♠ K J 8 7 ♡ K Q 9 3 ♢ — ♣ A Q 10 8 4

c) ♠ K J 8 7 ♡ K Q 9 3 ♢ — ♣ Q J 8 7 4

With hand (a) you don't want to risk partner's passing a double for a small penalty when you almost surely have a game or slam in hearts. Many players would double with hands (b) and (c), but hands with voids are not good on defense. With (b) you risk partner's passing the double with

♠ Q 5 ♡ J 8 7 4 ♢ K J 9 8 6 ♣ K 7

for probably a one-trick set (as partner gets endplayed in trumps several times) while you are cold for game in hearts. With (c) you risk not even setting 1♢ doubled when you are cold for at least a partscore your way. Note that the cuebid in fourth position does not guarantee another bid, and partner must jump to show some offensive values.

Partner should in general treat your reopening suit bids and doubles as being almost the same as a second-seat bid or double. With a good eleven points and a fit, he should cuebid when you overcall a suit. With about ten points and a five-card major, he should jump (after all, he could hardly hold much more having failed to overcall). Only with a four-card major or a weak five-card minor should partner take a slightly more conservative action than if you had doubled in second position.

Balancing over Preempts

When the opponents open with a preempt, it is bound to create problems. That, after all, is why people preempt. Unless either you or partner has opening bid values, it is unlikely that you will miss a game, so a good rule of thumb is not to bid over a preempt unless you have at least opening-bid values. This rule of thumb applies whether you are in second seat or fourth seat. There is a big difference between this situation and the balancing auctions that we have been discussing up to now. When a one-bid is passed around to you, you know that RHO is very weak and it is very unlikely the opponents can double you for penalties even when they can set you. Opener doesn't know whether his partner has zero points or a scattered five, and if he does double, it is for takeout. But when the bidding goes

WEST	**NORTH**	**EAST**	**SOUTH**
3♢	pass	pass	?

you can't assume that East is weak. He may have the best hand at the table, something like

♠ A Q 10 8 ♡ K J 10 6 ♢ 7 ♣ A J 8 6

and be just drooling at the prospect of your reopening the bidding. Of course, you should not base your decision whether to bid on the assumption that he actually does have such a good defensive hand, but you can't place partner with high cards simply because East passed. Suppose you hold

♠ K J 7 6 4 ♡ Q 10 6 ♢ A 6 ♣ J 8 5

Some players would balance 3♠ with this hand, but I think that is a losing bid. I wouldn't be surprised to discover that you can make 3♠, but there is no way to get there (and stay there!). If you bid 3♠ and partner has enough for you to make it, he will raise you to 4♠. At matchpoints you might do well, getting minus 50 instead of minus 110, but at IMPs you are risking a large loss for a very small gain — and (who knows?) they might not make 3♢. My choice would be to pass and defend.

An exception to the requirement of opening bid values to compete over a preempt is when the opponents open a weak two-bid and you have a good weak two-bid of your own in a higher-ranking suit. If RHO opens 2♢ or 2♡ and you hold

♠ K Q J 8 3 2 ♡ 8 ♢ J 7 5 ♣ Q J 7

you should bid 2♠. If partner has

♠ A 9 6 4 ♡ K 5 4 ♢ 8 ♣ K 9 8 5 2

you could lose a double game swing by passing. You may also recall a hand from the quiz in the first chapter: I recommended overcalling 2♡ over a weak 2♢ bid with:

♠ 6 ♡ AQ875 ◇ — ♣ 9876532

on the grounds that your playing strength compensated for your lack of high cards. But this was an extreme example.

Reopening When Both Opponents Have Bid

The term 'reopening bids' applies to two situations that have little in common. Thus far we have been discussing an opening bid on your left, followed by two passes — i.e. it was your first chance to bid. The second situation occurs when you and partner have both passed, but you have decided, since the opponents have bid weakly, that your side can make something, or perhaps that you can push the opponents one trick higher in the hope of setting them. I think it is clear by now that, in general, I prefer immediate action to 'backing in' later since immediate action is safer, and it makes it harder for the opponents to find their fit. However there are a few hands that are not appropriate for immediate action, but which justify action later, usually after the opponents have found a fit.

When the opponents have a fit, your side usually has a fit. Stated in terms of the Law, when the opponents have eight or nine trumps between them, they have fewer cards in the other suits, and you probably have an eight- or nine-card fit. When the opponents have found a fit, but still stop at the two-level, your side has about half the high cards — somewhere in the 18-22 point range — since if they had 23 points or more, one of the opponents probably would at least have tried for game. On auctions such as these

WEST	NORTH	EAST	SOUTH
1♡	pass	2♡	pass
pass	?		

WEST	NORTH	EAST	SOUTH
1◇	pass	1♡	pass
2♡	pass	pass	?

it is fairly safe to reopen. You should certainly bid 2♠ in either case with

♠ J8753 ♡ 873 ◇ A7 ♣ K93

But if the bidding has gone:

WEST	NORTH	EAST	SOUTH
1◇	pass	1♡	pass
1NT	pass	pass	?

the opponents' hearts could be 5-2 or even 4-2. Partner has some values, but they may be in the wrong spot. It is too dangerous to bid 2♠, although if the spade suit were strengthened to ♠J10973 you should probably risk it. Change the bidding to:

WEST	NORTH	EAST	SOUTH
1♢	pass	1♠	pass
2♣	pass	pass	?

and now it is extremely dangerous to reopen. The opponents haven't found a fit, and the deal looks like a misfit. Responder may well have 5-4-1-3 distribution to go with opener's 1-3-5-4 distribution, and anything you bid will be severely penalized.

Here are a couple of 'safe' sequences:

WEST	NORTH	EAST	SOUTH
		1♢	pass
1NT	pass	2♣	?

♠ K 8 7 5 3 ♡ Q 10 6 5 4 ♢ 7 ♣ 9 4

West won't have a four-card major very often here — most players would have bid a four-card major, no matter how weak, rather than skip over it to bid 1NT. East could have 4-1-4-4 or 0-4-5-4 distribution, but if he has length in one major, he must be very short in the other. You can't possibly be hurt at the two-level if you find the right major suit, and my recommendation is to bid 2♢. Might partner think you have a diamond suit? Not if he is half awake! For this sequence opener must have at least four diamonds, and will have five more often than four. Responder almost surely has two or more diamonds — 3+ on average. So if partner has three or four diamonds, he will know you can't possibly have a diamond suit, and therefore your 2♢ bid must show a weak, distributional major two-suiter.

The other 'safe' sequence is

WEST	NORTH	EAST	SOUTH
1NT[1]	pass	pass	?

1. 15-17.

♠ J 10 9 6 5 2 ♡ 6 ♢ K 8 7 3 ♣ 8 7

East's pass marks partner with a lot of high cards, and they are behind the notrump bidder so that most of your finesses will work. This is a 'safe' sequence so far as making 2♠ is concerned; however, the danger is that partner will think you have a better hand and invite game or jump to game.

The right hand for a penalty double of a strong notrump occurs very infrequently, and I suggest therefore that you use the direct-seat double to show something else. Kit Woolsey suggests that it be used to show a major and a longer minor, for example, while in some systems it is a transfer to 2♣, showing a one-suiter. But you have a good penalty double of a strong notrump even less frequently in fourth position than in second. Partner doesn't know what to lead and your strength is under the notrump bidder's. One possible way to play is that a balancing overcall guarantees a weak, distributional hand, like my example above. With a sound overcall you double, allowing partner to pass with a good balanced hand and otherwise to bid 2♣, over which you pass (with clubs) or bid your suit. This caters to the few times that you belong in game despite the strong notrump opening. The reopening bid itself is very safe when you have a good suit; the greatest danger is not from the opponents — it is from partner.

Even in 'safe' sequences, you need the right sort of distribution to make a reopening bid or double. In either of these auctions

WEST	NORTH	EAST	SOUTH
		1♡	pass
2♡	pass	pass	?

WEST	NORTH	EAST	SOUTH
1◇	pass	1♡	pass
2♡	pass	pass	?

there is virtually no danger in doubling with

♠ Q743 ♡ J ◇ A986 ♣ K1074

You were slightly too weak to double 1♡, and you couldn't even consider a double of 1◇, but the way the bidding has gone, you must have a fit in one of your suits. The same is true when you hold

♠ Q975 ♡ 6 ◇ K873 ♣ QJ74

Change your distribution to

♠ Q975 ♡ 65 ◇ K87 ♣ QJ74

and there is some risk involved. A double will gain slightly more often than it will lose (partner will realize that you are bidding his cards as well as yours, and he won't compete further without a remarkable distributional fit). At least your hand is 'pure' with no wasted high cards. Add the queen of hearts

♠ Q975 ♡ Q5 ◇ K87 ♣ QJ74

and, in my opinion, it is better to pass. Quite likely, your side has 18-22 HCP, and when you have the worthless ♡Q, partner is less likely to have a useful card to go with your hand! Change your hand to

♠ 986 ♡ Q74 ◇ KJ6 ♣ A1094

and a reopening double is sickening. It will often be punished, and it deserves to be punished.

Occasionally you can pass originally and plan to reopen later. If RHO bids 1♠ and you hold

♠ AJ54 ♡ 9 ◇ AK105 ♣ K983

you have no safe bid. So you pass and LHO bids 1NT and RHO bids 2♡. Now you can double to show a good hand with support for the other two suits. Or with

♠ J954 ♡ 8 ◇ AJ3 ♣ AJ873

you should pass a 1◇ bid on your right, hoping LHO will bid 1♡ and RHO will raise to 2♡. If the bidding goes that way, you will double. If the bidding goes

WEST	NORTH	EAST	SOUTH
		1◇	pass
1♡	pass	1NT	?

it is more dangerous to compete (since West is unlimited) but you still might double.

You should recognize that what I have been expressing is the 'conservative' view. Some players almost never allow the opponents to play a suit contract at the two-level, especially when the opponents have found a fit. Despite my recommendation, they wouldn't even consider passing here

WEST	NORTH	EAST	SOUTH
		1♡	pass
2♡	pass	pass	?

♠ Q975 ♡ Q5 ◇ K87 ♣ QJ74

In the November-December 1999 issue of *Bridge Today*, Matthew Granovetter called himself a chicken and apologized for his cowardice in not reopening with a double, vulnerable against not, (at matchpoints) with

♠ 1063 ♡ AK5 ◇ 1076 ♣ K952

when the bidding went

WEST	NORTH	EAST	SOUTH
		1♠	pass
2♠	pass	pass	?

Perhaps that is a winning tactic at matchpoints, but it looks terribly dangerous to me.

The following hand also made quite an impression on me. My partner (North) held

♠ Q754 ♡ K63 ◇ 87 ♣ AJ52

and I held as South:

♠ KJ96 ♡ A10974 ◇ Q94 ♣ 6

The bidding at matchpoints, with both sides vulnerable, went:

WEST	NORTH	EAST	SOUTH
1◇	pass	1♡	pass
1♠	pass	2◇	2♡
3◇	3♡	all pass	

Not knowing that spade ruffs were available, West led the ace of diamonds and a diamond to his partner's king (not the best defense, by far, on a double-dummy basis), and by playing West for a singleton honor in hearts, I made my contract for a very good score. I thought my 2♡ bid was a reasonable gamble at matchpoints, since West, who had bid two suits, was likely to have a singleton heart, and even if we were potentially in trouble, he might not pass my bid around to his partner.

After the hand was over, my partner, despite being pleased with the result, said, 'You don't need to bid my hands for me. If you had passed, I would have reopened with a double.' I tactfully expressed my opinion that no sane player would double with his hand. So we started asking around (this was at the Nationals). Most players agreed with me that partner shouldn't balance with a double since we would probably have to play the contract in one of the opponents' suits, and we could so easily be minus 200 or more (but they didn't necessarily agree with my 2♡ bid either). But Geir Helgemo and Tony Forrester, two of the world's top players, said that they *would* double with partner's hand.

Here is another hand, this time from the *Bridge World* panel. Again it is matchpoints, and with neither side vulnerable, the bidding goes:

WEST	NORTH	EAST	SOUTH
3♢	pass	pass	?

♠ K J 9 6 5 ♡ Q J 7 5 3 ♢ 4 ♣ Q 6

It seems to me that doubling is just begging for minus 470, or possibly minus 500 or minus 800 if partner bids 5♣ with:

♠ A 7 2 ♡ K 9 ♢ J 7 3 ♣ K 8 7 5 3

Game seems very unlikely, and if partner has enough for you to make a partscore, he will surely bid a game. Of course you might be minus 50 or minus 100 instead of minus 110 by taking action, but I don't like the odds. However, thirteen panelists doubled, compared with eight who passed and ten who took other action (three cuebid 4♢). So you can see that my recommendations are more conservative than average, perhaps because I usually play IMPs rather than matchpoints these days, or perhaps because I am more likely to take immediate action and don't expect so much 'protection' from partner. It could just be the pessimism of old age.

Except for the last two hands, I have tried to give clear-cut examples, but here is another borderline case:

WEST	NORTH	EAST	SOUTH
			pass
1♣	pass	1♡	pass
2♡	pass	pass	?

♠ 10 6 ♡ A J 5 ♢ J 9 8 6 5 2 ♣ 7 5

One player in an IMP game bid 3♢, reasoning as follows: 'Partner must have at least 12 HCP to account for the opponents' failure to make a game try. Why didn't he overcall 1♠? Because he has only a four-card suit. He probably has one or two hearts, leaving about seven cards in the minors. So he has a fit for my diamonds.' He gained a part-score swing since his partner held

♠ KQ83 ♡ K7 ♢ KQ4 ♣ 9862

The opponents were cold for 2♡ and his side was cold for 3♢. Within the framework of his bidding, the 3♢ bid figured to work more often than not (perhaps by pushing the opponents to 3♡, down one; perhaps by scoring minus 50 instead of minus 110). But partner could have held less useful cards, for example one of these hands

♠ Q943 ♡ K7 ♢ A7 ♣ QJ843

♠ QJ43 ♡ Q73 ♢ K73 ♣ KJ8

(after all, West might have raised hearts with only three-card support plus a ruffing value) and with the latter hand you just rescued the opponents from a hopeless contract into a dubious contract of your own. With partner's actual hand I like an immediate overcall better — despite the four-card suit. The bidding might go:

WEST	NORTH	EAST	SOUTH
			pass
1♣	1♠	dbl	2♣[1]
2♡	3♢	all pass	

1. I hope you remembered that 2♣ was a transfer to diamonds.

If East had passed, you might pass rather than introduce the weak diamond suit, but when East made a negative double, you could anticipate further competition.

In most of the examples so far, the player who had a decision whether or not to reopen was in fourth position, so after his RHO passed, the opponents' hands were limited. When the bidding by the opponents is relatively weak, you may anticipate a pass on your left, and it may be more logical for you than for partner to 'reopen'. In general, the player who is short in the opponents' suit should be the 'reopener', although three small of a suit bid and raised may be almost as good. When the bidding goes

WEST	NORTH	EAST	SOUTH
		1♡	pass
1NT[1]	pass	2♡	?

1. Forcing.

West will usually pass if you pass. I realize he may have a three-card limit raise or some other type of hand justifying further bidding, but if you have

♠ K876 ♡ 8 ♢ Q954 ♣ A875

you should double. It would be even safer to reopen (with a different hand, of course) if the opener had bid 1♢ and rebid 2♢ over a non-forcing 1NT response. Over

WEST	NORTH	EAST	SOUTH
		1♢	pass
1NT	pass	2♢	?

you would bid 2♡ with

♠ Q986 ♡ K98543 ♢ 86 ♣ J

(you didn't bid 2♡ immediately because the suit was too weak, and you didn't want to discourage partner from bidding spades).

When a suit has been bid and raised:

WEST	NORTH	EAST	SOUTH
1♡	pass	2♡	?

Larry Cohen and Marty Bergen recommend bidding or doubling with very light hands. Since the opponents have eight or nine hearts between them, they are not likely to double you. If they have extra values they will try for game instead. So Cohen-Bergen might double here with

♠ K876 ♡ 8 ♢ J954 ♣ A875

or bid 3♢ with:

♠ Q8 ♡ 95 ♢ KQJ874 ♣ J106

In fact, I doubt that they need the queen of spades or the jack-ten of clubs to bid with the latter hand. There are pros and cons to this style of bidding (where you simply assume that you have, at most, a partscore and so partner won't try for game even with a very good hand). Whether or not you would take action with these hands, you should tend to bid with skimpier values than you would usually expect for bids or doubles at this level. Conversely, when there is a two-over-one response, it is almost never safe to compete unless you have a very good, long suit or 6-5 distribution.

SUMMARY

1. You can balance with an overcall or double over an opening suit bid with about a queen less than you would have in second seat. A balancing 1NT should be played as 12-16 HCP over a major and 12-14 HCP over a minor.
2. Some bids (such as 2NT, cuebids, and jump overcalls) have a different meaning in fourth chair than when used in second seat.
3. Don't balance over a preempt without opening bid values or the equivalent in playing strength.
4. When both opponents have bid, reopening carries a higher risk. Some sequences are inherently much safer than others to come in against.
5. When the opponents have a fit, your side usually has a fit; however, immediate action is usually preferable to (and safer than) backing into the auction later on.

What is your next bid on each of the following hands?

1.

WEST	NORTH	EAST	SOUTH
3♡	pass	pass	?

♠ A J 8 7 ♡ 10 ◇ K 9 7 4 ♣ K 8 6 2

2.

WEST	NORTH	EAST	SOUTH
1◇	pass	pass	dbl
pass	1♠	pass	?

♠ A 10 8 6 ♡ K 9 8 ◇ 6 4 ♣ A Q 10 5

3.

WEST	NORTH	EAST	SOUTH
		1◇	pass
1NT	pass	pass	?

♠ A J 3 ♡ K 9 6 ◇ Q 8 4 3 ♣ K 7 2

4.

WEST	NORTH	EAST	SOUTH
		1♣	pass
1NT	pass	pass	?

You are playing a convention whereby you can show various two-suiters in this sequence, so 2♣ would show diamonds and hearts. Do you use your new gadget with:

♠ J 7 6 ♡ A 9 8 5 ◇ Q 10 5 4 ♣ 8 7

5. *Neither vul., IMPs*

WEST	NORTH	EAST	SOUTH
1NT[1]	pass	2◇[2]	pass
2♡	pass	pass	?

1. 15-17 HCP.
2. Transfer.

♠ K Q J 7 ♡ K 6 ◇ A 8 7 3 ♣ 9 5 4

6.

WEST	NORTH	EAST	SOUTH
1NT[1]	pass	pass	?

1. 15-17 HCP.

♠ 8 ♡ K Q 10 9 6 5 ◇ A J 10 8 ♣ J 6

7.

WEST	NORTH	EAST	SOUTH
2♡	pass	3♡	?

♠ A K J 7 5 ♡ 8 7 3 ◇ K 8 ♣ J 10 6

SOLUTIONS

1. Double. This is my idea of a minimum reopening double. If partner passes for penalties, his heart honors will be well placed. I realize that some players would double with a lot less, perhaps with the queen-ten of spades in place of the ace-jack. I don't know how their partners ever know what to do. Are they allowed to jump to game? Do they need the setting tricks in their own hand to pass?

2. Raise to 2♠. If you were in second position, you would need a bit more to raise, but since you could have doubled without the queen of clubs, and since partner hit your four-card suit, the hand is (barely) worth a raise. If partner held

   ♠ Q 8 3 2 ♡ Q 6 ◇ K 7 5 2 ♣ K J 2

   for example, he would not have jumped to 2♠ over your reopening double.

3. Pass. To me this isn't close. The best you can hope for is that you have twenty-one points to the opponents' nineteen, but they may have as many as twenty-four points to your sixteen. Some players invariably double 1NT contracts reached in this manner, but I think the odds are against them. With ◇QJ98, a double would be somewhat more tempting, but I would still pass. Partner will often run out, and you would rather defend than see partner declare when you hold this hand.

4. Pass. No, this is not the time to use your gadget. Even if you find a 4-4 fit, which you may not, this hand is too weak to justify competing. Save your gadget for something like

   ♠ 8 6 ♡ K Q 10 6 ◇ Q J 9 6 4 ♣ 7 5

   or, at worst, 4-4 in the reds but with more solid suits.

5. Bid 2♠. It is risky, but I think competing will gain in the long run. However, my suggestion is to bid 2♠ rather than double. There's a chance that West will lead the ace of hearts, and at least, if you are declarer, the opponents can't force you immediately. While you hope to find a 4-4 spade fit, you may not, and it would be safer to play a 4-3 spade fit at the two-level than a 4-3 club fit at the three-level. If you double, partner would probably bid 2NT with four of both minors, but he might have 3-3-3-4 distribution and have to bid clubs. Even if you find an eight-card minor fit, it may not be any safer or score any better than a 4-3 spade fit at the two-level. When an opponent opens 1NT you don't expect your suit to break badly, so when you wind up in a 4-3 fit, the trumps are more likely than usual to split 3-3. The reason for stating the vulnerability is that the best time to compete is when neither side is vulnerable. You don't lose as much if you are wrong, while you don't have any chance of setting the opponents for 200 if their contract is not making.

6. Double. If you adopt my suggestion, you will double and bid 2♡ over partner's semi-forced 2♣, showing a sound overcall. Game is still possible and you want to bid differently with this hand than you would with:

   ♠ 8 ♡ K Q 10 9 6 5 ◇ J 10 4 3 ♣ J 6

   Also, if there is further competition (East may bid 3♣), partner will have a better idea what to do if you show a good hand rather than a bad hand.

7. Bid 3♠. Having three small hearts is an advantage since partner is likely to be short in hearts, and likely to have some length in spades. You could easily have a game in spades when partner holds a hand like either of these:

   ♠ Q 8 4 ♡ 10 ◇ A 9 7 5 4 ♣ K 8 5 2

   ♠ 10 9 4 2 ♡ J 4 ◇ A J 7 5 4 ♣ K Q

   Even if you get to 4♠, down one, that still may be a better result than letting the opponents play 3♡.

CHAPTER 7

Problems of Opener's Side

When Not To Use a Negative Double

When the opponents compete, you have fewer bids at your disposal.

WEST	NORTH	EAST	SOUTH
	1♠	2♡	?

♠ Q 10 ♡ K 7 6 ◇ A 7 5 4 3 ♣ 8 5 2

Without the overcall, you would have bid 1NT, but what do you do now? Many players would make a negative double, but I think that is wrong. No matter what partner does now, you will have a problem. If he rebids 2♠, should you raise? Depending on how well the hands fit, you could either be cold for game, or too high in 3♠. If he rebids 3♣ with ♣AJ63 (regardless of the rest of his hand), you don't belong in clubs, but if you take him back to spades, he may again be too high. Or he may think you have a better hand for this sequence and bid a hopeless game.

To me, this is not a negative double, but a clear-cut 2♠ bid if you open five-card majors. You normally have three-card support for a raise, but when partner has a minimum opening, 2♠ will be the best contract nine times out of ten. This is not as radical a suggestion as it may appear. If East had passed, you would have bid 1NT and corrected a 2♣ rebid to 2♠ (and probably a 2♡ rebid to 2♠

to give partner another chance to bid, since partner would expect four-card support and a slightly better hand if you raised hearts). If you are willing to let partner play in a 5-2 fit without competition, why not let him play in a 5-2 fit after an overcall? If he has

♠ AJ8543 ♡ 93 ◇ KQ8 ♣ A7

he will bid 3♠ (or make some sort of game try, knowing there is no misfit) and you will bid game.

Take away your king of hearts or ace of diamonds and you should pass — you need compensating values to raise with a doubleton. With a strong doubleton in partner's major suit, you should at least consider a raise rather than a negative double that could lead to a high-level contract on a poor trump fit.

Now let's strengthen your hand to:

WEST	NORTH	EAST	SOUTH
	1♠	2♡	?

♠ Q10 ♡ KJ7 ◇ A7543 ♣ 852

Not only do you have ten points instead of nine, but all of your honors are working, and you have a double stopper in hearts. You should bid 2NT, which is nonforcing. While it is possible that partner has a singleton small club, the odds are that he has some values in clubs. When the opponents bid and you are considering a notrump bid, you should worry mostly about having strength in their suit since that is what they will usually lead. Besides, if partner has a singleton club, that leaves him with lots of spades or diamonds, and he may rebid his spade suit with six spades or his diamond suit with four or five diamonds.

With the same bidding, but this time holding

♠ 75 ♡ QJ7 ◇ 97 ♣ AQ10854

you again have a problem. My choice may not appeal to everyone, but I would again bid 2NT. It gives you a chance to get to the most probable game if you belong in game, and a chance to stop short of game when partner has a minimum hand. No, I don't really like the bid, but what are the alternatives? If you make a negative double, partner's most likely rebid is 3◇. Then what? If you pass instead, you may never get back into the bidding.

Free Bids

Let's continue examining responder's problems for a moment.

WEST	NORTH	EAST	SOUTH
	1♣	1◇	?

a) ♠ KQ985 ♡ J5 ◇ 76 ♣ 9854

b) ♠ QJ743 ♡ 8 ◇ K987 ♣ 654

To me it seems clear that you should bid 1♠, even without the jack of hearts in the first hand, or with ♠Q10974 in the second. In the first example, West may bid 3♢ or 4♢, and you will be glad you made your spade bid while you could. With the second hand you are afraid, if you don't bid 1♠ now, that the bidding may be up to the three- or four-level in hearts the next time you get a chance to bid.

When I first started to play bridge, Goren and Roth-Stone both said you needed nine points for a 'free bid'. I thought that style had gone completely out of fashion, but in the November-December 1998 *Bridge Today* magazine, Al Roth had South bidding 1♠ with

♠ QJ1072 ♡ J10876 ♢ — ♣ KJ4

in this same auction. There is nothing unusual about that, except that he implied that South barely had his bid, and that when the bidding continued 5♢ by West, 5♠ by partner, South had nothing to spare. Al said, 'I have always played that the bid of 1♠ in competition is a 'free bid.' This expression may be new to some of you. It goes back a long way. The idea works like this — when RHO passes partner's opening bid, the only way you can keep the bidding alive is to bid, so you must bid on some very light hands. But when RHO overcalls, partner has another chance! You don't have to bid to keep the auction going. When you have five spades and a poor seven- or eight-point hand, for example, you can pass, *because you cannot miss a game by passing.* [Italics are Roth's.] Partner will balance if there is enough strength for game or even a good partscore. Thus, your 1♠ bid after the overcall is a 'free bid' and shows values. One benefit of a free-bid style is that if LHO jump-raises the overcall, partner is much better placed to know whether to take the push.'

I didn't agree with this concept in the 1950s and I don't agree with it now, but obviously it has some merit, or a player of Al Roth's caliber wouldn't still be playing it. Opener's hand in Al's example was

♠ AK98 ♡ AK2 ♢ 82 ♣ 9873

and knowing that South had a reasonably good hand enabled him to bid 5♠ over the opponent's 5♢ bid. But suppose responder had a weaker hand, such as one of these

♠ Q10764 ♡ Q8764 ♢ 6 ♣ Q4

♠ J76432 ♡ 87 ♢ 6 ♣ A1065

and suppose West made the more likely raise to 3♢ or 4♢. Wouldn't you be glad you had bid your spades as South? So sometimes the free bid concept gains and sometimes it loses. I feel certain that, on partscore hands, where you can make more tricks in spades than the opponents can make in their suit, the light (I'd call it normal) response works better.

This leads us to the following auction:

WEST	NORTH	EAST	SOUTH
	1♢	1♠	?

What would you bid with these hands:

♠ K7 ♡ KJ87542 ♢ J6 ♣ 94

♠ J ♡ KQ10865 ♢ J652 ♣ 98

Both of these hands have a lot of playing potential in hearts, and of course, you play weak jump shifts in competition. In the old days you were supposed to pass and hope that partner would reopen the bidding. The trouble nowadays is that the bidding might be at the 3♠ or 4♠ level when it comes back to you, and then you would have to guess whether to bid hearts at the four- or five-level. Also, while the sequence

WEST	NORTH	EAST	SOUTH
	1♢	1♡	2♠

shows less than 6 HCP, a jump to the three-level is not exceptionally weak. The solution, then, is to bid 3♡ immediately, which shows a good, long suit and less than the high-card strength partner would expect for 2♡ followed by 3♡, a sequence which is invitational. If you do bid 3♡, partner will know not to sell out to 4♠ with this kind of hand:

♠ 84 ♡ A93 ♢ AK109843 ♣ 6

Higher-Level Responses

Many players today play two-over-one forcing to game. That is too rigid a system for me, and I prefer to play that a two-over-one response guarantees a rebid (unless partner jumps to game) and is forcing to 2NT. But however you like to play when the opponents stay out of the auction, in competition I think you should go back to the 1950s style of bidding where two-over-one is merely forcing for one round. Incidentally, that is what Mike Lawrence recommends despite advocating two-over-one forcing to game in uncontested auctions. The reason for the change is that you no longer have a forcing 1NT bid available. Although the negative double takes care of some of the weaker hands, it doesn't work well when responder has a long suit or an unbalanced hand. Let's see what the problem is.

WEST	NORTH	EAST	SOUTH
	1♠	2♡	?

♠ 75 ♡ QJ7 ♢ 97 ♣ AQ10854

Earlier, I suggested that you bid 2NT with this hand — not because you were too weak to bid 3♣, but because you were too weak to bid 3♣ followed by 3NT. Exchange your red-suit holdings, and I think you should bid 3♣ (since 2NT is no longer an option).

When you bid a new suit at the two- or three-level in competition, you are allowed to pass if opener rebids his original suit, raises your suit, or bids notrump.

WEST	NORTH	EAST	SOUTH
	1♠	2♢	2♡
pass	2♠/2NT/3♡	pass	?

♠ 74 ♡ AJ763 ♢ J4 ♣ KJ96

With this hand, you would pass any of these rebids, which means that partner should jump to game with slight extra values (if he knows where the hand should play) or cuebid or bid a new suit to force. Some players would make a negative double with this hand, but they would probably lose their heart fit if opener had only three hearts. I have no strong feelings about this hand, but I definitely think it is losing tactics to make a negative double on a hand with a six-card (or longer) suit, especially when that suit is a major. How can partner make an intelligent decision when you haven't shown your six-card suit?

Notice, too, that in this auction

WEST	NORTH	EAST	SOUTH
	1♠	2♣	2♢
pass	?		

2♡ should be forcing since it is awkward if North has to jump to 3♡ on a four-card suit, just to show slightly better than a minimum opening.

Four of a major is the most common game, but 3NT comes next. When there is room to explore all possibilities, you should do so, but when the opponents compete, there is less bidding room. If it appears that you have no major fit, you may go out of your way to try for notrump. For example, you open 1♠ and the auction develops as follows:

WEST	NORTH	EAST	SOUTH
			1♠
3♣	3♡	pass	?

♠ J9854 ♡ K ♢ AKQ106 ♣ Q6

What would you bid? It would be somewhat extreme to raise with a singleton, even if it is the king. If partner needs no more heart support than you have, he will probably rebid hearts himself. Your spade suit could hardly be weaker than it is, and if partner has three spades, he will probably offer belated support. The 'obvious' bid is 4♢, but that would bypass your most probable game, and over 4♢ with

♠ K7 ♡ A98642 ♢ 975 ♣ A3

partner would probably give you preference to spades with his doubleton honor. Your hand is great for notrump in all respects except for not having a sure stopper in clubs. If partner has ♣Ax or ♣Axx or ♣Kxx, you probably have a double stopper, but only when played from your side. So your percentage bid is 3NT.

Queen doubleton should be treated like a stopper in many sequences provided the suit has been bid on your left. As was mentioned in Chapter 4, Qx provides a double stopper when partner has Ax(x) or Kxx. You have a combined stopper when partner has Jxx, and sometimes when he has 10xx (if the jack is on your right, the opponents can't untangle and run the suit if it is distributed AKxxxx opposite Jx or AKxxx opposite Jxx or Axxxx opposite KJx, etc.). Even when partner has two or three small cards, LHO may lead low from the ace-king, letting your queen win (especially when he has no outside entry), or he may cash a high honor, then shift, waiting for his partner to gain the lead to lead through what he believes to be your guarded queen.

Bidding in Competition—the Good-Bad 2NT

If you opened 1♠ with

♠ A Q 10 5 4 ♡ K 8 7 ◇ 7 ♣ K 10 4 3

and partner raised to 2♠, you would pass, of course, since game is very remote. But in competitive auctions such as the following

WEST	NORTH	EAST	SOUTH
			1♠
pass	2♠	3◇	?

WEST	NORTH	EAST	SOUTH
			1♠
2◇	2♠	3◇	?

you are faced with a very different problem on the same hand. Game is still remote, but you would rather play 3♠ than let the opponents play 3◇. On an average, you have 8½ spades and the opponents have 8½ diamonds, making a total of seventeen tricks, according to the Law. Since you have no wasted values in diamonds, plus a singleton, you should adjust the trick total upward. Almost surely one side can take nine tricks and it is likely that both sides can take nine tricks. A singleton in the opponents' suit (or a sixth trump) is enough 'extra value' to compete to the three-level.

You should have some agreements regarding how to make a game try in this kind of auction (this is discussed in Chapter 11), so that partner will know that a bid of 3♠ here is just competitive. However, even if you have no way of inviting game 3♠ should be treated as competitive rather than invitational since competing is so important (with invitational hands, if there is no way to invite, opener should just bid game and hope for the best). With 5-3-3-2 distribution, on the other hand, you should tend to sell out since that distribution is poor for offense and good for defense. Partner will usually compete to the three-level himself with four-card support or a singleton in the opponents' suit, since that is what the Law tells him to do.

When you open a minor and the opponents compete, the situation is slightly different. Whether or not you play inverted minor-suit raises in an uncontested auction, you shouldn't play them in competition. The problem is that your jump raise really should have some distribution if you only have four trumps — failing that, you would probably normally bid 1NT instead. However, when they've overcalled, you may not have a stopper, and so this option may not be available. Thus

WEST	NORTH	EAST	SOUTH
			1♢
1♠	2♢		

should just show an old-fashioned single raise. However, this raise will almost never be made on only three trumps because you often open a four-card minor suit. So when you (opener) have a five-card suit and therefore a total of at least nine trumps, you can afford to compete to the three-level, even with 5-3-3-2 distribution.

WEST	NORTH	EAST	SOUTH
			1♢
1♠	3♢		

If 2♢ would have shown a weakish hand, then, should this auction show a limit raise or a preemptive raise? As a theoretical matter, I think the pros and cons just about balance each other, but I follow the usual expert practice of treating most jumps in competition, including this one, as preemptive.

It is very costly to let the opponents make a partscore when you could make a partscore. That is why it is so important to contest the partscore with unbalanced hands, even with minimum high card values. Suppose the bidding goes

WEST	NORTH	EAST	SOUTH
	1♢	pass	1♠
2♣	pass	pass	?

♠ AJ754 ♡ K8732 ♢ 98 ♣ 6

If partner had rebid 2♢, you would pass. The hand might play better in hearts if you find a fit, but game is unlikely, and you can't risk looking for a heart fit since a 2♡ bid would be forcing. But when the opponents have competed, and your partner has passed, your choice is not whether to let partner play in what might or might not be an inferior partscore, but whether you are going to let the opponents make 2♣ when you can probably make 2♡. As you will discover in a later chapter, partner almost surely does not have spade support since with four spades he would raise and with three spades he would make a support double. You would like to bid 2♡, non-forcing, and you are allowed to do that — 2♡ over the opponent's bid *is* non-forcing. What if you had a stronger hand and wanted to force? With a stronger, but more balanced, hand, you double, which is primarily for takeout, but allows partner to pass if his second suit is clubs. With the same distribution (5-5 in the majors) and another ace, you would bid 3♡, forcing. This is one of the rare situations where in competition, a jump is strong and a non-jump is weak.

Now, let's consider a more difficult situation. The bidding goes

WEST	NORTH	EAST	SOUTH
	1♣	pass	1♠
2♡	pass	pass	?

and you hold:

♠ K8754 ♡ 6 ◇ KQ862 ♣ Q4

With one more heart and one less diamond, you would double for takeout, not minding if partner left it in (with a four-card heart holding). But as will be explained later, your double under the bidder should show at least two cards in his suit. You don't want partner to leave the double in when the opponents have eight hearts between them. Nor do you want to bid a forcing 3◇ and have partner take a preference to spades with:

♠ Q6 ♡ 983 ◇ AJ5 ♣ AJ953

So what is the solution? When you start reading the next paragraph you may think I have forgotten this question, but you will eventually see how it ties in.

When the opponents have overcalled and presumably shown a long suit, 2NT is rarely a very desirable contract. It is unlikely that you can take exactly eight tricks in notrump — usually you take nine or ten tricks if they can't get their suit established in time, and only six or seven tricks if they do. Occasionally you will play in 2NT because you are inviting 3NT and partner has a bare minimum for his previous bidding and refuses your invitation, but in many competitive sequences 2NT is used as a conventional, rather than a natural bid. An early use of the bid was Lebensohl. (After partner opened 1NT and RHO overcalled, 2NT asked partner to bid 3♣, allowing you to sign off at the three level or to show or deny a stopper in the opponents' suit. Reverse Lebensohl is now more popular, with a bid of a new suit at the three-level being weaker than bidding 2NT first. There were two articles in the February 1999 *Bridge World* advocating this method.)

Largely through Marty Bergen's influence, a 'good-bad' 2NT bid is used in many other sequences. Marty originally suggested that 2NT should always start the weaker sequence. On this auction:

WEST	NORTH	EAST	SOUTH
			1♢
pass	1♠	2♡	?

♠ 97 ♡ J8 ♢ KQJ873 ♣ AJ8

you would bid 2NT, and partner would usually bid 3♣, allowing you to bid 3♢, showing a good diamond suit and a minimum hand. An immediate 3♢ bid would show the kind of hand where you would have jumped to 3♢ over a pass by East, something like:

♠ 97 ♡ J8 ♢ AKQJ87 ♣ AQ2

Now let's look again at the hand that preceded this discussion:

WEST	NORTH	EAST	SOUTH
	1♣	pass	1♠
2♡	pass	pass	?

♠ K8754 ♡ 6 ♢ KQ862 ♣ Q4

According to the original good-bad 2NT, you would bid 2NT with this hand, followed by 3♢ over partner's 3♣ bid, while with a stronger hand, you would bid 3♢ immediately, which is forcing. The modern tendency is to play it the opposite way — the immediate bid shows the weaker hand (and is non-forcing here) and 2NT, followed by a bid, shows a stronger hand. The reason for the change is that with a weaker hand, you want to get your bid in before the opponents compete further since you are too weak to show your suit at the four-level. When you hold the stronger hand, the opponents are not likely to compete further (and if they do, they may be sorry), so you will be able to finish describing your hand.

Let's consider the (reverse) good-bad 2NT by opener first. After:

WEST	NORTH	EAST	SOUTH
			1♢
pass	1♡	2♠	?

a) ♠ 97 ♡ J8 ♢ KQJ873 ♣ AJ8

b) ♠ 97 ♡ J8 ♢ AKQJ87 ♣ A92

c) ♠ 97 ♡ KJ74 ♢ AK952 ♣ J10

d) ♠ 97 ♡ KJ7 ♢ AK952 ♣ K108

e) ♠ 97 ♡ AJ92 ♢ AKJ92 ♣ K8

f) ♠ 97 ♡ 6 ♢ AK952 ♣ AQ843

g) ♠ 97 ♡ A ♢ AK952 ♣ KJ843

h) ♠ K7 ♡ 6 ♢ AKJ92 ♣ AQJ42

i) ♠ 7 ♡ A7 ♢ AKJ92 ♣ AQ842

On hand (a) you would bid 3♢ while with (b) you would bid 2NT, followed by 3♢ (this hand is strong enough, even with the nine of clubs in place of the queen in the earlier example). With (c) or (d) you would bid 3♡ (support doubles do not apply at this level, so a double to show three-card heart support is not an option). With (e) you would bid 2NT, followed by 3♡.

The only problem occurs when you (opener) have a minor two-suiter. With an average or skimpy 5-5, you would bid 3♣, as on (f) or (g). With a very strong minor two-suiter you would start with 2NT and then, over 3♣, bid 3NT with a spade stopper — hand (h) — or cuebid 3♠ without a stopper — hand (i). Both 3♠ and 3NT guarantee five clubs and a very good hand.

Over 2NT by opener, the 3♣ bid is forcing since opener hasn't shown which type of hand he has, so responder would normally bid 3♣ over 2NT to find out. With extra values, responder can bid more after opener finishes describing his hand, but with a minimum hand and a long, independent suit of his own, he should rebid his suit (non-forcing) instead of bidding 3♣. With

♠ 875 ♡ QJ10974 ♢ 86 ♣ K10

he would bid 3♡, which might enable opener to raise to game with a good hand, but skimpy heart support. Add a king to responder's hand and he would be too strong for a non-forcing 3♡ bid, so he would bid 3♣, followed by 3♡ (forcing), if opener rebid 3♢.

I suggest one extra gadget: a 3♢ bid over opener's 2NT means that responder is near minimum with a decent five-card heart suit or a weak six-card suit. He isn't strong enough to bid 3♣ and then 3♡ (forcing) over 3♢, so he shows this feature indirectly. Opener would pass 3♢ with:

♠ A8 ♡ 7 ♢ AQ107654 ♣ KJ8

He would bid 3♡ with

♠ A8 ♡ K75 ♢ AK10754 ♣ Q9

or bid 4♡ with:

♠ A8 ♡ K75 ♢ AK10754 ♣ A9

Now let us think about how we handle responder's problems in the same auction.

WEST	NORTH	EAST	SOUTH
	1♢	pass	1♡
2♠	pass	pass	?

♠ J8 ♡ AJ876 ♢ Q75 ♣ K87

Double on this hand! A double in front of the bidder is for takeout. You don't care whether partner bids 3♡ with three-card support, bids 3♣ (over which you will bid 3♢), bids 3♢, or passes (with four spades).

♠ J8 ♡ AJ87 ◊ Q75 ♣ K875

Bid 3◊. You can't stand to have partner bid 3♡ with three-card support (which he couldn't show by doubling 2♠ — you will see in Chapter 11 that support doubles are inapplicable at this level), so you have to gamble that partner has five diamonds or knows how to play 4-3 fits.

♠ J8 ♡ AJ87 ◊ 7 ♣ K87542

Bid 2NT, intending to pass partner's 3♣ bid.

♠ J8 ♡ AQJ875 ◊ 7 ♣ J875

Bid 3♡, expecting partner to pass.

♠ J8 ♡ AQJ875 ◊ 7 ♣ K875

Bid 2NT, followed by 3♡ to show the kind of hand where you would have bid 3♡, invitational, if LHO had passed.

♠ 8 ♡ AJ876 ◊ Q75 ♣ K875

Bid 3◊. Although a double would be for takeout, partner would pass with four spades. You don't like to defend doubled contracts at the two-level when the opponents have eight trumps.

The 'defenders' can use this kind of method also:

WEST	NORTH	EAST	SOUTH
2♡	dbl	pass	?

Almost everyone nowadays plays that 3◊ here is either stronger or weaker than bidding 2NT (which transfers to 3♣) followed by 3◊. As you will recall, I recommend playing that 2NT initiates the stronger sequence, showing a hand at least as good as

♠ 763 ♡ 52 ◊ AQ732 ♣ 643

and more high cards if you have no five-card suit. But however you play this auction, would you have the same agreements on this next auction:

WEST	NORTH	EAST	SOUTH
		1♡	pass
2♡	dbl	pass	?

I think you should, since the problems are similar. If a 3◊ bid can be made on anything from zero to nine points, partner will have to do some very good guessing.

Some people even play a good-bad 4NT! Partner opens 1♡ and RHO bids 4♠. Which do you think would be more useful, playing 4NT as Blackwood or to show extra values? If you choose the latter, 4NT transfers to 5♣, and if responder now bids 5◊ or 5♡, he is hoping to get to a slam, while an immediate 5◊ or

5♡ bid means that responder might be stretching. A direct 5♣ bid is natural and invitational to slam since with

♠ 10 ♡ Q 8 ◇ Q 8 7 ♣ K Q J 10 8 5 4

responder would have bid 4NT and passed 5♣. Similarly, in this sequence:

WEST	NORTH	EAST	SOUTH
4♠	dbl	pass	?

the 4NT relay is useful to distinguish between hands with slam interest and those where the five-level may be plenty high enough.

SUMMARY

1. With a strong doubleton in partner's major suit, you should at least consider a raise rather than a negative double.
2. Play jump shifts to the three-level in competition as showing less than invitational values, but a good, long suit.
3. Play two-over-one responses in competition as forcing for one round only, however you play them in uncontested auctions.
4. You need some method in competitive auctions to distinguish forward-going hands from hands where you merely do not want to sell out. (Reverse) Good-Bad 2NT is one method to accomplish this, and analogous agreements are useful in a number of situations.

What is your next bid on each of the following hands?

1.

WEST	NORTH	EAST	SOUTH
	1♢	pass	1♡
2♠	3♢	pass	?

♠ A 7 5 ♡ K 7 4 3 ♢ 8 6 ♣ Q 8 5 4

2.

WEST	NORTH	EAST	SOUTH
			1♢
1♠	2♡	pass	?

♠ 5 4 ♡ K J 9 6 ♢ A K J 10 4 ♣ 10 6

3.

WEST	NORTH	EAST	SOUTH
			1♢
pass	1♠	2♡	pass
pass	dbl	pass	2♠
pass	3♣	pass	?

♠ Q 10 ♡ K 6 4 ♢ A K 9 5 4 ♣ J 8 7

4.

WEST	NORTH	EAST	SOUTH
	1♢	pass	1♡
1♠	pass	2♠	?

♠ 10 ♡ A Q 10 4 ♢ J 8 7 ♣ A 8 5 3 2

5.

WEST	NORTH	EAST	SOUTH
	1♢	pass	1♡
2♠	2NT	pass	?

♠ A 6 ♡ Q J 9 8 4 ♢ 10 ♣ J 7 5 4 2

6.

WEST	NORTH	EAST	SOUTH
			1♡
4♠	4NT[1]	pass	?

1. Good-Bad.

♠ A 4 3 ♡ A K 8 6 5 2 ◇ 9 ♣ A 7 5

7.

WEST	NORTH	EAST	SOUTH
	1♠	3♡	?

♠ Q J ♡ 8 7 6 4 ◇ A 8 7 ♣ A 7 5 3

SOLUTIONS

1. Pass. If partner couldn't bid 2NT, game is remote. Without the Good-Bad 2NT convention, your correct call would be guesswork.

2. Bid 4♡. All your high cards are working and you have good distributional support. Partner would pass with either of these hands

   ♠ 983 ♡ AQ1054 ♢ 75 ♣ K87

   ♠ J3 ♡ A107542 ♢ 75 ♣ A87

   if you just bid 3♡.

3. Bid 3♢. Partner probably has 4-2-3-4 distribution. Your 2♠ bid was logical since partner could have a five-card suit, and he won't expect you to have better spades than this when you failed to make a support double the previous round.

4. Double. Usually you shouldn't double with a singleton, but when the suit has been bid and raised, partner will figure the opponents for an eight-card fit and will only pass with very good spades. The fact that he has a maximum of two hearts makes the defense quite promising if partner chooses to pass.

5. Bid 3♢ (see p.118!). You are not quite strong enough to bid 3♣ followed by 3♡ if partner bids 3♢. If partner has something like

   ♠ 1075 ♡ AK62 ♢ AK1072 ♣ 8

   and was planning to show a good raise to 3♡, he should now bid 4♡.

6. Bid 5♢! If partner was planning to pass your 5♣ bid, you want to force him to the six-level. If he had other intentions, the 5♢ bid shouldn't do any harm. In fact, if he holds

   ♠ 6 ♡ Q8 ♢ AKQJ1054 ♣ Q75

   he can bid 6♢. He knows you have good high cards, and since his diamonds are solid, he doesn't care whether you have diamond support.

7. Bid 3♠. Some players would pass, hoping partner would reopen with a double. But partner may not double at this level, and your hearts are not strong enough to make you lick your chops. The opponents probably have seven heart tricks and possibly another trick. Nor is double an attractive choice for you — you know partner won't be able to pass, and what will you bid if he rebids 4♢? Partner will probably make nine tricks in spades, even with a minimum hand, and if he bids 4♠, your hand should not be a great disappointment to him.

CHAPTER 8

Co-operative Doubles

The Twilight Zone

Until a few years ago, ACBL rules required you to alert most doubles that were not penalty doubles. Like many players, I found that a nuisance since only about one double in ten is clearly a penalty double — perhaps another six out of the ten are clearly for takeout, and the other three are hard to label. Suppose, for example, the bidding goes:

WEST	NORTH	EAST	SOUTH
	1♠	4♣	dbl

Your card may say you play negative doubles through 3♠, but no expert that I know would double here with:

♠ 86 ♡ 954 ◇ Q74 ♣ QJ1085

All doubles of preempts are supposed to show general strength so that partner can pass or bid, depending on his hand. Over a double partner would therefore bid 4♡ with

♠ AQ1054 ♡ KQ873 ◇ K62 ♣ —

In other words, the double of 4♣ is neither a clear-cut takeout double nor a clear-cut penalty double. It falls somewhere in between.

In the early days of contract bridge most doubles were for penalties and all doubles were clearly defined, but that is no longer true. Even before negative doubles became popular experts realized that 'sure' doubles (when you had, among other things, QJ1098 of trumps and wanted partner to leave the double in no matter what he had) occurred very rarely. Rather than wait for such a strong trump holding it was considered quite proper to make a penalty double at the two- or three-level with Q1074 of the opponent's suit, expecting partner always to pull the double with a void and usually to do so with a singleton. So even in the 1950s doubles were somewhat cooperative, except that then they were usually primarily for penalties while today they are usually primarily for takeout.

Some players are bothered by the concept of cooperative or optional doubles. Suppose partner bids 1♠ and the next player bids 4♡. When you hold

♠ 5 ♡ QJ1097 QJ10 ♣ 8742

you would like to double, fold up your hand, and ostentatiously write 4H^X in your private score. But you can't do that. If you double, partner would bid 4♠ with:

♠ KJ97653 ♡ — ♢ A87 ♣ AJ5

Or he might bid five of a minor with a freakish hand (he almost surely has a void in hearts). You just have to pass and hope partner will reopen with a double.

Another example:

WEST	NORTH	EAST	SOUTH
	1♠	pass	2♢
2♡	dbl	pass	?

♠ 87 ♡ 3 ♢ KQJ9854 ♣ QJ7

Partner made a penalty double here, but you have much less defense than partner expects, so you bid 3♢ anyway. If partner has

♠ AK542 ♡ KQ1093 ♢ 3 ♣ 108

all you can say is that you are sorry. Partner will not wait until he has the contract set in his own hand to double in this auction. It is perfectly reasonable for him to double with

♠ AQ963 ♡ AJ75 ♢ 62 ♣ K3

and, if you leave it in this time with your sub-par defensive hand, the opponents are likely to make their contract and score an undeserved game. Your partnership will make many more successful doubles if, instead of waiting for a sure thing, one player can double to suggest obtaining a penalty and his partner will leave it in unless he has much less (defensively) than the doubler expects. For the typical successful penalty situation, one hand has extra high cards and the other has good trumps:

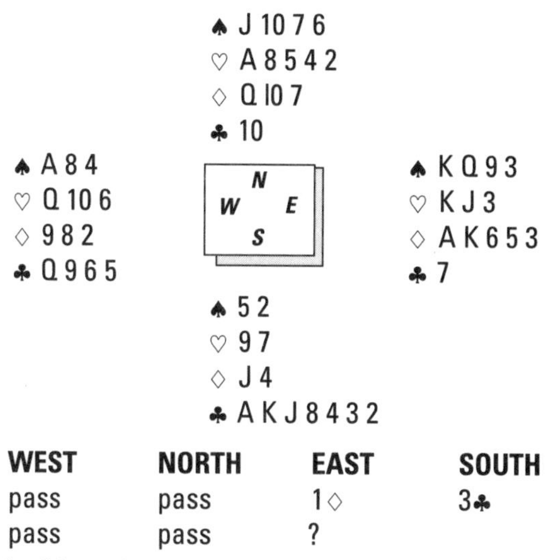

WEST	NORTH	EAST	SOUTH
pass	pass	1◇	3♣
pass	pass	?	

You should double with the East hand. You don't care whether partner bids or passes (with the appropriate hand, of course). Game is still possible and if partner holds something like

♠ A 10 8 6 5 ♡ Q 8 4 ◇ Q 7 ♣ 9 8 6

he might jump to game. This situation will be discussed further in a later chapter. On the actual hand, partner's trump holding and smattering of high cards, along with the extra high cards suggested by your reopening double at the three-level, are adequate for a penalty pass. Your side can make 3NT, but only because diamonds break and South has no entries. Your double is called a takeout double since you are short in clubs, but, because of the level, it is left in about a third of the time. The higher the level, the fewer tricks you need to set the contract and the more tricks you need to make a contract of your own. Therefore, doubles at the three- or four-level, whatever they are called, are more likely to be left in than doubles at the one- or two-level.

'Negative' Doubles at Higher Levels

The foregoing discussion should suggest a precaution.

WEST	NORTH	EAST	SOUTH
	1◇	3♡	?

What should you do with one of these hands:

♠ Q 8 7 4 ♡ 6 ◇ K J 5 4 ♣ J 10 8 5

♠ J 9 5 4 ♡ — ◇ Q 9 7 5 ♣ K 9 8 7 4

Many players would double, righteously pointing out that they play negative doubles through 3♠, but I think a negative double is too dangerous with either hand. What is partner supposed to do with:

♠ A 6 3 ♡ A 10 5 4 ◇ A 10 8 3 ♣ 6 3

He would almost surely pass, and you might set the contract and you might not. I know I am in a minority, but I think opener should pass a double at the three level with as few as three good trumps in a balanced hand. I would pass a double of 3♡ here with

♠ A 6 3 ♡ Q J 9 ◇ A J 4 2 ♣ J 6 3

If responder has a more normal double, like

♠ K 8 6 4 ♡ 7 6 ◇ K 8 7 ♣ A 10 5 4

a pass would be the winning action with the latter hand. Nor do I think responder has to have four spades for his double. What is he supposed to do with:

♠ K Q 8 ♡ 8 7 3 ◇ A 5 4 ♣ Q J 7 4

Pass with 12 HCP? Bid 3NT with no heart stopper and no source of tricks?

I had become afraid that I was almost alone in my concept of negative doubles, but I was reassured by a problem in the August 1999 *Bridge* magazine.

Neither vul., matchpoints

WEST	NORTH	EAST	SOUTH
	pass	pass	1♠
3♣	dbl	pass	?

♠ K J 9 7 3 ♡ A 9 6 ◇ A Q 4 ♣ 5 2

I was surprised to discover that 'pass' received the top vote among the panelists (two-thirds of them did something else, but the votes for other actions were scattered). Barry Rigal said, 'Pass. Negative doubles should be passed with balanced hands. I hope we can beat it, but guessing which red suit to bid is a fairly arid and unrewarding pastime.' Karen McCallum said, 'Pass. Partner has a good balanced or semi-balanced hand. Three clubs doubled may be our last plus score. This is a much easier decision if your agreements regarding negative doubles mandate balanced flexible hands, no two-suiters, and absolutely never contain a singleton in the opponents' suit (above the one-level).' Several panelists stated that they would only pass at matchpoint scoring. If you decide to pull the double (at IMPs), 3◇ would be safer than 3♡, both because your diamonds are stronger than your hearts and because partner would be less likely to raise diamonds than hearts. And with 5-5 in the red suits (which Karen and I say you shouldn't have), or five hearts and four diamonds, partner might have chosen 3♡ rather than a negative double.

Doubling Preempts

Suppose RHO opens 4♡. With which of the following hands would you prefer to double?

a) ♠ 82 ♡ KJ108 ♢ AK ♣ J9843

b) ♠ AJ84 ♡ A7 ♢ KQJ5 ♣ Q82

c) ♠ KJ98 ♡ — ♢ KJ765 ♣ KQ64

Of course, if partner were barred and you knew you were going to be able to defend 4♡ doubled, you would prefer (a). You have five potential defensive tricks, and partner might turn up with a trick or two. The trouble is that partner won't pass your double. He probably has a singleton or void in hearts and four or five spades. Some players say that doubles at the four-level are clearly for penalties (while others say they are for takeout). Forget about labels! Because of the level these doubles are left in more often than not. But when partner has

♠ KQ1075 ♡ 9 ♢ 764 ♣ KJ65

he would, or at least should, pull the double to 4♠. Or with

♠ Q7 ♡ 9 ♢ 7643 ♣ AK7632

he should bid 5♣. He needs a better hand (or a better suit and a more distributional hand) to bid at the five-level, as compared to the four-level. Pulling the double works well when you hold hand (b). It changes a plus to a minus when you hold hand (a).

Frankly, I don't know what I would do with hand (c). A double is very dangerous since with

♠ Q754 ♡ K52 ♢ Q64 ♣ J85

partner would pass, and the opponents would make a doubled overtrick — eight heart tricks plus three aces. At the risk of scaring you off completely before you even finish reading this book, I'll admit that non-vulnerable I might bid 4♠. If West doubled, I would then run to 4NT (obviously for takeout). Anyway, your choice of hands for a double would surely be (b).

All doubles of preempts are cooperative. This rule could be expanded to cover other situations where it is not obvious whether the opponents are bidding to make or to save. For example, you hold:

♠ — ♡ Q8 ♢ AKQJ1063 ♣ A874

RHO opens 1♠ and you bid 3♠, asking partner to bid 3NT with a spade stopper. LHO naturally bids 4♠. You don't know whether he hopes to make 4♠ or whether he intends it as a sacrifice, figuring you have a game your way. Almost any hand with five-card spade support (and many hands with fewer spades) would justify a 4♠ bid. Suppose partner doubles; he should not hold

♠ J9642 ♡ 74 ◇ 54 ♣ K963

but he might hold:

♠ J54 ♡ K954 ◇ 52 ♣ KJ63

With the former hand he has little to contribute offensively. With the latter hand he doesn't care whether you pass or bid your suit and since, in this case, your hand is better for offense than defense, you would bid your suit. With

♠ 7 ♡ AQ10 ◇ AKQJ76 ♣ 1063

you would be delighted to pass.

This is a similar situation:

WEST	NORTH	EAST	SOUTH
1♡	1♠	4♡	dbl

The 4♡ bid here may be a preempt or East may expect to make it (with distribution, not high cards). Even if East is grossly overbidding, West may have extra values. Without the double, North would have no indication whose hand it is. For his overcall he may have ♠Q8743 with values on the side, in which case he would gladly pass the double, or he may have

♠ KQJ1084 ♡ — ◇ KJ3 ♣ Q1065

with which he would be tempted to bid again (and indeed should bid 4♠ if his partner doubles). South should have general strength for his double, perhaps

♠ 96 ♡ J85 ◇ A1076 ♣ KJ83

but not

♠ 63 ♡ QJ108 ◇ Q74 ♣ J732

which has little to offer except on defense against 4♡.

Non-Co-operative Doubles

Now that I have told you most doubles are optional, let me show you a few cases where they are not — and explain why they are not.

WEST	NORTH	EAST	SOUTH
		1♠	pass
2♠	pass	4♠	?

♠ QJ1086 ♡ A95 ◇ 642 ♣ K8

On this deal, the opponents may have been bidding quite logically, expecting to make their contract with normal breaks. But you can see that their trump suit is splitting 5-0, and you almost surely have three trump tricks and one heart trick. Probably you also have a club trick since the ace should be on your right in the strong hand. There is no doubt that you want to double for penalties, but might partner pull the double? He may hold a beauty like:

♠ — ♡ 8743 ◇ 973 ♣ 1096542

No, he should trust you. Obviously you intended the double for penalties. You surely wouldn't invite partner to bid at the five-level when you couldn't double 1♠, which would have allowed him to bid at the two-level. Your exceptionally good trump holding is called a 'surprise' — the opponents had no reason to believe all of their outstanding trumps were in one hand.

When partner has bid, you don't need as big a surprise as when he has remained silent throughout the auction.

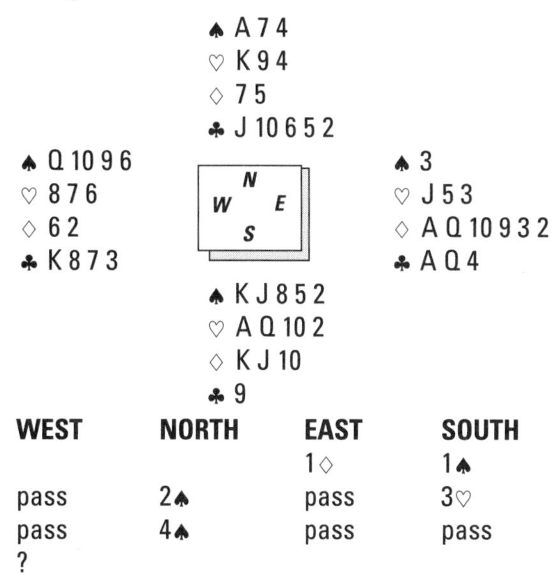

You (West) probably have two trump tricks. Even if the ♠J is in dummy you may get two trump tricks by overruffing the third round of diamonds, or declarer may be unable to ruff his losers in dummy if he picks up your trumps. Your king of clubs will often take a trick. Partner, for his opening bid, should have at least two defensive tricks since you are fairly short in his suit. So you double, hoping for a two-trick set, but not being greatly disappointed when you set it only one. Again, partner has no option but to leave your double in.

Since most doubles are co-operative, why did partner have no right to pull the last two doubles? Because they were late in the auction. When you fail to act until the opponents get to game on the second or third round of bidding, partner has to trust your judgment and pass since a rescue on his part would usually be suicidal. In the last example partner must be consistent. If he was considering bidding again, either constructively or to suggest a sacrifice, he should have taken action over 2♠. Once he decides to pass, he has no right to bid again without encouragement from you.

However, the last two hands were exceptions to the general rule. Often when you make a takeout double you are hoping partner can pass for penalties. On other occasions partner may properly take out your penalty double. I remember an old cartoon where a player lies dead on the floor while his (ex-)partner holds a smoldering pistol. 'He took out my penalty double,' the (ex-)partner exclaims. Today that would no longer be considered justifiable homicide. Most doubles show values useful for both offense and defense. What that means is that, with few exceptions, you should not double unless you are prepared both for partner to pass or to bid.

Suppose partner opens 1♢ and RHO overcalls 2♣. You hold:

♠ Q10965 ♡ K98754 ♢ 6 ♣ 3

Some players would make a negative double, but I think it is too dangerous. If partner's second suit is clubs, which is a strong possibility, won't he pass? He certainly would with

♠ 8 ♡ Q3 ♢ K8743 ♣ AK752

for example. I admit that I am rather conservative; some players would double with these hands despite the danger. They figure they will get enough good results when they find a fit to compensate for the bad results when partner passes.

Telling the Difference

Granted that most doubles are somewhat optional, how can you tell whether a double is primarily for takeout or primarily for penalties? Specific sequences will be discussed in the following chapters, but here are the general rules, some of which it must be admitted are in slight conflict with each other.

1) *A double is for takeout if partner hasn't bid. (Passes don't count as bids; redoubles do.)*

The same rules apply whether or not your side has opened the bidding. Thus the final double in each of the following auctions is for takeout:

WEST	NORTH	EAST	SOUTH
1♠	2♡	pass	pass
dbl			

WEST	NORTH	EAST	SOUTH
1♠	2♡	pass	3♡
dbl			

WEST	NORTH	EAST	SOUTH
1♢	1♠	2♢	pass
pass	dbl		

2) At the one- and two-levels, a double in front of the bidder is for takeout while a double behind the bidder is often for penalties.

WEST	NORTH	EAST	SOUTH
			1NT
2♡	pass	pass	dbl

Here double is for takeout, showing a maximum notrump and a doubleton heart. But in the following auction the opening bidder has hearts:

WEST	NORTH	EAST	SOUTH
1NT	pass	pass	2♡
dbl			

Both doubles are somewhat optional. Responder could pass the first double with

♠ K3 ♡ J953 ◇ Q87 ♣ 10952

and he would probably pull the second double with

♠ J643 ♡ 3 ◇ 108654 ♣ 973

Similarly in the following sequence:

WEST	NORTH	EAST	SOUTH
			1◇
pass	1♠	2♡	pass
pass	dbl		

North might hold:

♠ A865 ♡ J6 ◇ Q83 ♣ K964

We have already discussed this type of double.

3) One must consider the previous bidding to tell whether a double is primarily for penalties or takeout.

For example, in this sequence

WEST	NORTH	EAST	SOUTH
		1♠	dbl
2♠	pass	pass	dbl

your first double was obviously for takeout, and presumably no one slipped you three more spades between rounds of the auction. The second double is therefore also a takeout double, showing not additional spades, but more high cards than the first double guaranteed. Partner might leave the second double in, of course, with

♠ J1095 ♡ J43 ◇ J87 ♣ A62

but I can't imagine a hand where he should leave the double in with only three spades. Well, maybe with ♠KQJ.

4) *When you have preempted or made some sort of limit bid that has described both your strength and distribution, partner's doubles are for penalties.*

When you open 1♠, you may have a one-suiter, a two-suiter or a three-suiter; you may have 10 HCP with good distribution or as much as 21 HCP. As a result of this wide range of possibilities, partner needs to be able to use a negative double in competitive auctions both to describe his hand and to find out more about your hand. In contrast, when you open 2♠ (weak), he knows your approximate strength and you are unlikely to hold a second suit, so there is no need for a negative double. The double in this auction, then, is for penalties:

WEST	NORTH	EAST	SOUTH
	2♠	3♡	dbl

Likewise, most players play that when 1NT is overcalled, a double is for penalties since responder knows opener's approximate strength and distribution. The same is true when opener bids a Precision 2♣ or a Flannery 2♢. Responder knows enough about opener's hand to make a decision, and a double of an overcall is for penalties. Of course, if the Precision 2♣ bidder's hand is

♠ KQJ8 ♡ — ♢ 875 ♣ KQJ1054

nothing prevents him from removing a double of 2♡ to 2♠.

SUMMARY

1. All high-level doubles show general strength, and should not be made on a hand where the doubler is not prepared to have partner pass. This includes negative doubles at the three-level and above.
2. All doubles of preempts are cooperative.
3. Doubles late in the auction are for penalties, and indicate that you have a surprise for the opponents.
4. In general, a double is for takeout if partner hasn't bid, and is for penalties if partner has made some sort of bid that closely defines his strength and distribution. At the one- and two-levels a double in front of the bidder is for takeout while a double behind the bidder is often for penalties.

What is your next bid on each of the following hands?

1. *Neither vul., matchpoints*

WEST	NORTH	EAST	SOUTH
			1♣
3♡	dbl	pass	?

♠ Q 7 5 4 ♡ Q 6 2 ◇ A Q 7 ♣ K 8 5

2. *Both vul., IMPs*

WEST	NORTH	EAST	SOUTH
			1◇
2♣	dbl	pass	?

♠ A J 8 ♡ A K 6 ◇ A 10 9 4 ♣ 9 8 5

You are playing a weak notrump, which is why you opened 1◇. What action would you take now?

3. *Neither vul., IMPs*

WEST	NORTH	EAST	SOUTH
		1◇	1♠
1NT	2♠	pass	pass
3◇	dbl	pass	?

♠ K 10 9 7 5 ♡ J 10 8 ◇ 7 ♣ A J 8 4

4. *Both vul., IMPs*

WEST	NORTH	EAST	SOUTH
			1◇
1♠	dbl	3♠	pass
pass	dbl	pass	?

♠ 8 7 ♡ J 6 5 2 ◇ A J 6 4 ♣ A K 8

5. *Both vul., matchpoints*

WEST	NORTH	EAST	SOUTH
			1◇
4♠	dbl	pass	?

♠ — ♡ J 5 2 ◇ A K Q J 9 4 3 ♣ A 9 6

6. *North-South vul., matchpoints*

WEST	NORTH	EAST	SOUTH
			1♢
4♠	dbl	pass	?

♠ — ♡ A 7 6 ♢ A Q 8 7 5 4 ♣ K 6 5 4

7. *North-South vul., matchpoints*

WEST	NORTH	EAST	SOUTH
			1♢
4♠	dbl	pass	?

♠ — ♡ A Q 10 4 ♢ J 10 9 8 7 ♣ A K 10 4

8. *Both vul., IMPs*

WEST	NORTH	EAST	SOUTH
			2♠
3♡	dbl	pass	?

♠ K Q J 10 8 5 ♡ — ♢ J 9 5 4 ♣ 8 7 4

9. *Neither vul., matchpoints*

WEST	NORTH	EAST	SOUTH
	1♢	pass	1♠
4♡	pass	pass	?

♠ K 7 5 4 ♡ Q J 10 ♢ 8 2 ♣ K 10 8 3

10. *North-South vul., IMPs*

WEST	NORTH	EAST	SOUTH
2♡	pass	4♡	dbl
pass	5♣	pass	?

♠ K 9 7 6 ♡ A J 5 2 ♢ A K 7 ♣ A K

11. *Both vul., IMPs*

WEST	NORTH	EAST	SOUTH
			1♠
2♣	dbl	pass	?

♠ K Q 5 4 2 ♡ Q 10 ♢ A 8 ♣ 10 9 7 5

12. *North-South vul., IMPs*

WEST	NORTH	EAST	SOUTH
			1♢
4♣	dbl	pass	?

♠ A 7 5 ♡ A 8 3 ♢ A 10 9 6 4 ♣ J 5

SOLUTIONS

1. Pass. With a balanced hand and the wasted (for offense) ♡Q, it is unlikely that you can make 3♠, even when partner has four spades, which he doesn't guarantee. If you can take nine tricks in spades, partner will probably raise to 4♠. Your best chance for a plus score is to pass. This seems clear-cut at matchpoints, but I might take the same action at IMPs.

2. You should pass! You have four top defensive tricks, and your ♠J and ♢10 may take tricks. Your top tricks will promote partner's honors to winners — balanced hands often take more defensive tricks than you would expect. Partner may even win a trick with ♣Qx or ♣Jx — if declarer can get to the dummy to take a trump finesse. Besides, you have no good alternative. When this hand came up at the table, partner happened to have a balanced hand with three clubs to the queen, and you had an easy 800-point set on a hand that wouldn't make game your way.

3. Pass. Yes, partner has doubled 'under the bidder', but you should pass anyway. First, the bid is at the three-level, and the higher the level, the fewer tricks you need on defense. Second, in this sequence, it is hard to tell who has the better or longer diamonds, opener or responder. So partner may actually be doubling 'over the bidder'. Third, and most important, since you have already found your fit, partner does not need to double to look for a fit. Only a stack in trumps would justify the double, so you should trust partner and pass.

4. Pass. Partner's double was primarily for takeout, but with most of your honors outside your suit, your hand is better for defense than offense. It is hard to imagine that you can't set 3♠, and partner needs a very good hand with very good hearts to make 4♡. Most players would bid 4♡, but my preference is to pass.

5. Bid 5♢. The fact that you have a void in spades does not mean that partner has tricks in spades. He could easily hold:

   ♠ J 7 5 ♡ K Q 4 3 ♢ 7 2 ♣ K Q 7 5

   What could he do, except double? Since you have a solid suit with a void, and partner promises transferable values, you should bid either 5♢ or 6♢. Probably 5♢ is enough — some of partner's values could be in spades.

6. Pass. If you bid, you should bid 4NT, which implies long diamonds and shorter clubs. However, it is dangerous to look for a fit at the five-level, and I think the percentage action is to pass and hope for the best. Partner is not precluded from holding values in spades, and whether he does or not, you should easily set the contract with your combined high cards.

7. This is a very close decision. In a bidding panel of international experts the vote was nineteen for 4NT (obviously for takeout) and seventeen for a pass. At IMPs you have a clear-cut pass.

8. Bid 3♠. Yes, I know I told you that when you opened a weak two-bid, partner's doubles were for penalty. But with a solid suit, a void, and worse than normal defensive strength, I think your percentage action is to pull to 3♠. The whole hand was as follows:

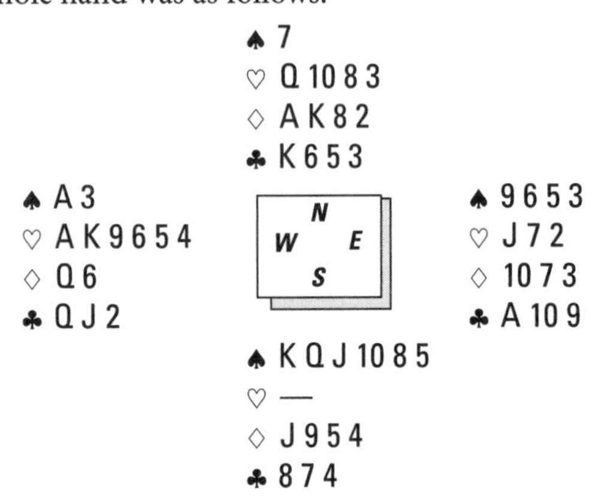

I don't blame partner for doubling since that is the action that will usually work out best. There is a saying that if your opponents never make a doubled contract, you are not doubling enough. Change your spades to ♠KQ9852 and you should pass and blame your minus 730 on bad luck (or on partner, of course!). But when you have both a very safe run-out and subnormal defense, you should not risk a disaster. Sometimes when you pull a double with this sort of hand, things work out very well indeed. If partner held

♠ 7 ♡ J 10 5 4 ◇ A K 10 4 ♣ A Q J 8

he would raise you to 4♠ since he would know you had good spades and short hearts.

9. Pass. You expect to set the contract, but just be happy the opponents did not bid only 3♡, which they might well make. The danger in doubling is that partner may bid 4♠ with one of these hands:

♠ A J 8 ♡ 7 ◇ A Q 7 5 3 ♣ A 7 4 2

♠ Q 8 6 3 ♡ 5 4 ◇ A K Q 6 ♣ Q J 7

He was tempted to bid 4♠ last round but refrained from doing so since you might have had a minimum response. If you show extra values, the temptation may become irresistible.

10. The decision is close, but I think you should bid 6♣. Remember, partner didn't have to bid at this level, and he shouldn't have bid unless he thought he could make it. Meanwhile, you have lots of extra values. Partner actually held

♠ QJ4 ♡ — ♢ 842 ♣ Q1098654

and the slam was cold.

11. Pass. Partner usually has a maximum of two cards in your suit, and he may hold 2-4-4-3 distribution. That's what he actually had, and you could be plus 500 if you passed and minus if you bid anything else. No, I wouldn't be overjoyed at the prospect of defending 2♣ doubled, but any bid by you risks a minus score, and it is not the end of the world if the opponents make their doubled contract since it isn't game.

12. Pass. Surely you will set 4♣; perhaps you will only get 300, but what is your alternative? Nick Nickell bid 4♢ with this hand in an international match, and with bad breaks, he was down five. So there is no assurance that you can make 4♢, and even if you can, it will score less than defeating 4♣ doubled. To be honest, I must tell you that many top experts approved of the 4♢ bid, since they visualized games and slams (where partner would bid over 4♢). But I would expect partner to have about ten or eleven points far more often than values for a five- or six-level contract. And if I were the responder with something like

♠ KQ62 ♡ KQ42 ♢ Q753 ♣ 4

or the same hand with the ♣A (the type of hands the 4♢ bidders had in mind), I wouldn't risk doubling 4♣; I would bid 5♢ with the hand shown, and 5♣ with the one that included the singleton ♣A!

CHAPTER 9

Doubles for Takeout

Traditional Takeout Doubles

The first topic we need to discuss in this chapter is the classical situation for a takeout double. It occurs when partner hasn't bid (passes don't count as bids; redoubles do) and the double is of a suit bid (not notrump) at the one-, two- or three-level. Those have been the rules for as long as I can remember. Suppose the bidding goes

WEST	NORTH	EAST	SOUTH
		1♣	1♠
3♣	pass	pass	?

and you hold either of these hands:

a) ♠ A Q 10 7 6 ♡ 7 5 ◇ K 9 8 5 ♣ 7 2

b) ♠ A Q 10 7 6 ♡ Q 7 4 ◇ A Q 9 6 ♣ J

With hand (a) you pretty much told your story when you overcalled 1♠, so you should pass. With hand (b) it is quite possible that you can make a contract your way since you have much better than a minimum overcall, so this time you double. Obviously, you intend your double for takeout, but if partner holds

♠ 5 2 ♡ A 8 4 3 ◇ 10 5 4 ♣ Q 10 8 6

he's allowed to pass since you show extra high cards by doubling at this level.

When the bidding goes

WEST	NORTH	EAST	SOUTH
		1♢	pass
1♠	pass	2♠	dbl

the double is still for takeout. You might have had a pretty good hand with a singleton spade and unbiddable hearts — for example:

♠ 5 ♡ Q875 ♢ AK94 ♣ AJ83

Of course there is some risk involved since partner has to respond at the three-level. In fact, rather than chance defending 2♠ doubled with

♠ J876 ♡ J62 ♢ 875 ♣ Q42

he should bid a confident 3♣.

Supposedly all doubles of natural notrump bids are for penalties. The justification for this 'rule' is that when you have the balance of power and the opening lead, you are supposed to be able to do better penalizing the opponents than playing a contract of your own. So when partner bids 1♡ and RHO bids 1NT, a double is for penalties, even though partner can and should take the double out with a weak, distributional hand. However, there are many exceptions to this 'rule'. The double in this auction

WEST	NORTH	EAST	SOUTH
1♡	pass	1NT	dbl

is equivalent to a takeout double of 1♡. Partner needs a good hand with heart strength behind the bidder to leave the double in. It is extremely unlikely that the doubler has a good enough hand to set 1NT all by himself, but he will often have sufficient values, including distribution, to compete for a partscore. It is uneconomical to save the double for, at most, one hand out of a hundred.

Likewise, it is poor strategy to double RHO's strong notrump opening for penalties on a strong balanced hand. You would need a hand at least as good as the opening notrumper's hand, and you would be gambling that partner, rather than LHO, has the balance of the outstanding strength. Besides, these hands are hard to defend. Since you don't know where partner's strength is, you won't know what to lead, and the opponents may take seven or eight tricks before you discover what suit you should have attacked. For those reasons, many players have given up the penalty double of 1NT; instead, they use the double to show other types of hands (such as a one-suiter, which they will show over a forced 2♣ response).

How about this sequence?

WEST	NORTH	EAST	SOUTH
1♢	1♠	1NT	dbl

To set 1NT you would surely need strength in diamonds, but your diamond strength is poorly placed, under the opening bidder. Meanwhile, the notrump bidder must have spades stopped, and he may have a double stopper. Partner's 1♠ overcall varies widely as to high-card strength and distribution, so you could almost never guarantee a set. So this double should just show a few high cards, enabling partner to compete with a second suit or rebid spades with a good suit of his own. Of course, he would be delighted to pass your double with

♠ KQJ106 ♡ A75 ◇ K9 ♣ J43

but how often will he hold a hand like that when the bidding goes this way? With

♠ KJ8754 ♡ 8 ◇ 95 ♣ KJ85

partner should rebid 2♠ and with

♠ AJ632 ♡ 85 ◇ J4 ♣ K1095

he should rebid 2♣.

Next, let us consider another exception to our general rules. A double is supposed to be for takeout when partner hasn't bid, and a pass is not considered a bid. But suppose the bidding goes like this:

WEST	**NORTH**	**EAST**	**SOUTH**
	1◇	1♠	pass
pass	dbl	pass	pass
2♡	dbl		

What is North's second double? According to the general rules, since partner has passed throughout, it is a takeout double. But partner's pass of 1♠ doubled was a penalty pass, equivalent to bidding spades himself. So the second double was a penalty double. This makes sense because North's first double showed a shortage in spades with presumably at least three hearts and maybe four. Besides, when three suits have been bid, a double is usually for penalties and does not say, 'Partner, please bid the fourth suit, I am too tired to bid it myself.'

Suppose instead of doubling, North passes the 2♡ bid in the sequence just shown. If East also passes, what should South do with:

♠ KJ985 ♡ AJ3 ◇ 7 ♣ J865

Having, in effect, made a penalty double himself already(by passing his partner's takeout double) he can make another penalty double here too.

To double or overcall?

With the major exceptions out of the way, let us consider the traditional takeout double. As we have already seen, it tends to deny a five-card major unless the doubler has a very good hand — because

♠ K 7 5 ♡ K J 8 4 2 ◇ A 5 ♣ K 8 3

is too weak to double first and then later voluntarily bid hearts, and if you don't bid hearts after doubling, you may miss a 5-3 heart fit. However, when the choice is between passing, overcalling at the two-level with a weak suit, or doubling, the double is usually the least of evils. Suppose RHO bids 1♠ and you hold one of these hands:

♠ J ♡ A 7 6 5 2 ◇ K Q 8 ♣ A J 5 4

♠ 6 4 ♡ K 9 6 5 4 ◇ A 10 ♣ A K 5 4

In either case, a 2♡ overcall is very dangerous with so weak a suit. Even if you don't get doubled, you hate to commit the hand to a heart contract when it is entirely possible that another contract will play several tricks better. So you double — perhaps you will miss a heart contract when partner has three, but at least you won't miss it when he has four.

The ideal distribution for a takeout double is 4-4-4-1, with a singleton in the opponent's suit. With that distribution you can double 1♣ with as little as

♠ A 8 7 6 ♡ K 9 5 3 ◇ K 7 3 2 ♣ 5

since you are almost bound to find an eight-card fit and should be safe at the one-level. (The reason for not bidding with an even weaker hand is that partner may take you seriously and bid too much or double the opponents.) A double of 1♠, probably forcing partner to the two-level, requires slightly more body to the hand; perhaps

♠ 5 ♡ A J 6 5 ◇ K 9 5 3 ♣ K 10 9 6

(which is marginally stronger)is a minimum. Some players say they will never double with 4-3-3-3 distribution; others say they will seldom double without at least one four-card major. These philosophies will cost them many partscore swings:

♠ A 6 5 4 ♡ 9 8 5 ◇ K Q 6 ♣ A 6 4

is clearly enough to make a takeout double of 1♡, since you have no wasted values in hearts. In fact, I believe

♠ A 6 5 ♡ 9 8 5 ◇ K Q 6 3 ♣ A 6 4

is (though barely) enough. If partner has

♠ K 9 8 7 3 ♡ J 3 ◇ J 8 7 ♣ K 8 2

you would rather have partner play 2♠ than let the opponents play 2♡, but it is safer for you to double than for partner to bid all by himself on his hand, even as a reopening bid. Or suppose partner has:

♠ Q 10 4 ♡ 7 2 ◇ A 9 8 5 2 ♣ Q J 7

Do you want to defend 2♡ or play 3◇? The only safe way to compete is for you to make a takeout double.

Likewise, you should double a 1◇ opening with

♠ A Q 6 ♡ Q 9 5 4 ◇ 8 7 5 ♣ A J 9

since all of your points are working. With

♠ A Q 6 ♡ Q 9 5 4 ◇ Q J 6 ♣ K 6 4

despite having one more point, you should pass over 1◇ since your hand is much better for defense than for offense. Give partner a typical, unexciting hand

♠ J 8 7 4 3 ♡ K 8 6 ◇ 9 4 ♣ Q 10 7

and you will see what I mean. Opposite the recommended double, partner can probably make 2♠. Opposite the other hand, he is probably going down in 2♠ while you have a good chance to defeat 2◇ (or 1NT).

Larry Cohen recommends a takeout double of 1◇ with

♠ A 7 5 ♡ A 5 3 ◇ 8 7 ♣ K J 9 5 4

and I agree 100%. Why put all of your eggs in one basket by overcalling 2♣? Even worse, why pass and try to guess what to do after the auction dies early, for example in a sequence like:

WEST	NORTH	EAST	SOUTH
		1◇	pass
1♡	pass	2♡	?

Responding to a takeout double

Everyone knows that the only forcing bid in response to partner's takeout double is a cuebid. Some players make a jump response any time they have eight to ten points and cuebid with eleven or more points. This doesn't make good sense to me. If partner doubles a 1◇ opening, then a hand like

♠ Q 7 5 ♡ Q 7 4 3 ◇ Q J 6 ♣ K 4 2

is only worth a 1♡ or 1NT response, not a jump to 2♡, because your diamond honors are probably worthless.

The following hand was used three times in bidding panels for *Australian Bridge* (1971, 1989 and 1994) since the moderator, the late Keith McNeil, felt so strongly about it. The bidding goes:

WEST	NORTH	EAST	SOUTH
			pass
1♣	dbl	pass	?

♠ K94 ♡ 10872 ◇ AJ53 ♣ Q10

Keith favored a 2♡ response, and he thought anyone who bid 1♡ was a wimp. Certainly, he had some support — 2♡ was the panel's choice by 27 to 9 over 1♡, with eight choosing a 2♣ cuebid! Nevertheless, I still believe that 2♡ is wrong, and that 2♣ is terrible (unless you play that a cuebid does not guarantee another bid). Your club holding is worthless unless partner has a club honor, and even if he has ♣Kx, the ace is likely to be onside anyway so your queen still isn't contributing. It is very unlikely that you will have a game in hearts (or anywhere else) if partner passes 1♡. I reserve the right to evaluate my hand, taking into consideration where my points are located, and whether I have a decent suit. Partner doesn't always have four-card support, and I don't like to play contracts, even at the two-level, with 10872 of trumps opposite Q54.

The following hand came up in a tournament, and almost everyone got too high.

WEST	NORTH	EAST	SOUTH
1◇	dbl	pass	?

♠ J7 ♡ Q1096 ◇ Q10 ♣ AK642

Your hand calls for a 2♡ response, not a 2◇ cuebid. (In response to a takeout double, you almost always bid a four-card major rather than a longer minor.) It is very awkward if the takeout doubler has to jump in a bad suit just to show extra values, so the cuebid should promise another bid. That is part of Bridge World Standard. With

♠ K875 ♡ Q974 ◇ J6 ♣ A72

you could cuebid and raise whatever suit partner bids. (You can afford to raise clubs since partner usually has a good hand and at least five of his minor when he doubles without a four-card major.) The raise is non-forcing, but a cuebid followed by a new suit is forcing. If you don't want to force, you jump in your suit in the first place. So if you cuebid with

♠ J7 ♡ Q1096 ◇ Q10 ♣ AK642

(which isn't nearly as good as your 12 HCP suggest), how will you ever stop below game? If partner bids 2♠, his most likely response, and you bid 3♣, forcing, you will probably get to 4♣, and, since you are now within one trick of game anyway, you may be tempted to bid again. For that matter, are you even sure that 4♣ is safe? Partner actually held

♠ KQ53 ♡ AJ4 ◇ 83 ♣ QJ83

and raised to 4♣ when your hand started with a cuebid (mistakenly, in my opinion). It was unlucky that the heart finesse failed, but since you weren't even close to belonging in game, getting to the four-level was an unnecessary risk.

This brings me to an important point about bidding 1NT in these takeout double auctions. Suppose the bidding goes

WEST	NORTH	EAST	SOUTH
1♢	dbl	1♠	?

and you hold:

♠ J6 ♡ Q94 ♢ Q1064 ♣ K652

You should bid 1NT. You don't need a spade stopper since partner's double implies spade length or strength. But you do need a diamond stopper since partner is usually short in opener's suit for his takeout double.

The doubler's next turn

When you make a takeout double, it is important to remember that partner may have nothing. He has to bid unless he is very strong in the opponent's suit — so strong that he welcomes a trump lead. Partner won't often have a Yarborough, but you have to proceed with some degree of caution.

WEST	NORTH	EAST	SOUTH
1♢	dbl	pass	1♠
pass	2♠		

Even this single raise, therefore, should show extra values, probably 16-18 points, counting points for distribution. But suppose the bidding goes:

WEST	NORTH	EAST	SOUTH
		1♢	dbl
pass	1♠	2♢	?

Should the doubler raise with a minimum double when there is competition? Some very fine players and theorists, like Kit Woolsey, Marty Bergen and Larry Cohen, say the doubler should raise whenever he has four-card support, since the Law protects you. If the opponents can slaughter you at the two-level when you have an eight-card fit, they could score more by playing the hand their way, and the possibility that partner was forced to respond on a three-card suit is too remote to worry about.

I don't agree. There is some danger in raising to the two-level when partner could be very weak. (Remember adjustment factors!) But a more serious problem is that partner will not know when to compete further. Suppose the opponents bid on over your raise:

WEST	NORTH	EAST	SOUTH
		1♢	dbl
pass	1♠	2♢	2♠
3♢	?		

Should partner bid 3♠ with:

♠ KJ74 ♡ Q43 ♢ 984 ♣ 852

After all, he could have held a Yarborough. But if your raise is automatic with four-card support, partner doesn't know whether you have extra values.

My solution is to stretch by no more than one point. In competition doubler is allowed to raise with fifteen support points instead of sixteen. Suppose the hands are as follows:

NORTH
♠ AJ95
♡ K984
♢ 87
♣ A95

SOUTH
♠ Q643
♡ A6
♢ J53
♣ J743

WEST	NORTH	EAST	SOUTH
1♢	dbl	pass	1♠
2♢	pass	pass	3♣
pass	3♠	all pass	

I think everyone will agree that North-South should compete to 2♠ and sell out if the opponents bid 3♢. But in this case the opponents did not push North-South to the three-level — they did it to themselves. This is why there is an argument for North to bid 2♠ with no extra values and for South to pass despite his extra values. But no matter how they work it, North-South will make the wrong decision some of the time if a raise with four trumps is automatic.

However, there is a good theoretical solution to this problem. North should pass over 2♢, but instead of bidding 3♣, South should double! The double merely says, 'I have enough strength to bid again, but only a four-card spade suit (and probably not a longer side suit).' With a five-card suit and fewer than four spades, North would bid his suit. With

♠ A87 ♡ KJ54 ♢ 86 ♣ KQ82

he would bid 2NT to let South choose between the unbid suits. Or, at matchpoints, he might even gamble on a pass.

What if your original double was based on a strong balanced hand? Suppose RHO opens 1♡ and you hold

♠ A 10 5 ♡ K Q 10 6 ◊ A K 10 8 ♣ K 3

You are too strong to overcall 1NT, so you double, planning to rebid 1NT over a 1♠ response or 2NT over a minor suit response. LHO bids 3♡ (preemptive) and the bidding is passed back to you. You are tempted to double again since you can easily set this contract by yourself, but you should resist the temptation. What does poor partner hold? Probably a Yarborough with a void in hearts! If you double, partner will bid 4♣ with

♠ 9 6 4 ♡ — ◊ 9 5 4 3 ♣ 10 8 6 5 4 2

and you will be minus instead of plus. Partner will expect you to hold something like:

♠ K Q 7 3 ♡ A 6 ◊ A K 6 2 ♣ K 7 3

For this sequence you would often hold a singleton heart, but when partner has a void, he will figure a doubleton is more likely — but certainly not three or four!

Doubles under the bidder

We have already discussed doubles under the bidder which are for takeout at the one- or two-level. After

WEST	NORTH	EAST	SOUTH
	1♣	pass	1♠
2♡	pass	pass	?

♠ A J 8 7 3 ♡ J 4 ◊ K 7 ♣ Q 8 7 6

you would double, planning to pass if partner bids 2♠ (probably with a doubleton honor). Although you will be happy if partner has the right hand to pass, your double is primarily for takeout. Suppose the bidding is

WEST	NORTH	EAST	SOUTH
	1◊	1♡	1♠
2♡	pass	pass	?

♠ A J 9 5 2 ♡ 7 ◊ 9 7 4 ♣ A J 4 3

You would like to double here rather than commit the hand to diamonds. I advised you not to double with a singleton in the opponents' suit for fear that partner would pass with four of their suit — and you don't usually like to defend low-level doubled contracts when the opponents have eight trumps. But it is permissible to double in this sequence because the suit has been bid and supported. Partner has been warned, and if he leaves it in, he should have very good trumps.

Doubles at the two-level in front of the bidder are for takeout. What about doubles in front of the bidder at the three-level? The following hand is from the Master Solver's panel of the March 1982 *Bridge World*:

WEST	NORTH	EAST	SOUTH
		pass	pass
pass	1♣	1♢	1♠
3♢	pass	pass	?

♠ A 10 8 6 3 ♡ J 8 5 ♢ J 10 4 ♣ A 5

The panel voted 24 for a double and 6 for a pass (I was one of the minority). If partner had three-card spade support or a six-card club suit, he was expected to remove the double, but the double was basically for penalties — at IMPs!

More recently *International Popular Bridge Monthly* had the following problem (I don't remember the vulnerability or the form of scoring).

WEST	NORTH	EAST	SOUTH
	1♡	pass	1♠
3♣	pass	pass	?

♠ A J 8 5 ♡ K 7 ♢ Q 8 7 6 4 2 ♣ 5

This time twelve panelists doubled, five bid 3♢, and only one passed! Whatever the double means, I don't approve — do you really want to hear partner bid 3♠, or have him pass with 2-5-3-3 distribution? However, it was obvious that a majority of the panel of international experts considered the double to be clearly for takeout. What this means is that now, eighteen years after the *Bridge World* hand appeared, most experts treat all doubles 'under the bidder' as showing extra values, but being basically for takeout. Whether partner can pass with a balanced hand or needs a stack in the opponent's suit is not clear. With:

♠ A J 8 5 2 ♡ K 7 ♢ Q 8 7 6 ♣ 5 4

I would double also, since I would welcome a 3♠ bid by partner and wouldn't mind if partner passed with:

♠ 7 5 ♡ A Q 6 3 2 ♢ K 5 4 ♣ K 9 7

So I agree that doubles at the three-level, in front of the bidder, should be primarily for takeout, but I require more of a safety margin than most, since I expect partner to leave the double in with a balanced hand and no safe rescue bid.

Bidding over the opponents' takeout double

Before advancing to a new topic, we should consider how the opening side bids after a takeout double. Suppose the bidding commences:

WEST	NORTH	EAST	SOUTH
	1♢	dbl	?

♠ 9 7 6 5 4 ♡ J 8 3 ♢ 5 ♣ 9 7 5 2

In the old days (even before my time) the accepted bid on this hand was 1♠. You didn't want to play 1♢ doubled, and you were trying to improve the contract. Your bid was not forcing since with all good hands you would start with a redouble. Players soon realized that the double was seldom left in (and when it was, partner could rescue himself). So it made better sense for your 1♠ bid to be at least constructive, and most players now play that a new suit at the one-level is forcing. Suppose, though, that you redouble to show a good hand with

♠ AJ642 ♡ 7 ♢ Q654 ♣ KJ3

and LHO bids 4♡, which is passed around to you. What call would you make now? Double? 4♠? 5♢? You would have to be very lucky to guess the right action. However, if you bid 1♠ instead of redoubling in the first place, LHO is slightly less likely to preempt, and if he does, you can show your extra strength by doubling. Partner can then bid 4♠ with:

♠ K93 ♡ 84 ♢ AKJ83 ♣ Q94

There is even more reason to bid immediately with a heart suit before the opponents can preempt you in spades. On the same auction

WEST	NORTH	EAST	SOUTH
	1♢	dbl	?

you should bid 1♡ with any of these hands:

♠ J7 ♡ KQ96 ♢ 987 ♣ K873

♠ 8 ♡ KJ754 ♢ Q9 ♣ K8542

♠ A4 ♡ Q10965 ♢ K8432 ♣ A

If you have extra strength you can show it later by doubling or cuebidding. Some players disregard the double completely (except for redoubling with good balanced hands). I suggest three minor deviations, as follows:

1) Don't bid a weak four-card suit with a balanced hand.

There are several reasons for this.

WEST	NORTH	EAST	SOUTH
	1♢	dbl	?

♠ K7 ♡ Q865 ♢ J87 ♣ Q643

On this hand, I would bid 1NT. Since RHO has made a takeout double, he probably has at least three hearts, perhaps four, which decreases your chances of finding a heart fit. If you do find a 4-4 heart fit, the hearts are likely to split 4-1, and if you find a 4-3 heart fit, you are almost sure to lose control. Unless partner has precisely 4-4-4-1 distribution, when you have a good heart fit the opponents probably have a good spade fit, and they can outbid you. A 1NT response instead has several advantages. First, West won't have a very good hand, and you might preempt him out of showing his spade suit. It is also quite likely that 1NT will be your best contract. Finally, if there is further competition, partner can make intelligent decisions since 1NT limits and describes your strength and balanced distribution. Bidding 1♡ only gains when partner has four hearts, and not always even then. (Incidentally, you should know that a majority of experts reject this exception — they would bid 1♡ on this hand just as though there had been no double.)

2) *While your new suit bid at the one-level is forcing, new suit bids on later rounds should not be forcing (unless you jump).*

Consequently, you can bid 1♡ and later bid clubs without it being forcing here:

WEST	NORTH	EAST	SOUTH
	1♢	dbl	1♡
pass	1♠	pass	?

♠ 7 ♡ KJ754 ♢ Q9 ♣ K8542

With a stronger hand, when you want your later bids to be forcing, you must either redouble right away (with semi-balanced hands) or jump on the next round.

3) *When you have a weak hand with support for partner's major, show it immediately.*

Over

WEST	NORTH	EAST	SOUTH
	1♡	dbl	?

you should bid 2♡ with:

♠ 86 ♡ K95 ♢ Q9852 ♣ 976

What if you have a better hand, though?

WEST	NORTH	EAST	SOUTH
	1♡	dbl	?

♠ A65 ♡ Q872 ♢ K107 ♣ 976

A redouble would just goad West into preempting, and if you do redouble and support hearts later, partner will expect a better hand. The solution is to pass and support hearts on the next round at the lowest possible level. When your hand is relatively balanced, with a good 8 to a bad 10 HCP, it is unlikely that the bidding will be at a high level when it comes back to you. Since you bid immediately when you are weak, provided you are able to bid at all, a pass followed by a bid shows a fairly good hand. (Of course, if partner bids again himself before it gets back to you, you have to jump to show your values.)

What about this hand on the same auction?

WEST	NORTH	EAST	SOUTH
	1♡	dbl	?

♠ A96 ♡ 84 ♢ J2 ♣ AQ10762

Without the ace of spades you would have a perfect 2♣ response (non-forcing at the two-level), but this hand is too strong. Suppose you redouble and the opponents bid 2♢ or 2♠ — now if you bid 3♣, it will be forcing. You would rather bid 3♣ non-forcing, and again the way to do that is to pass now and bid 3♣ next round. A recent Master Solver's problem in *Bridge World* showed that all players who learned to play bridge in California know about this pass-and-bid-later gimmick to show a fair hand, while players from other parts of the world are still living in the Dark Ages.

When you have four or more cards in partner's suit and a good, distributional hand, you want to show your hand-type immediately. If you have a great fit, the opponents also have a great fit, and if you redouble, the opponents may jump to the three- or four-level, which will create problems for you and your partner. So you should bid 2NT immediately to show an unbalanced limit raise or better. After an opening bid in a minor, many players prefer to play 'flip-flop', where 2NT is a preemptive raise and three of partner's minor is a limit raise. The argument is that partner is more likely to be able to bid 3NT over a limit raise than over a preemptive raise and it is better for partner, with the stronger hand, to be declarer in 3NT and have the takeout doubler on opening lead.

Negative Doubles

I can remember a time when all doubles by responder were for penalties, but in the late 1950s, Roth and Stone introduced the negative double. The expert community resisted the concept at first, but eventually everyone adopted it. Since successful penalty doubles at low levels are relatively rare, it made good sense, based on frequency, to use low-level doubles for offensive rather than defensive purposes. So all doubles of suit overcalls at the one- or two-level by responder are now for takeout, and even at the three-level they are primarily for takeout. Since negative doubles at the one-level are never left in unless opener has five of the suit (and how often will opener have five of a higher-ranking suit than the one he opened?), responder doesn't need to worry about doubling with a void or a singleton. At the two-level opener may well pass if the opponents happen to have bid his second suit, so responder should not make a negative double with a void or a weak two-suiter. At the three-level, responder should not double unless he is willing to have opener pass with a balanced hand.

As Roth and Stone first explained the negative double, it was made on balanced hands and there was no guarantee regarding major-suit length. The only 'guarantee' was that if partner bid naturally, the final contract would be reasonable. That basic concept still appeals to me. If partner opens 1♣ and the next hand overcalls 1♠, you would like to do something with

♠ 864 ♡ KQ6 ♢ Q7542 ♣ K7

and since no other action is attractive, you would make a negative double. You should double even though it implies four hearts. You hope partner will rebid 1NT or 2♣, but if he bids 2♡, he should make it, because your extra strength compensates for your disappointing distribution. If you pass now, because you require four hearts to double, you will have serious problems later. What will you do if partner reopens with a double or a 2♣ bid? (This is a rhetorical question since there is no way to catch up.) Some players guarantee four cards in an unbid major when they make a negative double. I prefer a more flexible approach: you *imply* support for a major suit, but you are allowed to double when you are strong enough to handle any rebid by partner.

When partner opens 1♣ and RHO overcalls 1◇, a negative double shows both majors and is my choice with:

♠ AQ62 ♡ Q10753 ◇ 75 ♣ 95

The advantage of doubling is that if LHO raises diamonds (perhaps to the three-level), you may find your fit when partner has either major, while if you bid your five-card suit, you put all your eggs in one basket. Nevertheless, I would also double on the same auction with:

♠ KQ5 ♡ 7652 ◇ 9762 ♣ A8

When every action is slightly misleading, you have to choose the one with the fewest defects, and neither passing nor bidding 1♡ has much appeal. Do you want partner to give you a heart raise with three-card support if LHO bids 3◇? Or double to show three-card support if LHO bids 2◇?

Suppose the bidding goes:

WEST	**NORTH**	**EAST**	**SOUTH**
	1◇	2♣	?

♠ K4 ♡ Q984 ◇ J853 ♣ J42

The only bid you can make is 2◇ (remember, we don't play inverted raises in competition!). You aren't strong enough to make a negative double and correct a 2♠ or 2NT response to 3◇. But if RHO had overcalled 1♠ you would double, as you would with

♠ A87 ♡ Q874 ◇ 109653 ♣ 9

since in that case you could correct any club bid by partner to diamonds. When there is only one unbid major, an immediate raise of partner's minor should deny four cards in that major.

Experts are in violent disagreement regarding one sequence. When partner opens a minor and RHO overcalls 1♡, should a double show or deny four spades? One group says the 1♡ bid doesn't raise the bidding level, so if you had planned to bid 1♠ over a pass, you should bid it anyway, even with a four-card suit. Since you don't need to make a negative double with four spades, a negative double should therefore deny four spades. Another group says that you can take advantage of the negative double by doubling to show exactly four spades and bidding one spade to show five or more.

I don't agree with either group. I think a negative double should *imply* four spades, but when the bidding goes

WEST	NORTH	EAST	SOUTH
	1♢	1♡	?

I would double with either of these hands:

♠ KQ8 ♡ 984 ♢ J64 ♣ A852

♠ QJ7 ♡ 98 ♢ 864 ♣ AQ642

since partner should make whatever he bids, including a low-level spade contract on a 4-3 fit. Similarly, with

♠ J652 ♡ 874 ♢ Q6 ♣ AJ54

I don't want to respond 1♠ with so weak a suit and have partner raise (or make a support double) in competition with three-card support. Besides, the hand may play much better in clubs. If I bid 1♠ and West raises hearts, partner will be forced to pass with

♠ 97 ♡ A3 ♢ KJ742 ♣ KQ83

while if I had doubled, he could have competed in clubs. Since my hand is only worth one bid, why not show a flexible hand rather than bid such a weak spade suit?

By contrast, though, I prefer a 1♠ bid to a negative double with

♠ KQ106 ♡ A654 ♢ 83 ♣ 952

I don't mind if partner raises with ♠A72 (and probably only one or two hearts). I am not anxious to hear him bid either minor, especially at the three-level. Maybe he will bid it anyway, but I don't want to encourage him in case of further competition. So in deciding whether to bid 1♠ or double, I consider at least two factors:

1) Is it likely the hand will play better in some other contract than in spades?

2) If I bid 1♠, will I mind being raised with three-card support?

What about negative doubles on stronger hands? The following problem was presented to the bidding panel for the March 1998 *Bridge World.*

WEST	NORTH	EAST	SOUTH
	1♣	2♡	?

Vulnerable against not, you hold:

♠ AQ10 ♡ A1074 ♢ QJ3 ♣ AQ8

Despite holding only three spades, nineteen panelists chose a negative double compared to eleven who chose a cuebid. They felt that the negative double was more likely to coax a revealing rebid from partner than a cuebid would have been. In a more mundane sequence

WEST	NORTH	EAST	SOUTH
	1♠	2♢	?

I again prefer a negative double to a cuebid with:

♠ J 5 4 ♡ Q 9 4 ♢ A 10 5 ♣ K J 10 6

A cuebid, showing a limit raise or better in spades, will commit you to a spade contract. A negative double gives you a slight chance of getting to notrump, which might be a better contract if partner has a balanced hand with a diamond stopper to go with yours. If partner trustingly bids hearts at the two- or three-level, you will show a jump preference for spades.

Opener's rebid over a negative double

Negative doubles may cause a serious rebid problem when opener has a minimum balanced hand. What would you bid here?

WEST	NORTH	EAST	SOUTH
			1♢
2♣	dbl	pass	?

♠ A J 6 ♡ A J 8 ♢ K 7 5 2 ♣ 9 8 2

Many experts would bid 2♡, but my inclination is to pass. Balanced hands often take more tricks than you would expect, and partner might well win a trump trick with the doubleton queen or jack. I am not happy about passing — it is just that everything else looks worse, and 2♣ doubled is not game if they make it. The problem is more serious when partner doubles a 2♡ overcall and you hold:

♠ A J 6 ♡ 9 8 2 ♢ K 7 5 2 ♣ A J 8

Now if they make it, it is game, so my recommendation is to pass at matchpoints and bid 2♠ at IMPs.

Clearly, opener often does not have an easy rebid in these auctions. If he has a stopper in the opponents' suit, he may have to rebid 2NT despite holding a bare minimum. That is why negative doubles at the two-level with a balanced hand should show at least 9-10 HCP; even then, they are dangerous.

Even when you open a five-card major and partner makes a negative double, you may still have problems. You open 1♠ with

♠ A K 7 5 2 ♡ Q 6 4 ♢ 9 8 ♣ K 9 6

and RHO overcalls 2♢. If partner doubles, what would you bid? You have already shown a five-card spade suit, so if you rebid spades partner may think, or at least hope, that you have six. But 2♠ is the least misleading bid. Worse, suppose you hold:

♠ J7642 ♡ AQ6 ◇ 86 ♣ AQ4

With such a weak spade suit, 2♡ is my choice. But I don't like to bid a three-card heart suit since, if partner worries about that possibility, he won't know whether to raise, or how high, when he has four-card heart support. I want partner to assume I have a four-card suit when I bid it. With

♠ AK1076 ♡ 875 ◇ A6 ♣ J64

you should bid 2♠ despite your diamond stopper since you have fairly good spades and a poor hand for notrump. With

♠ AJ642 ♡ Q10 ◇ K75 ♣ Q98

2NT seems like the least of evils, and it illustrates why partner should not make a negative double with a hand like either of these:

♠ 87 ♡ K853 ◇ 96 ♣ K6542

♠ 76 ♡ A642 ◇ 983 ♣ K642

With a known fit, however, opener can bid confidently. After this auction, for instance

WEST	NORTH	EAST	SOUTH
			1♣
1♡	dbl	2♡	?

♠ K985 ♡ K8 ◇ Q54 ♣ AJ43

you should bid 2♠.

When partner makes a negative double and you have four of the major he implies, you should bid your suit in competition at the two-level with no extra values. You can't afford to let the opponents play their eight-card fit at the two-level when you could outbid them in your own eight-card fit at the two-level. If East passed the double, of course, you would need something like

♠ AQ54 ♡ A7 ◇ KQ876 ♣ J4

to jump to 2♠ — the sort of hand you on which would have raised to 3♠ if partner had responded 1♠. Remember, a negative double should imply support for any unbid suit or the ability to return to your first suit. So after

WEST	NORTH	EAST	SOUTH
			1◇
1♠	dbl	pass	?

you should rebid 3♣ with

♠ A7 ♡ 9 ◇ AJ7643 ♣ AK104

If you merely bid 2♣, partner would pass with

♠ J63 ♡ AK54 ◇ 93 ♣ J876

Your jump is merely invitational — a cuebid is the only way to force. When opener fails to jump, responder needs something like

♠ AJ73 ♡ 85 ◇ Q87 ♣ K843

to raise spades or

♠ A875 ♡ J7 ◇ Q87 ♣ KQ42

to raise clubs. (If the opponents compete, responder can raise with slightly less.)

What about rebids by the negative doubler? In the following sequence, what should South's 2♡ bid mean?

WEST	NORTH	EAST	SOUTH
	1◇	1♠	dbl
pass	2◇	pass	2♡

The answer depends upon your agreement. Some very fine players treat a direct 2♡ bid over 1♠ as non-forcing (this is called a 'negative free bid'), and with a good hand they double first and bid their suit next round, the sequence shown above. But most pairs play just the opposite — for them, the double followed by a suit bid means that South was too weak to bid 2♡ (forcing) right away. He probably has 8-10 HCP and a good five- or weak six-card suit.

I don't like negative free bids since they require you to do strange things with good hands. After

WEST	NORTH	EAST	SOUTH
	1◇	2♣	?

since a cuebid would agree diamonds, you would be forced to start with a double holding

♠ AK652 ♡ K9874 ◇ K87 ♣ —

This is risky in two respects. First, partner might pass the double when you are cold for a game or slam. Second, if West preempts in clubs, you won't be able to bid both suits, while if your system had permitted you to bid 2♠, you could bid hearts later.

Responsive Doubles

These are classic 'responsive double' sequences:

WEST	NORTH	EAST	SOUTH
1♡	dbl	2♡	dbl

WEST	NORTH	EAST	SOUTH
1♡	dbl	3♡	dbl

What sort of hand would justify the last double in these auctions? For the first sequence the opponents should have eight or nine hearts, and any hearts the second doubler holds are unfavorably located. How often would he want to make a penalty double under these circumstances? In the second example the opponents almost surely have nine or more hearts, and a penalty double is even more unlikely. So the double should be primarily for takeout. For the first sequence the second doubler might hold as little as:

♠ K 10 4 ♡ J 7 5 ◇ Q 7 5 4 ♣ Q 10 8

To double at the three-level, he needs to be stronger; perhaps a hand like this

♠ K 10 4 ♡ 8 5 ◇ K 9 8 5 ♣ Q J 9 2

would be the minimum since partner may be forced to bid at the four-level. However, at this level partner may pass with a balanced hand, relying on the Law to protect him. When forced to make a responsive double with an off-shape hand, responder must apply some common sense to the subsequent proceedings:

WEST	NORTH	EAST	SOUTH
1♡	dbl	3♡[1]	dbl
pass	3♠	pass	?

1. Preemptive.

♠ Q 7 ♡ 8 7 4 ◇ A 10 8 5 ♣ A 7 5 2

Here you should bid 4♣, asking partner to pass or correct to diamonds. This is much more logical than trying to guess which minor to bid at the four-level.

After responder has made a negative double, opener can also make use of a responsive double.

WEST	NORTH	EAST	SOUTH
			1◇
1♠	dbl	2♠	?

♠ 6 ♡ A Q 5 ◇ A K J 8 6 ♣ Q 10 6 4

Here again, you should double — you are too strong just to bid 3♣. You could jump to 4♣ to show your values, but that would risk missing a 5-3 heart fit (or even a 4-3 heart fit!).

Most experts play responsive doubles after an overcall as well as after a double:

WEST	NORTH	EAST	SOUTH
1♢	1♠	2♢	dbl

WEST	NORTH	EAST	SOUTH
1♢	1♠	3♢	dbl

Again, in both these auctions South's double would either be a takeout double for the remaining suits or would 'show cards', meaning enough high cards to constitute the balance of strength. I am in the minority, but by no means alone, in suggesting there is a better meaning for this bid — the 'good raise' or 'cuebid' double, which has already been mentioned (see Chapter 2).

There is one more sequence related to responsive doubles that I should discuss.

WEST	NORTH	EAST	SOUTH
1♢	dbl	1♠	dbl

Here South's double is not a responsive double — it is a penalty double. In an international match many years ago Bob Hamman psyched a spade bid with a weak hand, knowing that the Italians played the double in this situation as responsive. Since they had no way to expose the psyche, they were talked out of a game in spades. The Italians were smarter and less stubborn than most players, and they immediately changed their system so that the double of East's new suit in this auction was for penalties. Perhaps your opponents don't psyche very often, but if they are aware of a weakness in your system, they might take advantage of it. Even if they don't psyche, some players bid very weak four-card suits over a double, so you should have a way to prevent them from 'stealing' your suit.

'Action' Doubles

As we have seen, doubles at the one- or two-level in front of the bidder are primarily for takeout. Several examples have already been given, usually when only suits have been bid. I think the same principle should apply in some other situations such as this one:

WEST	NORTH	EAST	SOUTH
	1NT	pass	pass
2♡	pass	pass	dbl

♠ A 8 7 5 ♡ 10 6 ♢ Q 9 8 3 ♣ J 10 5

You are really hoping partner has four spades or four hearts (he would pass with the latter holding). But the partnership can probably make something unless opener has specifically 3-3-3-4 distribution, and with four of both minors, opener can bid 2NT. You (responder) won't often have a good penalty double, but you hate to concede a partscore swing when partner has something like either of these hands:

♠ KQ43 ♡ A85 ◇ KJ10 ♣ Q87

♠ K104 ♡ J87 ◇ A7 ♣ AK965

Doubles of Two-Suited Artificial Bids

When partner opens a major and RHO bids 2NT (showing the minors), what should a double by you show? The standard agreement is that it shows good defense against at least one of the minors. You might hold

♠ 75 ♡ A854 ◇ KQ1065 ♣ J8

So if the opponents bid diamonds, you can double, and there is the hope that if they bid clubs, partner can double. That seems reasonable, doesn't it? But what if the bidding continues

WEST	NORTH	EAST	SOUTH
	1♠	2NT	dbl
3♣	pass	pass	?

A majority of experts say that you are forced to take some action here, but what should it be? It is likely that the opponents are going down in 3♣ since, if trumps are led, dummy will probably have some diamond losers. So if partner has three clubs, you will probably set the contract one or two tricks; but if partner has only one or two clubs, the opponents may easily make the contract. So it is dangerous to double — but if you don't double, what can you do? I think you should pass, but the majority of experts say you are not allowed to pass, which means you probably shouldn't have doubled 2NT.

Before discussing the pros and cons of obligating yourself to take further action, let's consider the related issue of doubling a Michaels cuebid. Most of the players who think that a double of a 2NT overcall guarantees further action of some kind play the same way over a Michaels bid. Again, the double shows good defense against at least one of the cuebidder's suits, and the doubler promises not to pass if opener passes. The argument in favor of guaranteeing further action is that if partner can't double the opponent's bid, he will pass to give you a chance to double — and he can safely pass with extra values, knowing that you will do something. And if the bidding goes

WEST	NORTH	EAST	SOUTH
	1♠	2NT	dbl
pass	pass	3♣	?

you can pass, knowing opener is obligated to take action. Yes, this approach sounds like a good idea, but it really isn't. When you hold

♠ 75 ♡ A854 ◇ KQ1065 ♣ J8

it is a cinch that the opponents will run to clubs. North has at least five spades; he may not have a four-card side suit, and when he does, it will usually be hearts, not clubs.

There was a similar problem in the December 1998 *Bridge World*. The sequence under discussion was:

WEST	NORTH	EAST	SOUTH
	1◇	2◇	dbl
2♠	pass	pass	?

♠ J103 ♡ A984 ◇ 106 ♣ KQ102

Kit Woolsey (and other panelists) suggested that perhaps the previous double had been ill-advised. South might instead have passed and then doubled at his next turn, suggesting some values, but since he did double in the first place, he was now obligated to take some action over 2♠.

Even with a better hand, you can run into some serious difficulties. The following hand is from the bidding panel for *Australian Bridge:*

WEST	NORTH	EAST	SOUTH
	1♠	2NT	dbl
3♣	pass	3◇	?

♠ 964 ♡ AQ62 ◇ AQ32 ♣ J6

You are playing the 'standard' method, so your double of 2NT showed defensive strength, after which a double by either you or partner would be for penalties. I suppose East has extra values to show the minors and take 3♣ out to 3◇, but even so, doubling 3◇ seems pretty clear-cut to me. Nineteen of the panelists doubled and five passed. The director recommended a pass, commenting, 'Pass is certainly forcing'. I'm sure you have by now realized that I don't think a pass *should* be forcing, but even if it is, I can't see any reason not to double. Unless partner has an unusual hand, with which he would pull the double, you should set 3◇. And if you pass, how can you expect partner either to double or to bid 3NT with one or two small diamonds?

The basic problem with agreeing that the double guarantees another bid is that it often prevents responder from taking immediate action with nine- or ten-point hands like this one (which occur much more frequently than twelve- or thirteen- point hands), because he may be too weak to take action on a later round.

There is another factor to consider, though. It is dangerous to pass and then double the opponents at the three-level with a mediocre hand. Partner may have neither a safe penalty pass nor a safe bid at that level (since his suits will usually break badly, and he doesn't know your exact distribution). But if you double a

2NT bid or a Michaels cuebid in the first place, he doesn't have to do anything. If your left hand opponent passes, partner can pass with absolute safety. So it makes good sense to have the immediate double show some values, although not necessarily enough to guarantee later action.

Over a 2NT bid, this is my suggestion: with nine or more HCPs and four or more of both minors, simply pass and then double when the auction comes back to you (the responder). You would bid this way with

♠ 84 ♡ A87 ◇ QJ83 ♣ K972

but your pass over 2NT implies either a singleton in partner's suit or less than 9 HCP. An immediate double shows a balanced hand (typically 4-4-3-2 or 5-3-3-2 with the doubleton in partner's suit and not four of both minors). Opener can then double freely with three cards in the opponents' suit or with a good defensive hand and a doubleton in the opponents' suit. Responder can leave in a double by opener with a good three-card holding. This enables the partnership to double the opponents in 3♣ and know what it is doing with

♠ AK864 ♡ K73 ◇ J8 ♣ Q54

opposite:

♠ 52 ♡ A965 ◇ K1054 ♣ K103

Also, this approach helps you if you want to bid on. Knowing that the double shows a balanced hand, opener can bid 3♠ over 3♣ with

♠ KJ10854 ♡ A87 ◇ A943 ♣ —

or jump to 4♠ with a slightly better hand. Both players can draw inferences regarding the distribution. Suppose opener has

♠ AQ1054 ♡ AK108 ◇ 74 ♣ 73

and the bidding goes

WEST	NORTH	EAST	SOUTH
	1♠	2NT	dbl
3♣	?		

Opener knows his partner doesn't have four of both minors (with which he would have passed) and the opponents have presumably bid their longer combined length. Responder's distribution is quite likely 2-4-4-3, so opener can bid 3♡ with relative safety, and he could bid 4♡ with hearts as good as ♡AKQ8.

Useful inferences can be drawn from this agreement here, too:

WEST	NORTH	EAST	SOUTH
	1♠	2NT	?

♠ J7 ♡ K9754 ◇ A83 ♣ Q105

Since 3♣ (Unusual over Unusual) would show a forcing 3♡ bid, 3♡ would be just competitive and non-forcing. This would be accurate as to values, but a dangerous bid, nevertheless, because the suit is so weak. What if opener has a singleton or doubleton heart? So South doubles and the bidding continues:

WEST	NORTH	EAST	SOUTH
	1♠	2NT	dbl
3♢	pass	pass	?

North would have doubled with three diamonds, so he probably has 5-3-2-3 distribution. South can now bid 3♡ with relative safety, and if North holds

♠ K 10 8 6 3 2 ♡ Q 3 ♢ K 4 ♣ A 7 6

he can correct to 3♠, knowing he will find a doubleton spade in dummy and only a 5-2 heart fit.

So, what is the drawback to this approach? It will lose when responder holds four of one minor and opener has four of the other because the opponents will escape the penalty double — but how often will opener have a side four-card suit to go with his five-card major? And when he does have a side four-card suit, how often will it be the other minor? We give up that less frequent combination to cater to the hands where responder has four of one minor and three of the other (to go with opener's three or his doubleton with good defensive values). Or perhaps both players have three of each minor, such as

♠ A K 5 4 3 ♡ K 9 ♢ Q 10 4 ♣ Q 8 2

opposite:

♠ 9 7 ♡ A 7 6 5 4 ♢ K 9 3 ♣ K 10 3

It is much easier to bid over 2NT (presumably showing the minors) than over Michaels cuebids for the majors, when the opponents are only forced to the two-level. I still think that responder should pass with a pure defensive hand, planning to double on the next round, and that an immediate double should show a fairly balanced hand. It is a bit more scary to try to double with three trumps in each hand when the opponents are at the two-level, but there is a much greater chance that opener will have a side four-card major after a minor-suit opening than that he will have the crucial four-card minor when he opens a major. Also, if the player in fourth position can't make a penalty double, he can bid more safely at a lower level (possibly 2NT).

Perhaps the standard method is best, with the double guaranteeing further action, but I don't think so. I think, again, that the double should just show 9+ HCP and deny a singleton in partner's suit. A double by either partner thereafter is for penalties but now it shows at least four cards in the suit bid. Responder's double, showing values and denying a singleton or four of both majors, enables the partnership to compete effectively for the partscore and occasionally to extract a penalty.

After a major-suit opening and a Michaels cuebid, the situation more closely resembles that after a 2NT overcall. Over a spade cuebid the opponents are forced to the three-level and often will get that high over a heart cuebid also. As well, when opener has a five-card major he is unlikely to hold four of one of the opponents' suits. So I recommend the same general defense as over a 2NT overcall. Of course, responder won't know what the overcaller's minor is (unless the opponents are playing 'top and bottom' instead of Michaels) so, unless he has 1-4-4-4 distribution, he can't always pass knowing that he can safely double anything they bid. However, a pass followed by a double should show a singleton in opener's suit with a stack in their major (and perhaps no more than a good three-card holding in the minor bid) while an immediate double should show a more balanced hand.

SUMMARY

1. Doubles of suit bids below the four-level, where partner has not yet bid, are traditionally for takeout. There are some exceptions to this rule, which are fairly obvious if you think about them.
2. With a decent hand, a takeout double is often the only sensible way to get into an auction, even if your shape is not ideal.
3. Most doubles 'under the bidder' are for takeout, and show extra values.
4. You should agree on the requirements for the takeout doubler to raise responder's suit in competition.
5. Show support for opener's major immediately over their takeout double with a weak hand.
6. Negative doubles should imply but not promise the unbid major(s). At higher levels, they are often the only way for responder to show values, and opener should seriously consider passing on a relatively balanced hand. As a result, you should not use a negative double with a weak two-suiter.
7. Responsive doubles are useful to show values in competition, and again can be passed at higher levels with the right hand.
8. Play the double of a two-suited overcall to show a balanced hand with a doubleton in partner's suit. Doubles thereafter by either hand are for penalties.

What is your next bid on each of the following hands?

1.

WEST	NORTH	EAST	SOUTH
1♠	pass	1NT	pass
2♡	dbl	pass	?

♠ A 5 ♡ 7 5 4 2 ♢ K J 8 5 4 ♣ Q 3

2.

WEST	NORTH	EAST	SOUTH
		1♣	dbl
pass	1♠	2♣	pass
pass	2♢	pass	?

♠ A K 9 ♡ Q 8 7 4 ♢ A J 3 ♣ 9 7 6

3.

WEST	NORTH	EAST	SOUTH
	2♣[1]	pass	2♢
2♡	dbl	pass	?

1. Strong and artificial.

♠ K 8 6 5 ♡ 9 5 ♢ 9 8 5 4 ♣ 7 6 3

4.

WEST	NORTH	EAST	SOUTH
4♢[1]	dbl	pass	4♡
pass	4♠	pass	?

1. Natural.

♠ Q 6 ♡ A 9 8 5 ♢ 9 7 3 ♣ J 7 4 2

5.

WEST	NORTH	EAST	SOUTH
	1♢	1♡	?

♠ K Q 9 6 ♡ 8 7 6 4 3 ♢ Q 7 ♣ 9 7

6.

WEST	NORTH	EAST	SOUTH
1♡	dbl	3♡	?

♠ K Q 6 4 ♡ 9 5 2 ♢ A 8 7 ♣ 8 6 4

7.

WEST	NORTH	EAST	SOUTH
		1♢	dbl
1♠	dbl	2♢	?

♠ Q 10 7 5 ♡ A J 8 ♢ J 4 ♣ A K Q 6

8.

WEST	NORTH	EAST	SOUTH
			1♢
2♣	pass	2NT	pass
3NT	4♣	pass	?

♠ K 7 ♡ K Q J 6 ♢ Q J 10 7 3 ♣ 9 8

9.

WEST	NORTH	EAST	SOUTH
			1♠
2♠[1]	dbl	2NT[2]	?

1. Michaels.
2. Asks for partner's minor.

♠ A Q 6 5 4 ♡ A 9 7 6 ♢ A 8 ♣ 9 6

10.

WEST	NORTH	EAST	SOUTH
1♠	2NT	pass	3♣
?			

♠ K J 9 6 5 3 ♡ A Q 7 ♢ A J 10 ♣ 5

11.

WEST	NORTH	EAST	SOUTH
	1♠	2NT	pass
3♣	dbl	pass	?

♠ J 7 ♡ Q J 8 6 ♢ A 8 3 ♣ 10 5 4 3

SOLUTIONS

1. It is close between bidding 4♢ and 5♢. I slightly prefer the latter. Partner's typical hand:

   ♠ KJ72 ♡ 6 ♢ A1062 ♣ AJ83

2. Pass. In response to a takeout double partner strains to bid a four-card major ahead of a longer minor. It is almost a cinch that partner has longer diamonds than spades. With four of both suits, partner would have doubled 2♣.

3. The rules I stated tell you to bid, but common sense tells you to pass. Partner's 2♣ bid created a force (to game in most sequences), and if he wanted you to bid, he would simply pass — with

   ♠ AQJ4 ♡ 7 ♢ AKQ3 ♣ AQJ3

   for example. So partner's double is basically for penalties. Perhaps he is showing up a psyche; more likely, he has a strong balanced hand with good hearts:

   ♠ AQ4 ♡ KJ107 ♢ AK7 ♣ AQ3

4. On the previous round you had a close decision whether to pass or bid 4♡. However, to solve the problem at hand, you must determine what this sequence means. There are two possibilities:

   1) Partner, by doubling before bidding 4♠, shows a better hand than by bidding 4♠ immediately. He is still hoping you can bid a slam.

   2) Partner has a hand that is hard to describe, with both clubs and spades — either a weak five-card spade suit or a four-card spade suit and longer clubs, something like these hands:

   ♠ AK105 ♡ K8 ♢ J8 ♣ AKQ63

   ♠ AKJ7 ♡ K8 ♢ Q ♣ AQ9863

   Your 4♡ bid does not deny four spades, and partner would hate to commit the hand to clubs when you might hold:

   ♠ Q984 ♡ A9652 ♢ 974 ♣ 4

   Based on frequency, you and partner should agree upon the latter meaning, in which case you would bid 5♣.

5. Bid 1♠. Your hearts are not nearly good enough for you to pass, planning to pass a reopening double. Nor should you make a negative double with such poor support for the minor suits.

6. Bid 3♠. A responsive double might get you to four of a minor on a 4-3 fit. Even if you have only a 4-3 spade fit, you are one level lower and can ruff hearts in the dummy, preserving your four-card length. As well, the 3♠ bid will get you to a good game when partner holds:

♠ A863 ♡ 6 ◊ KQ104 ♣ KQ73

On this hand, he would be reluctant to jump to 4♠ over a responsive double since he couldn't be sure you have a four-card spade suit.

7. Bid 3♠. You would bid 2♠ without the ace of clubs.

8. Bid 4♡. You shouldn't assume partner is crazy. Either he has a major two-suiter or a three-suiter with a void in clubs. And he must not have many high cards, both to account for the opponents' strong bidding and for partner's failure to make a negative double last round. Two possible hands are:

♠ A96543 ♡ 109754 ◊ 8 ♣ 6

♠ Q10654 ♡ 107532 ◊ K62 ♣ —

Your hand is ideal, with your strong major holdings. In real life, partner held the first hand and figured his 4♣ bid had two ways to gain — you might make four of a major, or you might have a good sacrifice.

9. Double. This is a more flexible call than 3♡ since it encourages partner to double either minor with a good three-card suit. You might miss a 4-4 heart fit, but 4♡ is not likely to make since West should have a singleton in one of the majors, and your heart suit is weak.

10. Double. If partner has a decent hand, he must have a singleton spade, which should discourage you from bidding 3♠. If partner was planning to double either minor, he will be delighted to pass your double. Even if he was too weak to take action on his own, he will be delighted to pass with good clubs and 6 or 7 HCP. Also, he might be able to jump to 4♡ with something like:

♠ A8 ♡ K10943 ◊ 43 ♣ 7432

11. Bid 4♣. Your hand is not particularly good for defense since you only have one trick in the minors (and partner probably has a singleton club). But you have a good offensive hand since partner probably has either four hearts or a six-card spade suit.

CHAPTER 10

Penalty Doubles

Typical Penalty Doubles

One of the reasons for abandoning penalty doubles early in the bidding in favor of takeout doubles and negative doubles is that, at that stage, partner hasn't finished describing his hand. When his high-card strength and distribution are still relatively unknown, you usually need more information before you can make an intelligent decision. This is especially true when you haven't yet found a fit. However, there are a number of situations where you do want to double for penalties, and where this action is available to you.

You have found a fit

Once you have found a fit, particularly a major-suit fit, you seldom need to ask partner for more distributional information — and when you do, you can obtain it by bidding suits you are interested in. For example, in an earlier chapter we looked at this sequence:

WEST	NORTH	EAST	SOUTH
		1♢	1♠
1NT	2♠	pass	pass
3♢	dbl		

Since your side has already found a spade fit, partner has no need for a negative double (does he really want to find out how many clubs or hearts you have?), so his double is for penalties.

John Mohan has suggested using an unusual type of penalty double which looks quite logical to me. The bidding goes

WEST	NORTH	EAST	SOUTH
	1♠	pass	2♠
3♣	pass	pass	?

and you hold

♠ J 9 8 ♡ A 10 6 5 ◇ A 9 6 2 ♣ 10 7

With a maximum raise, you have enough to bid again, but your hand is very good defensively. All you lack is good trumps. So you double — a penalty double without trumps (actually you need at least two). Opener needs either a slow trump trick or four of the opponents' suit to leave it in — one of these hands, for example:

♠ K Q 5 4 3 ♡ K 3 2 ◇ K 4 ♣ Q J 4

♠ A K 5 4 3 ♡ K 3 ◇ K 4 ♣ 10 6 3 2

Without club length or strength opener will bid 3♠, and will very probably make his contract.

The opening bid defines the hand

Many people play undisciplined weak two-bids these days, but at one time a weak two-bid was guaranteed to look something like this:

♠ A Q 10 7 6 5 ♡ 8 7 ◇ K 5 4 ♣ 9 4

If you opened 2♠ and LHO overcalled 3♡, there was nothing more partner needed to find out about your hand — you had already described it. So a double by partner, instead of being negative, was for penalties. While all preempts vary in strength and suit quality these days, and may not follow the traditional Rule of Two and Three (you can take within two tricks of your bid vulnerable and within three tricks not vulnerable), we still figure that an opening preemptor has more or less described his hand and has nothing more to say. Consequently, any doubles made by his partner are for penalties. The same is true for other bids which closely describe one's high-card strength and distribution. For instance, after an opening Flannery 2◇, showing 11-15 HCP with four spades and five hearts, doubles by responder are for penalties. A negative double would be pointless.

Responder shows strength

When responder bids a suit at the one-level, he may be very strong or very weak. Opener will assume responder is weak until he shows, by his subsequent bidding, that he has more than minimum values. Responder's wide range is the reason that we had to adopt rules regarding what bids were forcing in competition, what a double in various circumstances would show, and what 2NT (Good-Bad) would mean. But after a two-over-one response the rules are different, since presumably opener's side has the balance of strength.

Whether you play two-over-one as forcing to game or merely as guaranteeing a rebid, opener can pass an overcall by RHO, knowing that his partner will take some action when the auction gets back to him. So there is no need for opener to have a negative or takeout double available, and therefore his doubles are for penalties. Nor does he need extra values for this — if the opponents bid his second suit, he can double. For example:

WEST	NORTH	EAST	SOUTH
			1♠
pass	2♢	2♡	?

♠ AK862 ♡ KJ54 ♢ 87 ♣ J3

Opener should double with this hand. He can assume that his side has at least twenty-three points to the opponents' seventeen, and he has hearts behind the bidder. What more does he need? Of course, if responder has an unexpected hand, like

♠ J9 ♡ 3 ♢ KQJ106532 ♣ Q10

he will pull the double to 3♢.

Suppose the bidding goes:

WEST	NORTH	EAST	SOUTH
	1♠	pass	2♢
2♡	pass	pass	?

♠ 4 ♡ J93 ♢ AQJ87 ♣ K985

By making a 2/1 response, you have promised to bid again, but what should you bid? You should double. The hand looks like a misfit, and if opener holds

♠ AQ976 ♡ K84 ♢ 64 ♣ A74

for example, the defenders will do very well — and they can't make much of anything their way. This is a penalty double, even though you have no trump tricks. If opener has a bad defensive hand , say

♠ AKQ83 ♡ 74 ♢ 964 ♣ QJ7

he should pull the double to 3♢ rather than gamble that his spade honors and partner's diamond honors will all take tricks.

Here's another situation where you can help partner out:

WEST	NORTH	EAST	SOUTH
			1♠
2♣	2♡	4♣	?

♠ A K 10 9 5 ♡ 3 ◇ K J 3 ♣ 10 7 6 4

Even vulnerable against not, you should double. Partner won't assume the opponents are crazy and that you can obtain a bigger score by doubling them than you could make by bidding game. He will assume that you are doubtful about making game. If you pass, partner will bid 4♡ with

♠ Q 5 ♡ A J 9 8 7 5 4 ◇ Q 10 6 ♣ 8

but now, your penalty double may dissuade him. However, if he has an independent heart suit:

♠ Q 5 ♡ K Q J 10 8 5 4 ◇ Q 10 6 ♣ 8

he will bid 4♡ anyway, since he doesn't care whether or not you have heart support.

When you or partner has bid very strongly, a double is a penalty double, and it suggests either a bad hand for offense or a very good hand for defense.

WEST	NORTH	EAST	SOUTH
			1♠
pass	3◇[1]	3♡	?

1. Strong, game-forcing, and suggesting a slam.

♠ Q 10 7 6 4 ♡ K Q 8 ◇ 7 ♣ K J 10 5

You don't know whether partner has spade support for you or just a good diamond suit, but whichever he has, you don't like your hand. Your spades are fairly weak, you have a misfit for partner's suit, you are aceless, and your heart values are very dubious on offense. If partner has two or three hearts, there is a great danger of a heart ruff, while if he has a singleton heart, your king-queen will be mostly wasted. You should double to show that a) you don't have a good hand for slam purposes, and b) with the combined high card strength (probably 28+ HCP) and your heart holding, you would probably set the contract for more than the value of game. Partner doesn't expect you to set 3♡ for more than the value of a slam, and if he has

♠ A K J 5 ♡ — ◇ A K Q 9 6 5 4 ♣ 10 3

he will disregard your double and continue to investigate slam prospects. With a somewhat balanced hand and with less than overpowering strength, he will be glad to pass.

The following hand from the 1995 US Team Trials is worth looking at here, because it involves some interesting inferences:

WEST	NORTH	EAST	SOUTH
	pass	pass	1♡
pass	2♣[1]	2♢	4♡
5♢	5♡	6♣	dbl
6♢	pass	pass	?

1. Reverse Drury — limit raise.

♠ 3 ♡ AKQ754 ♢ 1075 ♣ A75

You bid 4♡ because you wanted to play 4♡ opposite heart support and a near-maximum passed hand (which is what Reverse Drury shows). It is very unusual for partner, after showing a Drury-type hand, to bid to the five-level by himself since you might have been gambling or stretching to bid 4♡. Usually he would double to discourage you from bidding more or pass to encourage you to go on, so to bid 5♡ he must have an exceptionally high ratio of offense to defense. Then when he didn't double 6♢ (obviously a sacrifice bid) either, he was seriously suggesting that you bid 6♡. How can he be so optimistic with bad trumps? He actually held:

♠ A9764 ♡ 1098 ♢ — ♣ KQ642

Even though the opening club lead was ruffed (the 6♣ bid was lead-directing), North-South were cold for 6♡. The point is that you should trust partner to have an unusually good hand to go with your solid trumps. He could have held:

♠ AK964 ♡ J9852 ♢ — ♣ J82

A void in diamonds is almost a certainty once partner did not double 6♢.

You have redoubled at the one-level.

After partner opens one of a suit and RHO doubles, if you redouble, any doubles by either you or partner are for penalties. This situation will be discussed in detail in a later chapter, but what I want to emphasize now is that you don't need to wait for a sure thing to double them. Suppose the bidding goes

WEST	NORTH	EAST	SOUTH
	1♠	dbl	rdbl
2♡	pass	pass	?

♠ 76 ♡ QJ75 ♢ A96 ♣ KJ54

you should double. Of course, if partner has

♠ AKJ1094 ♡ 3 ♢ KJ102 ♣ 87

(or even worse, a void in hearts) you may not set them, or you may set them one trick when you are cold for 4♠. Is that your fault? No, partner should not leave the double in when he has a hand of this type. In fact, you shouldn't even have had a chance to double because partner should have bid 3♠ over 2♡ or, with a slightly weaker hand, 2♠ over 2♡. When partner has a more balanced hand, like

♠ AK854 ♡ 64 ◇ KJ4 ♣ Q62

your best result will come from defending 2♡ doubled. The opponents are probably on a 4-3 trump fit, and if you don't double, who will?

Exposing a psyche

There is one more penalty double that doesn't fit into the usual pattern.

WEST	NORTH	EAST	SOUTH
3◇	pass	3♠	?

♠ AQ1096 ♡ AJ ◇ 9 ♣ K8752

You should double for penalties!

Why is this a penalty double? Let's consider the types of hands on which East would bid 3♠. He must have either a very strong hand with which he is trying to get to game or slam, or a very weak hand with which he is trying to confuse the issue (planning to return to diamonds, if doubled). If he has the strong hand, you surely don't belong in the bidding. If he has the weak hand — perhaps

♠ 82 ♡ Q10954 ◇ K874 ♣ J6

— you don't want to let him steal the pot with his psyche. Nor do you want partner to 'respond to your takeout double' by bidding 4♡ with:

♠ K873 ♡ K873 ◇ 74 ♣ A94

So the double of a major-suit response to a preemptive opening bid is a penalty double.

Inferential Doubles

Listen to the auction — it can give you valuable clues as to when a well-timed double will pay off handsomely. Here, for example:

WEST	NORTH	EAST	SOUTH
		1♠	pass
3♠	pass	4NT	pass
5♣	pass	5♠	?

♠ QJ108 ♡ 109 ◇ 10874 ♣ J53

you should double! Why would East bid Blackwood and stop at 5♠ if all the aces were accounted for? If your opponents are a reliable pair, they must be missing two aces, or, if they are playing Roman Key Card Blackwood, perhaps one ace and the king of trumps. If so, your teammates will probably be down one in 4♠, and failure to double will give away 4 to 6 IMPs, depending upon the vulnerability.

Notrump games, too, offer a fruitful field for the alert defensive bidder:

WEST	NORTH	EAST	SOUTH
		1NT	pass
2♣	pass	2♡	pass
2NT	pass	3NT	?

♠ J 10 9 5 ♡ K J 10 6 ♢ 3 ♣ Q 10 8 4

With this hand you should double. If West had bid 3NT over 2♡, it would have been too dangerous to double since he might have thirteen or fourteen points. Since he only invited game, the opponents have twenty-five points or twenty-six, at most, between them. None of the opponents' suits are breaking well for them, and you have a safe lead. Indeed, if a gambling opponent offered to settle for down one before the opening lead, you should reject his offer; down two is the most likely result.

The logic is similar here:

WEST	NORTH	EAST	SOUTH
		1♢	pass
1♡	pass	1♠	pass
2♠	pass	2NT	pass
4♠	pass	pass	?

♠ 7 ♡ 9 7 4 ♢ K J 10 8 ♣ A K 5 4 2

Again, you should double. You have a good lead, diamonds are locked up, and partner should have four spades — what more could you ask?

These last three hands have one thing in common. You don't have the setting tricks in your own hand, and partner has not bid. But you can infer from the opponents' bidding that partner has sufficient values, combined with yours, to lead to a substantial set.

SUMMARY

1. A double of an overcall is for penalties if opener has defined and limited his hand, if responder has shown a good hand, or if responder has redoubled at the one-level.
2. In obvious situations, a penalty double can be used to expose a psyche.
3. Sometimes you can make a profitable 'out-of-the-blue' penalty double since you can infer from the auction and your own hand that the cards do not lie well for the opponents.

What is your next bid on each of the following hands?

1. *Neither vul., IMPs*

WEST	NORTH	EAST	SOUTH
	2♣	2♡	?

♠ A 10 ♡ J 10 8 7 ◇ K 7 3 ♣ J 8 5 4

2. *North-South vul., IMPs*

WEST	NORTH	EAST	SOUTH
			1♣
dbl	1♡	1♠	3♡
pass	4♡	4♠	?

♠ 10 5 ♡ A J 6 5 ◇ A K 5 ♣ A Q 7 2

3. *East-West vul., IMPs*

WEST	NORTH	EAST	SOUTH
1◇	pass	1♡	pass
1NT	pass	pass	?

♠ A K 7 ♡ A K 10 8 ◇ 9 6 ♣ A Q 9 4

4. *East-West vul., matchpoints*

WEST	NORTH	EAST	SOUTH
		1♠	pass
2♣	pass	2♠	pass
3♣[1]	pass	3♡	pass
3♠	pass	4♠	?

1. Invitational, not forcing.

♠ Q J 9 8 ♡ A J 7 ◇ J 8 7 6 5 ♣ 10

5. *Neither vul., IMPs*

WEST	NORTH	EAST	SOUTH
			1♡
pass	2NT[1]	3♠	?

1. Jacoby, four or more hearts, game-forcing.

♠ Q J 9 ♡ A 8 6 5 2 ◊ K 7 5 ♣ Q 10

6. *Neither vul., IMPs*

WEST	NORTH	EAST	SOUTH
	1♡	dbl	2♡
pass	pass	dbl	pass
3◊	pass	pass	?

♠ A Q 9 ♡ 8 7 6 ◊ Q 10 5 ♣ 9 8 4 2

SOLUTIONS

1. There are three popular treatments of a double in this situation:

   1) strictly for penalties;

   2) any very weak hand (double negative);

   3) positive response with a balanced hand.

   I used to play (1) but now prefer (3) since (1) seldom came up, but I have no strong feelings one way or another. But if you do play (1), you definitely should not double with this hand. A double should show a terrible offensive hand with nothing but trump winners — something like:

   ♠ 7 4 ♡ Q J 8 6 ◊ J 5 4 ♣ 9 7 5 2

   If you do habitually double for penalties with as much as an ace and a king, partner would never dare to pass for fear of missing a slam.

2. You should double since your hand is balanced and as good for defense as offense. Many players make the mistake of passing, thinking they have already described their hand. But the hand you should pass with is something like:

   ♠ 8 ♡ A 10 7 5 ◊ A 7 3 ♣ A Q 9 8 6

Suppose partner has:

♠ 75 ♡ KQ983 ◇ J3 ♣ J1032

If you double, he should pass. If you pass, he should bid 5♡. (If the club finesse is off, you will be down one, but the opponents can probably make 4♠). You may argue that you are vulnerable and the opponents are not, but partner is also aware of that fact. With the right sort of hand (probably including a singleton spade) he will bid 5♡, but if he has a close decision, you want him to pass. Incidentally, I disapprove of East's bidding, whatever he has. He probably should have bid 3♠ the first time instead of 1♠, allowing his partner to decide whether to 'save', but even bad bidders sometimes get good results.

3. This hand has an interesting history — it actually came up in an OKbridge match. West had opened with a terrible, aceless eleven-point balanced hand and East had responded with ♡Qxxxx and nothing else. So if you doubled, partner could have left it in and, with good defense, scored 1400 points! But I think it unlikely that partner would leave the double in, and most of the time you would settle for a partscore instead of plus 300.

4. You should double with three sure tricks, and a good chance to win the jack of hearts. Partner will usually have a trick or two. Sometimes dummy has ♠K10x, or a double helps declarer to play the trump suit, but the former is surely impossible on this bidding. So you should double and lead the queen of spades. Most players would expect to defeat 4♠ but some might be afraid the opponents would run to a better spot. That is extremely unlikely after four rounds of bidding, and you will feel foolish when partner, with a club holding similar to your spade holding, asks you why you didn't double.

5. You should double. As I recall, Larry Cohen recommends doubling any time you have 5-3-3-2 distribution. (Partner should also have balanced distribution since he didn't splinter, but if he has a singleton spade, he will surely pull the double.) I'm not sure I would always double with 5-3-3-2 distribution (especially with a doubleton in the opponents' suit), but surely with this hand it is a good idea — a slow winner in spades, a weak trump suit and a minimum opener. If partner has

♠ 643 ♡ KQ94 ◇ A8 ♣ KJ52

the opponents defending 4♡ will take two top spades and a ruff plus the ace of clubs. If he has

♠ 64 ♡ K973 ◇ AJ8 ♣ A542

you are down one in 4♡ with a 3-1 heart split, while if hearts split 2-2, you should do extremely well on defense, probably at least plus 500. East may have stuck his neck out quite a bit, thinking you wouldn't double with a nine-card heart fit, so you should teach him a lesson. If you get plus 300 instead of plus 420, you lose 3 IMPs; if you get plus 300 instead of minus 50, you gain 8 IMPs; I like those odds; and best of all, if you get an inadequate penalty, you can always blame partner for not pulling your double!

6. Double. If partner had a six-card heart suit or a singleton diamond, he probably would have bid 3♡ over 3♢, so partner probably has a balanced hand. East must have the strongest hand at the table, and your honors, behind him, are well placed. On this bidding, West's most likely distribution is 3-3-4-3, perhaps 3-4-4-2. I wouldn't be surprised if the whole hand was something like this:

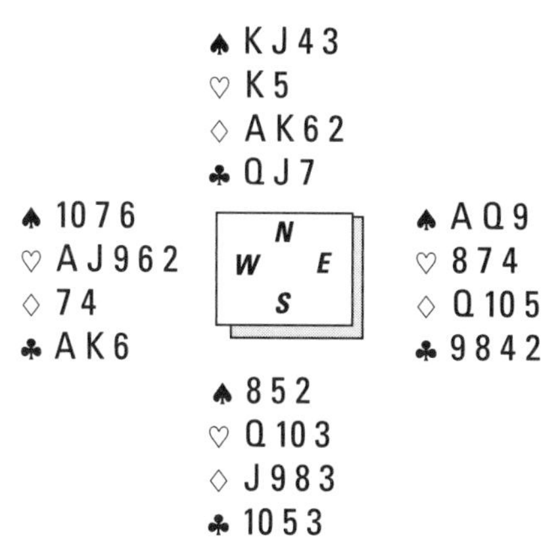

I mentioned a similar sequence where responder would double with a good defensive hand and a doubleton in the opponent's suit (and partner wouldn't leave it in without length or strength in the opponent's suit). The need for trump length or strength by the partner of the doubler only applies when the bidder has shown a long suit and is bidding without encouragement from his partner. The situation is different when the bidder has responded to a takeout double.

CHAPTER 11

Conventional Doubles

Support Doubles

Consider the following sequences:

WEST	NORTH	EAST	SOUTH
			1♣
pass	1♡	1♠	dbl

WEST	NORTH	EAST	SOUTH
			1♣
1◇	1♡	2◇	dbl

In the first sequence, how often would South have a good penalty double? Almost never! For one thing, he needs a very strong hand (in addition to good spades) since North's one-level response doesn't promise much in the way of high cards. We have already seen that successful penalty doubles at the one-level are rare since the Law says you can do better in a contract of your own unless there are lots of adjustment factors. In the second sequence the opponents almost surely have eight or more diamonds between them, and any diamond honors you have will be poorly placed. For all these reasons it is once again more useful to have the double describe your offensive values than to save it for the rare occasions when you want to penalize the opponents.

Most experts play 'support' doubles in this type of sequence to show exactly three cards in partner's suit. In case of further competition it helps partner a lot to know whether you have three- or four-card support. Now in this sequence

WEST	NORTH	EAST	SOUTH
			1♣
1♢	1♡	2♢	2♡

South shows four hearts, and partner can compete over 3♢ with as little as

♠ 87 ♡ KQ64 ♢ 7532 ♣ KJ7

because of the double fit. If South shows only three-card support by making a support double instead, North's offensive prospects become worse and his defensive prospects better, so he will pass and defend.

In the two sequences shown at the start of this chapter, where the opponents have bid at the one-level or have bid and supported a suit, it is clearly better to use the double to show three-card support. It is a closer question when the opponents' first bid is at the two-level:

WEST	NORTH	EAST	SOUTH
			1♢
pass	1♠	2♣	?

Now you might want to make a penalty double, but most players treat any double below the level of two of partner's suit as a support double. You might think by doing this, you are giving up a chance to penalize the opponents (as compared to the way people played twenty-five years ago when a double by either partner would have been for penalties). Not true! You get to defend doubled contracts more often than before — but on different hands. Look at this example:

WEST	NORTH	EAST	SOUTH
			1♢
pass	1♠	2♡	?

♠ 75 ♡ K984 ♢ AK84 ♣ A87

Would you like to double for penalties? You might be tempted, but since 2♡ doubled would be game if it made, you would be afraid to double it even if you had a penalty double available. So whether or not you play support doubles, you have to pass now. But partner, being a modern player, will double when it comes back to him with

♠ AK842 ♡ 74 ♢ Q53 ♣ J104

and you will be very pleased to leave the double in. It's harder to penalize them when South has a very strong hand like

♠ 6 ♡ KJ107 ♢ AK843 ♣ AJ6

but when the strength is more evenly divided, you still get to double them. Actually partner does the doubling, and you leave it in.

Strength and shape considerations

You don't have to make a support double just because you have three-card trump support — there may be a different message you want to send partner. Suppose the bidding starts:

WEST	NORTH	EAST	SOUTH
			1♢
pass	1♡	1♠	?

♠ KJ6 ♡ J74 ♢ Q954 ♣ AQ10

With this flat a hand, you should rebid 1NT. Partner has various ways to check back for heart support if he really wants to know. Likewise, with

♠ 76 ♡ 1087 ♢ AKQJ84 ♣ AQ

you should bid 3♢, hoping partner can bid 3NT. With a hand as bad as

♠ Q82 ♡ 642 ♢ KQJ7 ♣ KJ10

you should pass since you have a very dubious opening and a terrible hand for offense. But 90% of the time when you fail to double, you don't have three-card support, and partner should alert the opponents that you tend to deny three hearts.

Nor does the double necessarily mean that you would have given partner only a single raise if East had passed. After

WEST	NORTH	EAST	SOUTH
			1♢
pass	1♡	1♠	?

you would double with

♠ 96 ♡ AQ5 ♢ AKJ963 ♣ Q10

and then bid 3♢ if partner bids 2♡. With

♠ 96 ♡ AQ6 ♢ AJ873 ♣ AK5

after doubling, you would raise 2♡ to 3♡.

Responder's rebids

Whenever you make a support double, partner, with five or more of his suit, should rebid it at the appropriate level. If he has responded 1♡ and you make a support double, he should go straight to 4♡ with

♠ A7 ♡ KJ753 ♢ Q984 ♣ K5

but without the ♣K he should bid only 3♡ to invite game. The only times he should be tempted to bid a new suit are (a) when he is interested in a slam, (b) in competition, or (c) when he has only a four-card suit and thinks there might be a better place to play the hand, possibly 3NT.

An example of bidding a new suit in competition would be:

WEST	NORTH	EAST	SOUTH
			1♢
pass	1♡	1♠	dbl
2♠	?		

Here a 3♡ bid would be merely competitive, so if responder wants to invite game, he should bid 3♣.

Similarly, when the bidding goes

WEST	NORTH	EAST	SOUTH
			1♢
pass	1♡	1♠	dbl
pass	?		

a 2♢ bid is natural and weak, and denies a five-card heart suit, while 2♣ here should also be weak and non-forcing. North might hold, for example:

♠ J4 ♡ J854 ♢ 8 ♣ KJ9653

With a potential slam hand or a strong hand with only four hearts, North would either cuebid or bid a new suit at the three-level (whether or not it is a jump). Incidentally, 2NT would always be natural, not 'good-bad.'

An exception

Before leaving the subject, I should mention one sequence that most experts do not play as a support double.

WEST	NORTH	EAST	SOUTH
	1♣	pass	1♢
1♠	dbl		

The double in this sequence shows four hearts, not three diamonds. Opener might hold

♠ Q7 ♡ KJ87 ♢ A6 ♣ KJ864

a hand on which he is too weak to risk a 2♡ bid since that would force the bidding to the three-level if his partner lacked heart support (and partner would expect a much stronger hand).

'Maximal' Doubles

Suppose the bidding goes:

WEST	NORTH	EAST	SOUTH
			1♡
2◇	2♡	3◇	?

♠ K 8 3 ♡ A Q 9 8 5 ◇ 6 ♣ A Q 7 4

North could have a pretty skimpy raise in competition, so 4♡ might have no play. But a 3♡ bid here should be strictly competitive and would be justified even if your spade holding were three small. So how can you invite a game? By doubling! This is called a 'maximal' double. It only applies when the opponents have bid and raised a suit (making it unlikely you would want to double for penalties with the suit length on your left and the opponents in at least an eight-card fit) and when you have no room to make a normal game try. Thus, this auction is different:

WEST	NORTH	EAST	SOUTH
			1♡
pass	2♡	3◇	dbl

Here the double is for penalties, since diamonds have not been supported — diamonds might be opener's second suit.

In this similar auction you have a little more room:

WEST	NORTH	EAST	SOUTH
			1♡
2♣	2♡	3♣	?

You still have room here to bid 3◇ as an all-purpose game try (regardless of your diamond holding). I like to play that a double here is still a game try, but in contrast to the 3◇ game try, shows some interest in defending 3♣ doubled if partner has a suitable hand. This raises the point that whenever you make a maximal double, partner might decide to leave it in. So a maximal double should only be made with a high-card invitation, not with a hand like:

♠ 8 ♡ A K J 8 7 5 ◇ 9 ♣ Q 10 7 5 2

With a primarily offensive hand like this one, opener should just gamble by bidding game.

Doubling Slams

In a competitive bidding sequence, a double of a slam says you think you can beat it and you don't want partner to bid more, either in the hope of making it or as a sacrifice:

WEST	NORTH	EAST	SOUTH
	1♡	pass	4♡
5◇	5♡	6◇	?

For all partner knows when he bids 5♡, your 4♡ bid could be based on either

♠ 654 ♡ KJ9862 ◇ 5 ♣ 1085

(a hand with negative defense) or something as good as:

♠ Q1096 ♡ J10754 ◇ 6 ♣ A86

At this point, you don't know whether the opponents were sacrificing or whether partner was sacrificing (and might consider sacrificing at the six-level too). I think you should double with the latter hand, and it shouldn't be a Lightner double, but simply tell partner that you have some defensive prospects. Yes, you might hold instead

♠ Q9654 ♡ J98642 ◇ J7 ♣ —

in which case you would like to make a lead-directing double, but you can't have it both ways, and it is more important in a fiercely contested auction to show extra defensive strength for your previous bidding.

When the opponents bid a slam in a non-competitive auction (or where your side stopped bidding at the three-level or below, so that it is very unlikely you would consider sacrificing), a double does ask for an unusual lead. If it is a suit slam, your double often means that you can ruff something. However, if partner can tell from the auction and his own hand that a ruff is improbable, he has to figure out what lead you are calling for. In cases of doubt, he should lead dummy's first bid suit.

Usually the failure to double a suit slam denies a void, other than in trumps. So, if dummy has bid diamonds and opening leader holds

♠ J10 ♡ 74 ◇ J87642 ♣ Q85

he should lead a spade or a club, rather than a diamond, when the 6♡ contract is not doubled. The player with a void should double, even when he has no other possible defensive trick. The probability of setting a slam is greatly increased if you get the ruff. Since the opponents stopped short of a grand slam, quite likely they were only going to make six with a neutral lead, and the ruff, combined with another trick in partner's hand, will be enough to set them. We have all read about hands where, after a double, the slam bidders ran out to 6NT and made it, while if partner had guessed right, he could have set the suit slam. But these are exceptional cases. Usually the opponents avoided 6NT in the first place because they needed to do some ruffing, and they will run out of steam before taking twelve tricks at notrump.

Of course, almost any rule has exceptions. Recently my opponents got to 6♠ when I had a void in hearts plus ♠Q1054, but I decided not to double for the heart lead, since I might simply be ruffing a loser with a natural trump trick. The bidding sounded as though the opponents were quite distributional and, without a warning, declarer might play hearts himself, perhaps from the wrong hand, so that I could ruff one of his honors instead of a low card. Anyway, passing was the right decision, or I would have forgotten the hand along with all my other bad results.

Sometimes you *think* you would prefer a certain lead, but the preference is very slight, and a double could be costly (usually 6 IMPs, possibly 12 IMPs if the opponents redouble). Suppose the bidding goes:

WEST	NORTH	EAST	SOUTH
		1♢	pass
1♠	pass	3♠	pass
4♣	pass	5♠	pass
6♠	pass	pass	?

With this hand

♠ 8 6 ♡ 9 7 5 4 ♢ A Q 7 ♣ K 10 9 5

it is tempting to double for a diamond lead, but is it really necessary? If declarer has two small diamonds, he will almost surely lose two diamond tricks sooner or later. What will he discard his diamond losers on? If declarer has a singleton or void in diamonds, he may redouble. Even if he doesn't, your double will lose several IMPs for nothing.

By contrast, on the same auction, with

♠ 7 ♡ 8 7 5 ♢ K Q 10 5 ♣ J 7 6 4 3

a double is a good gamble since a heart or club lead might be costly, and a diamond lead can't hurt. There is no assurance that a diamond lead will set the hand, but any other lead may be fatal.

Here's a situation in which a double is much more likely to gain than lose:

WEST	NORTH	EAST	SOUTH
pass	pass	1♣	pass
1♠	pass	2NT	pass
3♡	pass	4♠	pass
6♠	pass	pass	?

♠ 9 6 ♡ J 8 6 ♢ 9 7 6 4 ♣ A Q 9 6

What kind of hand can West hold? He passed originally and then jumped to slam opposite a balanced 18 or 19 HCP. He must be 5-5 or 6-5 in the majors. If a club isn't led, he may get rid of a club loser on the ♢AK, possibly two club losers on the ♢AKQ. The odds favor a double, whether it works or not.

Doubling 3NT

Traditionally, a double of 3NT insists that partner lead your suit if you have bid. I think the traditional rule is wrong, since partner usually leads your suit without a double. A double should ask for an unusual lead. If you and partner have both bid, he should lead his suit, not yours. When you have bid a suit and partner hasn't, the double should ask partner to lead something else.

WEST	NORTH	EAST	SOUTH
			1♠
2♢	2♠	3♢	pass
3NT	pass	pass	?

♠ J9854 ♡ AKQ6 ♢ K7 ♣ 94

Here, a double is a good gamble since the opponents are almost sure to make 3NT with a spade lead. Fortunately, partner holds:

♠ A62 ♡ J9652 ♢ 8 ♣ 10754

so he doesn't need to try to guess which suit you have — he can lead the ♠A and look at the dummy. Without the double he would lead a low spade and the opponents would take the first eleven tricks.

When the bidding goes

WEST	NORTH	EAST	SOUTH
1NT	pass	3NT	dbl

your double asks partner to lead your suit. Usually, you have a solid suit like AKQJ6 or possibly KQJ107 with an outside ace. Fortunately, you have a smart partner, and he will usually be able to figure out what your suit is. Suppose the bidding has gone that way and partner holds

♠ 865 ♡ K974 ♢ Q873 ♣ 74

What should he lead? Obviously, not a red suit. That couldn't be your solid or semi-solid suit. So he has to lead either a spade or a club. Other things being equal, he will tend to lead his shortest suit, but other things are not equal in this case. Responder could have a long minor suit, but with as many as four of a major, he might have bid Stayman, and with five of a major, he would have shown it to suggest an alternative to 3NT. So, in this case partner should lead a spade. Even if your suit is clubs, partner may still win a trick in time to shift to a club. Some players play the double here to show a specific suit (hearts is the most popular choice), but that way you won't get to use your convention very often — maybe once every seven years instead of once every two years.

Other Unusual Doubles

The bidding has gone:

WEST	NORTH	EAST	SOUTH
			1♣
1♡	1♠	3♡[1]	4♣
pass	5♣	dbl	all pass

1. Preemptive, of course.

What would you (West) lead from:

♠ J 8 7 4 ♡ K J 9 6 3 ◇ A 10 6 ♣ 9

It is very unusual for partner to preempt and then double. Often it is because he has a void, but it seems unlikely that he has a void in this sequence. (Have the opponents overlooked their nine-card spade fit?) Partner couldn't count on heart tricks since one of the opponents must be short in hearts. He couldn't count on diamond tricks unless he has the ◇AK (which he can't have, since you have the ace), because declarer probably has a tenace over him. The only reason he can have for his double is that he has spade strength behind the dummy, either ♠AK or ♠AQ. In fact, this was the whole deal:

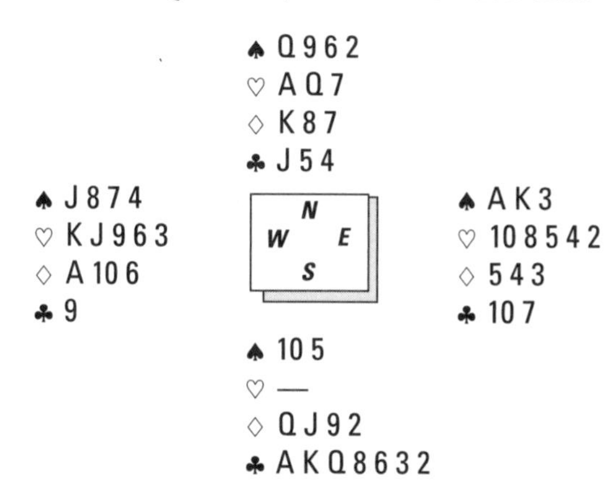

A heart lead would have allowed declarer to make an overtrick. Yes, I would have made a negative double with the North hand instead of bidding 1♠, but that is no excuse for your not leading a spade. If North had made a negative double, partner's double of 5♣ would still suggest leading spades, the suit North implied. Incidentally, many unenlightened players would bid 2♡ with the East hand (thinking they were too strong for a preempt). South would bid 3♣ and North would bid 3NT. Please excuse the commercial break!

There are other conventional doubles I could mention, like doubles of splinter bids to ask for the lead of the lower unbid suit, and Rosenkranz doubles to show a high honor in partner's suit, but there are pros and cons to all of them. Whether or not you play them is therefore more a matter of personal style than anything else.

SUMMARY

1. Many experts play support doubles at the one- and two-levels to show exactly three-card support for partner's suit. This allows more decision-making accuracy in competitive situations.
2. 'Maximal' doubles are useful in competitive auctions where you have little bidding room, and wish to distinguish a game try from a competitive bid.
3. Doubles at the slam level ask for an unusual lead (if only one side is bidding), or show extra defensive values if both sides are still in the auction.
4. A double of 3NT often asks for an unusual lead.

What is your next bid on each of the following hands?

1.

WEST	NORTH	EAST	SOUTH
	1♢	pass	1♠
2♣	dbl	pass	?

♠ K 8 6 5 4 ♡ A Q 10 6 5 ♢ Q 10 ♣ 6

2.

WEST	NORTH	EAST	SOUTH
	1♢	pass	1♡
1♠	dbl	pass	2♢
2♠	3♡	pass	?

♠ 7 5 4 ♡ A J 10 7 ♢ Q 10 6 5 ♣ J 8

3.

WEST	NORTH	EAST	SOUTH
		1♠	2♠[1]
3♠	dbl	pass	?

1. Michaels.

♠ A ♡ K 10 7 5 4 ♢ 8 ♣ A Q 10 6 5 2

4.

WEST	NORTH	EAST	SOUTH
	1♠	2♡	2♠
3♡	dbl	pass	?

♠ 9 6 2 ♡ Q 9 4 2 ♢ A 8 ♣ J 6 5 2

5. *North-South vul., matchpoints*

WEST	NORTH	EAST	SOUTH
	1♢	pass	2♠
3♣	dbl	pass	?

♠ A K 10 8 4 ♡ A Q 6 ♢ Q 7 6 5 ♣ 8

6.

WEST	NORTH	EAST	SOUTH
			3♣
pass	3♡	3♠	?

♠ K6 ♡ 6 ♢ J84 ♣ AJ98654

7.

WEST	NORTH	EAST	SOUTH
1♠	pass	2♢	pass
2♠	pass	3♣	pass
3NT	pass	pass	?

♠ 5 ♡ 9854 ♢ KQ109 ♣ A652

8.

WEST	NORTH	EAST	SOUTH
1♠	pass	3♠	pass
4NT	pass	5♣	?

♠ 532 ♡ A9764 ♢ — ♣ KQ1096

9.

WEST	NORTH	EAST	SOUTH
1♠	pass	3♠	pass
4NT	pass	5♣	pass
5♠	pass	pass	?

♠ 97 ♡ — ♢ Q108743 ♣ J9542

SOLUTIONS

1. Bid 3♡. You may have a 5-4 heart fit, which would be better than a 5-3 spade fit, so it is a good idea to bid hearts. However, 2♡ would be non-forcing and potentially very weak — a hand like:

   ♠ Q 6 4 5 2 ♡ Q J 10 7 5 ◇ 4 ♣ J 6

2. Bid 4♡. Although you only have four hearts, they are good (much better than ♡A642). Partner knows you have only four hearts, so he must be very strong to raise hearts to the three-level with three-card support. Also, he must be short in spades, and he probably figures you can ruff spades in his hand, retaining your four-card trump length. A typical hand for partner's bidding is:

   ♠ 10 6 ♡ K Q 6 ◇ A K 5 4 ♣ A Q 7 5

3. Partner's double asked you to bid your minor. You have a very good offensive hand opposite a known minor fit and probably a doubleton heart. So you should jump to 5♣.

4. Pass. A typical hand for partner's game try is:

   ♠ A K 8 4 2 ♡ 6 ◇ K 10 9 5 ♣ A 10 4

   If he had better distribution and fewer high cards, he would simply guess whether to bid 3♠ or 4♠.

5. The decision is close, but I think you should pass. A jump shift is frequently based on a fit for opener's suit, so just having a misfit in spades would not cause partner to double — probably he has bad diamonds also. If he has one of these hands, for example

   ♠ 6 ♡ K 8 7 ◇ A J 4 2 ♣ K J 9 7 4

   ♠ 6 3 ♡ K J 5 ◇ A 10 4 3 ♣ K Q 10 6

   you have two chances for an excellent result. First, you may score more points on defense than you could on offense. If not (and if you belonged in 3NT) you will still do better than some pairs who get too high in diamonds.

6. Double. You have an exceptionally good defensive hand, much more than partner can count on for your preempt. Your primary purpose is to suggest penalizing the opponents, but if partner holds:

   ♠ 5 4 ♡ A K Q 9 5 3 ◇ K 7 ♣ K 7 2

   he may bid 3NT.

7. Double. It is somewhat dangerous since either opponent (or both) might have extra values. However, you like your diamond holding, and any spade honors declarer is missing should be well placed for your side in partner's hand. With a diamond lead and probably a heart shift through declarer you should have a good chance to set the hand, and a much poorer chance with any other lead.

8. Pass. It would be a mistake to double since you want a diamond lead, not a club lead.

9. Double! Don't just sigh with relief that the opponents didn't bid a slam. If they are reliable bidders, partner should have two aces or one ace plus the king of trumps. He should realize your double is based on a void in hearts. Even one ace should be enough to set the hand since partner should show you where his entry is by the heart spot he leads.

CHAPTER 12

Other Doubles

Showing Extras

When you have already described your distribution, a double shows extra values. With either of these hands

♠ AJ54 ♡ 72 ♢ KQ87 ♣ Q106

♠ AJ54 ♡ 72 ♢ AQJ8 ♣ AJ6

you would, of course, double an opening bid of 1♡. If LHO now bid 2♡, which was passed around to you, you would pass with the first hand, having already told your story. However, you would double again with the second hand to show your extra values.

Likewise, if partner opened 1♣ and RHO overcalled 1♡ you would make a negative double with either of these hands:

♠ K954 ♡ J7 ♢ K873 ♣ J94

♠ AQ95 ♡ J7 ♢ K873 ♣ Q107

With the first hand, you intend to pass next round unless something unusual happens. With the second hand, you will double again if LHO bids 2♡ or 3♡ and partner passes.

The same considerations apply if you have made a bid that has a wide range:

WEST	NORTH	EAST	SOUTH
		1♠	2NT
3♠	pass	pass	?

♠ 8 ♡ A6 ◇ AKJ94 ♣ KQJ73

Here you would double to show your extra values. Conversely, with

♠ 8 ♡ — ◇ KQJ975 ♣ QJ10962

you would either bid 3NT or 4♣ since you don't want to risk partner leaving in a double.

This situation is similar:

WEST	NORTH	EAST	SOUTH
		1◇	4♡
pass	pass	5◇	?

♠ K4 ♡ AKQ98543 ◇ 6 ♣ KJ

On the first round, you decided that a slam was improbable after an opponent had opened the bidding. However, now you could double to show a strong hand rather than a typical preempt. With this kind of hand though, I think Jim Robison has the right idea. Over 1◇ he would bid 4♣ (a Namyats *overcall*, showing a good 4♡ bid). Partner *could* hold the two black aces!

Doubling Artificial Bids

Many types of artificial bids are in use these days: some are extremely common — Stayman, transfers in various auctions, splinter bids, Bergen Raises, and responses to Blackwood. What should it mean when you double an artificial bid?

The general rule, which has many exceptions, is that you 'have the suit' which you double. Does 'having the suit' mean that you want to compete in the suit or are merely asking for the lead of that suit? The answer depends upon many factors — vulnerability, the level at which you are doubling, and the probability that it is 'your' hand. For example, if you have never bid before the opponents use Blackwood, your double of an artificial response merely suggests a lead, not that you want to bid at the six- or seven-level. (I can remember a hand where a player doubled a Blackwood response with a void, and his partner, thinking it showed something like KQ10x, took a 3200-point sacrifice.) If the opponents are playing a strong notrump and responder bids 2♣ (Stayman) or 2◇ or 2♡ (transfer), it is very unlikely that you can outbid them, so a double is primarily lead-directing. However, since you don't know yet whether the opponents will get to a suit or notrump contract, you would never double with a void (even though you would like that lead against a suit contract). Consequently, about one time out of ten, partner may be able to compete in the suit.

A similar theoretical problem in some situations is whether a double of an artificial bid should just show that suit or should show general strength. Suppose an opponent opens 4♣, Namyats, showing a good 4♡ opening. Not everyone agrees on how good the hand has to be — any 8½ playing trick hand may be good enough, or perhaps

♠ 5 ♡ AKQ109654 ◇ KJ6 ♣ 7

is a typical minimum. Even when your opponent's hand is as good as this example, it is quite possible that your side belongs in 4♠ or 5♣. I think, therefore, that it shows mistaken priorities to double 4♣ with:

♠ Q87 ♡ 74 ◇ J5 ♣ KQJ984

Yes, you can definitely set 4♣, but the opponents are not going to play 4♣, and you don't really wish to suggest that partner should bid 5♣ over 4♡. By the same token, if the opponents have thought out their post-Namyats auctions at all, partner is not going to be on lead against a heart contract anyway. It is more useful for the double to show a takeout double of hearts, but it could be fairly light. For example, either of these hands would qualify:

♠ AJ92 ♡ 7 ◇ KQ87 ♣ Q742

♠ Q9875 ♡ 10 ◇ AQ106 ♣ K83

It is much safer to double 4♣ than it would be to double a 4♡ opening. If you had doubled a 4♡ opening with a hand of this type and partner had

♠ 863 ♡ 97 ◇ J543 ♣ J965

he would have a choice of passing and letting the opponents score a doubled overtrick, or of risking an astronomical set. But when you double 4♣, he can safely pass; even if the opponents can make 4♣ doubled, they won't know to play it there. After having doubled 4♣, you can double again later with a good hand, something like

♠ AJ92 ♡ 7 ◇ AKJ8 ♣ K1093

but with a skimpy double, you simply pass. You give yourself a chance to get to a good contract opposite

♠ K10643 ♡ 83 ◇ 95 ♣ A1065

(good because it will either make or be a cheap sacrifice), and when you don't find partner with the right hand, your enterprise will almost certainly cost nothing.

Finally, with a hand such as

♠ A6 ♡ QJ8 ◇ AK43 ♣ Q1087

you can pass the 4♣ bid and then double for penalties when the opponents finally bid hearts. Isn't this great? You can show a light takeout double, a good takeout double or a penalty double, all with little risk. Maybe the opponents will quit playing Namyats when they discover how effective your defense is.

Doubling responses to 1NT

It is worth pointing out that you do not have to wait until you are sure of setting the doubled contract before you can double an artificial bid. After

WEST	NORTH	EAST	SOUTH
1NT	pass	2♣	?

you should double with either of these hands:

♠ 985 ♡ 74 ◇ K96 ♣ KJ1085

♠ A6 ♡ 9754 ◇ 873 ♣ KQJ6

Perhaps one time out of thirty the opponent will redouble and score an overtrick. (This is one time partner has no obligation, or even right, to pull the double if he doesn't like his hand.) But the rest of the time a club lead will usually gain a trick, perhaps a crucial trick, against the opponents' final contract.

By the way, how do the opponents manage to play 2♣ redoubled on that one hand out of thirty? They play that a redouble by opener shows five clubs or a very strong four-card suit, which allows responder to pass with a balanced hand.

There is less risk in doubling a transfer bid. The bidding has gone:

WEST	NORTH	EAST	SOUTH
1NT	pass	2◇[1]	dbl
?			

1. Transfer to hearts.

Opener passes with a doubleton heart, bids 2♡ with three, and may take stronger action with four. Only with two hearts and five diamonds is it logical for him to redouble. Suppose opener passes, showing a doubleton heart — can responder redouble? Of course he can, but many people play (and I recommend) that a redouble now insists that opener bid the suit transferred to, in this case hearts. If responder next bids 2NT or 3NT, he shows a stopper in the suit that was doubled, while if he bids 2NT or 3NT directly, without redoubling first, he denies a stopper. Since the suit doubled will almost surely be led, the notrump bidder and his partner need to know about stoppers. If they fail to locate a stopper, they may decide to play in their 5-2 major suit fit.

Since opener's pass of 2◇ doubled showed a two-card holding in hearts, responder may wish to play in another suit if he has one, even if it is one level higher. After:

WEST	NORTH	EAST	SOUTH
	1NT	pass	2♢[1]
dbl	pass	pass	?

1. Transfer to hearts.

responder can bid 3♣, non-forcing, with

♠ 87 ♡ J8754 ♢ 7 ♣ KQ1075

With a good hand, where he wants the new suit to be forcing, responder redoubles, forcing opener to bid 2♡, and then bids the new suit. A similar procedure can be followed after a 2NT opening and a double of a transfer bid — a 3NT bid without a redouble would deny a stopper; a redouble followed by a new suit is a slam try; a new suit bid, even without a redouble, is forcing, but presumably responder is looking for the best game.

Incidentally, if the bidding goes

WEST	NORTH	EAST	SOUTH
1NT	pass	2♢[1]	?

1. Transfer to hearts.

since a double just shows diamond strength, when you have a good enough hand to make a takeout double of hearts, you simply 'cuebid' 2♡. That is what you would bid with:

♠ AQ65 ♡ 9 ♢ KJ84 ♣ KJ106

Any time an artificial bid shows five or more of a specified suit, a bid of the specified suit is equivalent to a takeout double. With a weaker hand, say

♠ A865 ♡ 9 ♢ KJ84 ♣ J1064

you would pass and plan to reopen with a double if opener bids 2♡ and responder passes.

What if the opponents are playing a weak notrump? If they have any larceny in their soul (and most of them do), they may purport to show an interest in game in order to conceal weakness. When responder has two points and a balanced hand opposite (let's say) an 11-14 point notrump, he may bid Stayman, simply because if he passes, he is pretty sure the next hand will double, while some people wouldn't double 2♣ without clubs. So in this case a double of either a Stayman or transfer response should show a good hand, one that would double 1NT. The holding in the suit doubled is not important.

Negative inferences from a failure to double

Suppose the bidding starts as follows:

WEST	NORTH	EAST	SOUTH
			1♡
1♠	pass	2♡	?

Some people say that failure to double here means that you don't want a heart lead (against the probable spade contract). Others say that a double asks partner not to lead a heart. If the double here is used for lead-directing purposes, it seems logical to me that the double of a major would ask partner not to lead the major, since that is what partner would probably lead without a request to the contrary. However, a double of your minor suit should ask partner to lead it. (You wouldn't want to double a club bid to say 'Don't lead my suit' when you hold ♣Jxx. The opponents might conceivably play it there, either doubled or redoubled.) But I think playing the double to show a desire to compete, at least when the bid is at the two-level, is more useful than a lead-direct in the long run. A light overcall opposite a good raise doesn't necessarily mean you can't outbid the opponents when you hold something like:

♠ 6 ♡ AK742 ◇ KQ5 ♣ KJ63

So my suggestion is to double a cuebid of your suit at the two-level on the same hand on which you would double a raise of LHO's suit.

The 'Automatic' Reopening Double

You may recall a hand from Chapter 8 where the bidding went

WEST	NORTH	EAST	SOUTH
			1◇
3♣	pass	pass	?

♠ KQ93 ♡ KJ3 ◇ AK653 ♣ 7

It is clear that you should double, but I said that you might get to game if partner had a five-card major and eight or nine points because your double at the three-level shows extra values. I still think it should, but there are many players who play what I call a 'full court press', a term from basketball. These players would double here even with:

♠ Q932 ♡ Q83 ◇ AK653 ♣ 7

All they require is a singleton club, or perhaps even a doubleton. They don't need extra values. I will admit that partner could be drooling at the prospect of your making a reopening double, but what if he has:

♠ J86 ♡ J74 ◇ 96 ♣ K9642

He has no alternative to passing your double, and the opponents will probably make their doubled contract when you have doubled with a minimum opening. Or if he bids 3♡ with

♠ 874 ♡ Q764 ◇ 98 ♣ K654

he will lose control, and be down three or four, perhaps doubled. Partner also has a dilemma when he has a fairly good hand. With something like these hands

♠ AK864 ♡ J93 ◇ 98 ♣ J82

♠ A8 ♡ Q10875 ◇ J108 ♣ 985

does he dare jump to game?

Players who double in this auction simply because they are short in clubs cannot stand the thought of letting the opponents play an undoubled contract that might be set several tricks. To me, this is like calling the pot in a no-limit poker game any time you might have the best hand, and, as poker players know, that is a sure way to lose in the long run. I think an automatic reopening double at almost any level, just because you are short in the opponents' suit, is losing bridge. However, many of the aggressive tactics I will mention in the next section do have a lot of merit.

Other Doubling Situations

WEST	NORTH	EAST	SOUTH
		1♡	1♠
4♡	pass	pass	?

♠ AJ10964 ♡ 6 ◇ A106 ♣ A87

What action would you take here? Many players would double, asking partner to bid or pass, depending upon his hand. I can't say this is necessarily wrong. Partner could hold

♠ Q73 ♡ 984 ◇ K8 ♣ 109643

with which he would bid 4♠, probably making. Or partner could decide to pass holding

♠ 73 ♡ 97 ◇ Q9742 ♣ K952

and probably obtain a one- or two- trick set. But sometimes partner will have little or nothing, and declarer will make 4♡ doubled. Worse still, partner, faced with a decision, may guess wrong and bid 4♠, down two doubled, when the opponents would have been down one in 4♡. What do you think should partner do with:

♠ Q83 ♡ 97 ◇ J83 ♣ 96542

Aggressive players like Meckstroth and Rodwell would argue, 'Sometimes aggressive action gets us to a good contract. Sometimes it should be costly, but the opponents make the wrong decision — they may not double when they can set us two or three tricks, or they may bid too much themselves.'

This next hand is from a bidding panel in *Australian Bridge*.

Neither side vul., IMPs

WEST	NORTH	EAST	SOUTH
		pass	1♣
4♡	pass	pass	?

♠ A 9 5 4 ♡ — ♢ K J 6 ♣ A J 10 9 8 4

The panel voted for a double by a ratio of 2 to 1 over a pass. Several panelists pointed out that North could easily hold

♠ K Q 7 6 3 ♡ 6 5 4 ♢ Q 5 2 ♣ 7 2

True, but he could also hold many less suitable hands. My guess is that doubling will lose more often than it will gain, but when it gains it will gain a lot. So a double is probably the best action.

Here's a very tricky real-life problem. Your partner is Jim Robison, who is a top expert and a very imaginative bidder.

East-West vul., IMPs

WEST	NORTH	EAST	SOUTH
1♢	2♢[1]	6♢	pass
pass	dbl	pass	?

1. Michaels.

♠ J 5 4 ♡ 9 7 5 ♢ 9 7 3 ♣ 9 6 5 4

You should bid 6♡! It is very unlikely the opponents will be down two. Given the unfavorable vulnerability, East must be bidding 6♢ to make, not as an advance sacrifice. Partner can hardly have a stack in trumps — if he had a sure set, he would simply pass and accept his 100 points. His actual hand was:

♠ A Q 10 7 2 ♡ A J 10 8 4 3 2 ♢ — ♣ 8

He expected the opponents to have a void in one of his suits, probably hearts, and therefore only one of his aces would cash. But he would feel stupid taking a sacrifice if his partner had a defensive trick (maybe ♢QJx). Logically, his double could only mean, 'If you have a defensive trick in the minors, you should pass. If you have no defense, bid a major. With my hand, I know the sacrifice will be cheap.' Would you trust your partner enough to double with Jim's hand?

It bothers me when partner decides ahead of time, 'I am going to describe my offensive strength, then double if the opponents outbid us. Partner can either bid more or pass, depending upon his hand.' Then partner pursues his plan without regard for any nuances he could draw from the subsequent bidding. Unless I have a much worse hand than I have shown, I expect partner to be able to set the opponents when he doubles on a late round of bidding. The following hand, ironically, was against Meckstroth and Rodwell. The event was the Reisinger with board-a-match scoring, where doubling for a one trick set is excusable.

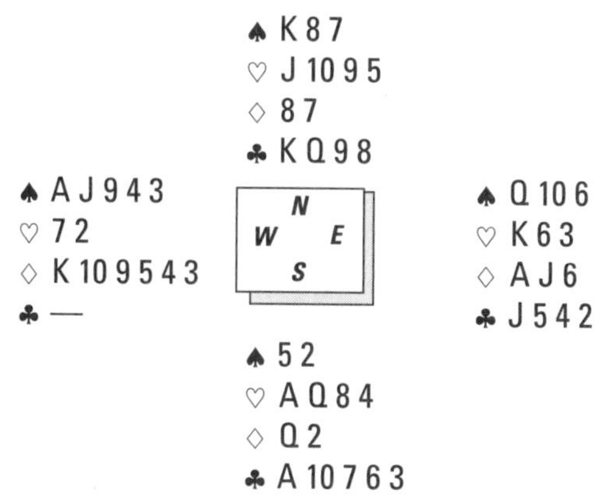

WEST	NORTH	EAST	SOUTH
			1◇[1]
1♠	1NT	dbl	pass
2◇	2♡	2♠	3♡
pass	pass	dbl	all pass

1. Precision, could be short.

I was West. Frankly, I thought the opponents' bidding was a bit peculiar, but they landed on their feet, as usual. This was many years ago and, not knowing better, we played the double of 1NT as penalty. Several players gave me part of the blame for passing the double, but I thought I had shown a weak, distributional hand already by pulling the double of 1NT. I also thought I had a 'good' hand for the bidding with diamonds behind the bidder, and that partner would have his values in hearts and clubs for his second double. In fact, once I showed spades and diamonds, partner's values were great for offense, (justifying a 3♠ bid over 2♡) while the only sure defensive trick he had was the ace of diamonds. His black suit honors were worthless, and the king of hearts was poorly placed under the opening bidder. So I think he made a terrible double. But partner was thinking, 'I have shown a good raise in spades, and if partner doesn't think we can set 3♡, he can bid 3♠.' That was his original plan, and the later bidding did not persuade him to change it.

SUMMARY

1. When you have already described your distribution, a double shows extra values.
2. A double of an artificial bid usually shows the suit, and is lead-directing. However, in my view it makes more sense to treat doubles of Namyats as takeout.
3. Doubling Stayman responses to 1NT is relatively safe, and doubling transfers even safer.
4. Double a cuebid of your suit at the two-level on the same hand on which you would double a raise of LHO's suit.
5. It is, in my view, losing bridge to make a reopening double as opener any time you are short in the opponent's suit. The reopening double should show at least some extra values.

What is your next bid on each of the following hands?

1.

WEST	NORTH	EAST	SOUTH
4♣[1]	pass	4♡	pass
pass	dbl	pass	?

1. Namyats.

♠ QJ764 ♡ 6 ◇ K10984 ♣ 75

2.

WEST	NORTH	EAST	SOUTH
		2◇[1]	?

1. Flannery.

♠ AQ87 ♡ 6 ◇ AJ54 ♣ KJ52

3.

WEST	NORTH	EAST	SOUTH
	1◇	2♣	2♠
5♣	dbl	pass	?

♠ KQJ9643 ♡ K86 ◇ Q76 ♣ —

4.

WEST	NORTH	EAST	SOUTH
1NT[1]	pass	2♡[2]	?

1. 15-17 HCP.
2. Transfer.

♠ 6 ♡ KQJ8752 ♣ K1085 ♣ J

5.

WEST	NORTH	EAST	SOUTH
4♡	4♠	4NT[1]	?

1. Blackwood.

♠ A8 ♡ 72 ◇ K653 ♣ Q10765

SOLUTIONS

1. Pass. Partner has made a penalty double, and your hand is not freakish enough to overrule him.

2. Bid 2♡. This shows a distributional takeout double of hearts (while a double would show a balanced strong notrump hand which partner might leave in with four hearts). This is similar to bidding 2♡ in the following auction:

WEST	NORTH	EAST	SOUTH
1NT	pass	2◇[1]	2♡

1. Transfer.

3. Bid 5♠. It is unlikely that partner expected to beat 5♣ for more than the value of game. He doubled because he has a misfit for spades and doesn't want to encourage you to bid 5♠. But in this case, your spades are good enough to bid without encouragement.

4. Bid 4♡ (or 3♡ vulnerable against not). A double is too timid and won't interfere with the opponents' bidding. Imagine the opponents' dilemma when you bid 4♡. Opener cannot logically bid 4♠, no matter what he has, opposite a possible Yarborough. If responder has a broken five-card suit, he can't bid 4♠ when his partner might have a doubleton. Even if you have no larceny in your soul and are only concerned with constructive bidding, you should bid 4♡. Partner doesn't need much for you to make it, and if he has nothing, the opponents can probably make 4♠. Besides, you cannot expect any cooperation from partner if you just double 2♡. He will never bid hearts with a singleton or worthless doubleton. For all he knows, you might be doubling for the lead with ♡KQJ10 and not much else.

5. Double. East could be bidding Blackwood as a bluff, hoping to escape into 5♡, undoubled. Alternatively, it could be partner who has a weak hand — perhaps he is sacrificing with:

   ♠ KQJ9854 ♡ 3 ◇ Q107 ♣ 98

   A double will tell partner you have a few high cards. If he has a good hand, he will bid 5♠ or double when the opponents return to hearts. If he has a weak hand, he will simply pass, happy to have pushed the opponents one trick higher. The opponents are extremely unlikely to stay in 4NT doubled, so you are glad you can show your values without risk. Incidentally, if you had a defensive hand and no desire to have partner bid 5♠ — something like

   ♠ — ♡ KQJ ◇ J7654 ♣ 98642

   — you would pass 4NT and double when the opponents bid hearts.

CHAPTER 13

Redoubles

The Meaning of a Redouble

The original meaning of a redouble was, 'I think the opponents made a mistake when they doubled us. Let's increase our score.' However, most doubles these days are for takeout, as we have seen, and not made with any intention of letting you play the contract, either doubled or redoubled. Consequently, it makes sense that most of the time a redouble should serve some purpose other than trying for an extra bonus. Frequently a redouble just suggests that your side has the balance of power, knowledge which may be helpful to partner on a later round of bidding, but there are other possible meanings such as:

1) I have a useful control in the suit which the opponents have doubled for a lead. Don't let the double dissuade you from bidding a slam.
2) I think we are in trouble. Let's try to find a better contract.
3) For goodness sake, don't run. I think we can make this contract.
4) Although the opponents doubled 3NT, asking for the lead of your suit, don't worry about not having a stopper in the suit because I've got one.
5) I have three-card support for your suit.

Since a redouble can convey diametrically opposed messages (to run or not to run), you must resort to logic to determine what partner means.

After a takeout double

First, let us discuss the most common situation: partner bids a suit, RHO doubles and you redouble. At one time this redouble showed the balance of power (roughly ten or more HCP) and a failure to redouble denied the balance of power. As stated in an earlier chapter, that concept is no longer accepted. With a good offensive hand it is better to bid your suit and show your extra values later, either by cuebidding or doubling; if you redouble and LHO preempts, you now have to guess what to do. So a redouble today tends to deny a five-card or longer major. Actually a redouble shows one of three types of hand:

1) a very strong offensive hand, where slam is possible (very unlikely after takeout double);
2) a good balanced hand with support for partner's suit;
3) a hand far better suited for defense than offense.

WEST	NORTH	EAST	SOUTH
	1♡	dbl	?

You might redouble here with

♠ A Q 8 ♡ J 9 8 5 4 ◇ Q 7 ♣ A K 3 (Type 1)

♠ A 10 6 ♡ J 9 7 ◇ A 9 ♣ Q 8 6 4 2 (Type 2)

♠ K J 9 8 ♡ 6 5 ◇ A Q 7 4 ♣ J 10 7 (Type 3)

The last type of hand is by far the most common. You plan to double if the opponents run to 1♠, 1NT, or 2◇, and you hope partner can double if they run to 2♣. You don't usually try for a penalty at the one-level with only four of the opponent's suit, but this is an exception. As you saw earlier, a takeout double is seldom made with a five-card major. So if you double 1♠ and partner leaves it in (with a doubleton), the opponents are probably in a 4-3 fit. In fact, when the opponents make a takeout double and don't find a fit, you will often have a lucrative penalty double.

Many years ago, the late Ed Manfield suggested a way to penalize the opponents most of the time when your side had the balance of strength and six trumps, however those trumps might be divided. In this method, a redouble shows at least 10 HCP and two unbid four-card suits. You plan to double if the opponents bid either of your four-card suits, and you hope partner can double if they bid the other suit. If you don't have two four-card suits, you pass and then double, which only promises three cards in the opponents' suit if it was bid at the two-level or higher, so partner won't leave the double in without three of their suit. Here's an example of how this works:

WEST	NORTH	EAST	SOUTH
	1♡	dbl	pass
2♣	pass	pass	?

♠ K J 8 ♡ 9 6 ◇ K J 7 6 4 ♣ K 10 5

At this stage you could double, showing 10+ HCP and at least three clubs. If partner holds

♠ Q 6 4 ♡ A K 10 4 3 ◇ 8 3 ♣ A 9 4

he will gladly leave the double in, and a three-trick set is almost assured. A side benefit of this style of bidding is that, by not redoubling in the first place, you didn't let West off the hook. With

♠ 9 7 3 ♡ J 7 5 2 ◇ 8 2 ♣ Q 8 7 3

he would bid 2♣ in this auction, while if you redoubled, he would pass and East would bid 1♠. Not only would the opponents be one level lower, but neither of you has a logical reason to double them in 1♠.

Theoretically you could be in trouble if you redouble with a singleton or void in partner's suit, especially when that suit is a minor.

WEST	NORTH	EAST	SOUTH
	1♣	dbl	?

♠ A J 10 8 ♡ Q J 9 4 ◇ K 9 5 4 ♣ 7

You should redouble here; usually your high cards will be enough for partner to make 1♣ should he be left there, but if he has a three-card club suit, he might go down. However, the opponents won't be very likely to pass out 1♣ redoubled even when they can set you. West's pass over your redouble isn't for penalties (unless they have a specific agreement to that effect) and East, who presumably is short in clubs, cetainly will not leave 1♣ redoubled in.

The following are two controversial hands that will give you an idea of how expert opinion on these matters is often divided. You hold:

♠ K Q 8 7 4 ♡ A 9 7 ◇ Q 10 4 ♣ 7 6

You and LHO pass, and partner opens 1◇. What call do you make when RHO doubles? About a third of the experts I polled would redouble. They didn't expect to double the opponents for penalties unless they got to a high level, but they were afraid, being a passed hand, that partner would pass 1♠ with something like

♠ A 9 3 ♡ J 5 ◇ A K 9 8 3 ♣ J 9 4

while if they redoubled and later bid spades, partner would know to raise. The other two-thirds said that partner would not play you for a five-card spade suit if you redoubled and later bid spades, so you should bid 1♠, followed (unless the next three players passed) by strong action later, which would imply that you had a five-card suit. For a change, I don't recommend one method over the other. Both ways have merit.

This is the other hand: it is IMPs scoring, the opponents are vulnerable and you are not. The bidding goes:

WEST	NORTH	EAST	SOUTH
	1♢	dbl	?

♠ J 10 9 6 5 ♡ A Q J 8 ♢ J 6 ♣ 8 4

If your only concern is to find the best offensive contract, you should bid 1♠, but I think you should redouble. The chances are very good that you can catch the opponents for a big penalty. The only thing that is likely to go wrong is that the opponents may find a club fit, but even when they have eight clubs, if they are 4-4 they may not find their way to the suit. West won't want to bid a four-card suit, preempting his partner out of a major-suit fit, and East will be reluctant to bid clubs without five of them. You hope, of course, that if the opponents do bid clubs, partner can double.

The downside of a redouble is that West may bid 2♣, which is passed around to you. You surely can't pass, but if you now bid 2♠ it is forcing, and you are likely to get too high. Some players thought the chances for a 500- or 800-point set were good enough to risk this sequence. My view is that if a 2♣ bid is passed around to you in fourth position, you should bid 2♢, which won't be the ideal contract if partner passes, but will probably make. Most of the experts were willing to give up a chance for a killing to avoid the possibility of getting to an inferior partscore contract. In my opinion, that is a matchpoint, not IMP, philosophy.

How far is a redouble forcing?

A redouble is forcing to the two-level in partner's suit. So if the last bid by the opponents is on your right, you can always pass and give partner a chance to double. However, when opener has a distributional hand, he should bid right away.

WEST	NORTH	EAST	SOUTH
			1♡
dbl	redbl	1♠	?

Whether East bids or passes, you should bid 2♢ with

♠ J ♡ A J 9 8 5 ♢ A Q 10 7 5 ♣ 10 6

or 2♡ with

♠ 7 6 ♡ K Q J 9 7 6 ♢ K 6 ♣ Q 10 7

Change the clubs in the last hand to ♣A107 and you should jump to 3♡. You have no intention of passing a double of 1♠, so you might as well finish describing your hand. If you bid 2♢ or 2♡ right away and the opponents still bid 2♠, you can pass partner's double having warned him that your hand is better for offense than for defense. Some players say that after

WEST	NORTH	EAST	SOUTH
			1♡
dbl	rdbl	2♣	?

if opener bids right away, he is distributional and weak, since he can pass and bid his second suit later to show extra values. I am personally not persuaded that an immediate rebid (other than a minimum rebid of opener's first suit) should be weak. In this last sequence you (opener) should bid 2♢ with:

♠ K 7 5 ♡ A Q 6 5 3 ♢ A Q 9 8 4 ♣ —

Your bid is forcing and you don't want to leave in a double of clubs at any level before having shown your distribution. Unless your partner knows that diamonds are your second suit, he would double 3♣ (or even 2♣) with:

♠ A Q 2 ♡ 6 ♢ K 7 6 3 2 ♣ Q 10 9 5

Once you have shown your second suit, you will be delighted to pass if the opponents persist to 3♣ and partner doubles — perhaps with:

♠ A J 9 2 ♡ 9 7 ♢ K 7 ♣ Q 10 8 7 5

Bidding over their redouble

Let's change sides for a moment and discuss how the bidding should go after the opponents redouble. After an opening bid, a takeout double, and a redouble, if you are fourth hand you will usually be very weak. It follows from this that all jump bids are preemptive, and you therefore have an easy decision when you hold a six-card major.

WEST	NORTH	EAST	SOUTH
1♢	dbl	redbl	?

♠ J 8 7 6 5 2 ♡ 7 2 ♢ J 5 3 ♣ 10 6

Here you would bid 2♠. However, with more distribution, say with:

♠ J 10 8 5 4 2 ♡ 9 ♢ 8 7 ♣ J 9 5 4

you should bid 3♠. Holding a five-card major you usually bid it at the one-level, although you might jump to 2♡ with:

♠ 8 6 ♡ K J 10 7 5 ♢ 9 8 7 4 ♣ 5 2

A pass, however, does not indicate a desire to defend the redoubled contract. It merely says, 'I have nothing worth showing. Rescue yourself.' With no suit longer than four cards, you have to consider how strong your suit is, what suits you are bypassing, and what partner might do if you pass. Let's look at some of the possibilities:

WEST	NORTH	EAST	SOUTH
1♢	dbl	redbl	?

1) ♠ J 7 5 4 ♡ 10 6 5 4 ♢ 8 5 3 ♣ J 2

Pass. If partner has a four-card major, he will bid it ahead of a five-card club suit So why guess which major partner has?

2) ♠ 7 5 ♡ Q J 9 6 ♢ 9 8 6 4 2 ♣ 5 2

Bid 1♡ since you don't want partner to rescue himself to 1♠ or 2♣.

3) ♠ J 9 4 ♡ 10 7 5 4 ♢ 9 7 5 3 ♣ Q 6

Pass. There is too little difference between your majors to suggest one over the other. Besides, partner will run to his cheaper four-card major if he has both.

4) ♠ 10 7 5 4 ♡ J 9 4 ♢ 9 7 5 3 ♣ Q 6

Pass. If partner rescues himself to 1♡ and that gets doubled, you will have a close decision whether or not to bid 1♠. But it is unlikely that you will have to make that decision, and unless you are doubled, you won't try to improve the contract.

5) ♠ Q 10 8 5 ♡ Q 9 5 2 ♢ 8 7 ♣ K 9 5

Pass, and when partner bids a suit, give him a raise. This is a very unlikely hand for you to hold, and it looks as though someone is very light for his bidding.

6) ♠ J 5 2 ♡ Q 10 9 5 2 ♢ 8 7 ♣ A Q 8

Pass, then jump in hearts on the next round. Someone must be psyching, and this is the way to expose the psyche since an immediate jump bid would be preemptive. This is better than cuebidding 2♢ since, after 2♠ or 3♣ by partner, 3♡ would be forcing, and you are not quite strong enough to force to game.

Notice, however, that this next auction is quite different from the ones we have been discussing so far:

WEST	NORTH	EAST	SOUTH
		1♢	pass
pass	dbl	redbl	pass

Does South's second pass in this sequence mean that again he has nothing to say? No, it means he wants to defend 1♢, whether doubled or redoubled! The reason is this: the player in fourth position almost never has the proper hand to pass when his partner doubles. Since he is under the bidder, he needs very solid diamonds, and he is asking his partner to lead diamonds to prevent declarer from winning tricks with small diamonds. I don't have any statistics, but my estimate is that North has the right hand for a penalty pass about one time out of a hundred (and after a redouble, about one time out of two hundred). But when West can't keep the bidding open, North is short in diamonds, and South's honors are over declarer's, he has a penalty pass much more frequently, perhaps one time out of ten. Since North almost never has a penalty pass, we don't need to devise a system to take care of that remote possibility at the cost of not being able to describe other types of hands. But since South has a penalty pass relatively frequently, his pass should still be for penalties.

The same thing is true when there is a weak two-bid. A second-hand double is seldom left in while a fourth hand or reopening double is left in fairly frequently. So the rule is that, after a redouble, a pass in front of the bidder shows no desire to defend, while a pass behind the bidder would be for penalties, despite the redouble (although what sort of hand could justify a redouble by the opening two-bidder after his partner passes?). Preempts at the three- or four-level are frequently left in by either hand, so here a pass over the redouble should be for penalties. We need to have definite rules to avoid disasters and also to avoid being bluffed out of a penalty by a random or psychic redouble.

Redoubles after high-level openings

One reason for redoubling when partner opens one of a suit is to prevent him from rescuing the opponents by bidding again with a marginal hand. However, after he has made a preemptive opening bid a disciplined partner will not come in again without encouragement from you. Suppose with neither side vulnerable, the bidding goes:

WEST	NORTH	EAST	SOUTH
	3♠	dbl	?

♠ J 5 ♡ K J 8 5 ◇ A K 7 5 ♣ K 10 4

If you pass and West bids, partner is bound to pass. When the auction comes back to you, what will you do? My guess is that you will double. If partner's hand is

♠ Q 10 8 7 5 4 3 ♡ 9 ◇ 8 4 ♣ Q J 5

defending will work out best, but if he holds

♠ K Q 10 8 6 4 3 ♡ 9 ◇ 8 4 ♣ Q 9 3

you would do better to play in 4♠. So, rather than guess what to do on the second round, you should solicit partner's cooperation by redoubling immediately. That would allow him to bid 4♠ with a good offensive hand. With a purely defensive hand like

♠ 5 ♡ K Q 9 6 ◇ K Q 7 4 ♣ A J 7 5

you simply pass the double and then double anything West might bid. When partner is barred (by his own preempt), the redouble serves the opposite purpose from usual. It encourages partner to bid!

Suppose partner opens 4♣ (Namyats — a strong 4♡ opening) and RHO doubles. What should a redouble mean? That you want to play 4♣ redoubled? Hardly! Let us consider your alternatives. You could bid 4♡, but now if LHO bids, partner will not be able to do anything. He would have to leave all decisions to you, since he knows nothing about your hand. Also, if you do bid 4♡ and either opponent competes further, you will again have to make the decision whether to pass, double, or bid more. Logically, a redouble should ask partner to participate in the final decision. For your redouble you might hold

♠ Q 9 4 ♡ K 9 ◇ A 10 5 4 ♣ J 8 4 2

People differ in their views on how good a hand Namyats shows, but if you redouble I think partner should bid 5♡ over 4♠ with

♠ 5 ♡ A Q J 10 7 5 4 2 ◇ K Q 6 ♣ 7

With a hand such as

♠ K 8 ♡ A Q 10 9 7 5 4 2 ◇ Q 8 ♣ K

he should double 4♠, but most of the time, after your redouble, he should pass and leave the decision to you.

The 'stolen bid' redouble

A redouble can take the place of a double which, of course, it is no longer possible to make:

WEST	NORTH	EAST	SOUTH
			1♣
pass	1♡	dbl	redbl

This is a 'support' redouble, showing exactly three hearts, just as a double would have if East had overcalled 1♠.

Similarly, suppose the bidding goes:

WEST	NORTH	EAST	SOUTH
		1♣	1♠
pass	pass	dbl	?

♠ A K 10 7 5 ♡ Q 10 7 ◇ A J 4 3 ♣ 6

If East had rebid 2♣ you would have doubled for takeout. A redouble for takeout serves the same purpose, and it would be useful several times as often as a redouble to say, 'At a spade contract, I have seven tricks in my own hand.' This redouble, just like most doubles, is optional. With three-card spade support, partner can pass, and with

♠ J 6 2 ♡ K 8 ◇ 8 6 4 2 ♣ 8 5 3 2

partner can compete to 2♠ if the opponents bid 2♡.

To Run or Not to Run

In the next series of hands the redouble has one of two opposite meanings:

1) We are in trouble. Please rescue me,

2) I think we are in our best contract; don't run.

Of course, it is fairly important to know which meaning partner intends to convey in a given situation! Before I state the general principles by which you can determine what partner means by his redouble, try to figure them out for yourself.

Even when it is obvious that a redouble can't suggest playing a contract redoubled, you still may have to decide esxactly what partner wants you to do. This sounds more difficult than it actually is. Look at this hand:

WEST	NORTH	EAST	SOUTH
	1NT	2♠	3♠[1]
dbl	pass	pass	?

1. Stayman without a spade stopper.

♠ 6 ♡ Q984 ◇ AJ54 ♣ A873

North probably has a single spade stopper. With a double stopper (and fewer than four hearts) he would have bid 3NT himself. With no spade stopper he would have bid a five-card minor if he had one, and with no long suit he would have redoubled to ask you to bid your suit. You are pretty sure you don't belong in 3NT opposite a single spade stopper when you know you are getting a spade lead. The person who held this hand bid 4♣ and his partner raised to 5♣ with 3-3-4-3 distribution, thinking 4♣ must show at least a five-card suit. Down one, while 5◇ was cold. Surely a redouble in this auction by either you or partner would not suggest playing in the opponents' suit. It would ask partner to choose a suit to play in. What else could it mean?

The next one, too, is easy to work out. Suppose the bidding goes:

WEST	NORTH	EAST	SOUTH
			1♣
dbl	pass	pass	redbl

What can the redouble mean? East's pass says that he wants to defend 1♣ doubled. His clubs are good enough that he wants his partner to lead them so as to draw your trumps. Admittedly, the opponents sometimes make the wrong decision, but since his clubs are strong, yours are probably weak, perhaps even a three-card suit. In any case, you surely prefer to play some other contract. Remember, partner would not bid immediately with

♠ 9854 ♡ J10653 ◇ 875 ♣ 5

since his one-over-one response would be constructive and forcing for one round, so if you held

♠ A62 ♡ K94 ◇ K96 ♣ A864

you would be much better off in hearts. Almost never would you hold a hand with which you would like to play 1♣ redoubled — if you thought you could make it, wouldn't you just be content to play 1♣ doubled instead? You can't have a hand that would make seven tricks in clubs and be able to set any contract the opponents might run to.

But suppose the bidding goes:

WEST	NORTH	EAST	SOUTH
			1♣
pass	pass	dbl	redbl

In the last sequence East had already passed for penalties, but in this case there is only a possibility that West will pass for penalties. There is a lot of difference between a possibility and a sure thing (furthermore, partner can still run if West passes). A redouble immediately over the double should show a good hand, where despite partner's pass, you might be able to outbid the opponents. The redouble urges partner to compete if he possibly can. It should also deny a two-suiter since you would tend just to bid your second suit with a 5-4 or 6-4 hand.

What about this one:

WEST	NORTH	EAST	SOUTH
			1♢
pass	1♡	pass	1NT
pass	3NT	dbl	?

♠ 10 9 4 ♡ K 5 ♢ A K J 10 5 ♣ Q 9 2

You should redouble since you expect to make 3NT, and it is conceivable that partner, with no heart stopper, will run to another contract if you pass. Some players play that, if South and West pass the double, a redouble by North says, 'I have no heart stopper. Run if you don't have one either.' The general rule is that a redouble in fourth position suggests doubt, while a redouble immediately over the double shows extra values. But the higher the redoubled contract, the less likely it is that the redoubler is suggesting a runout. The hands might be:

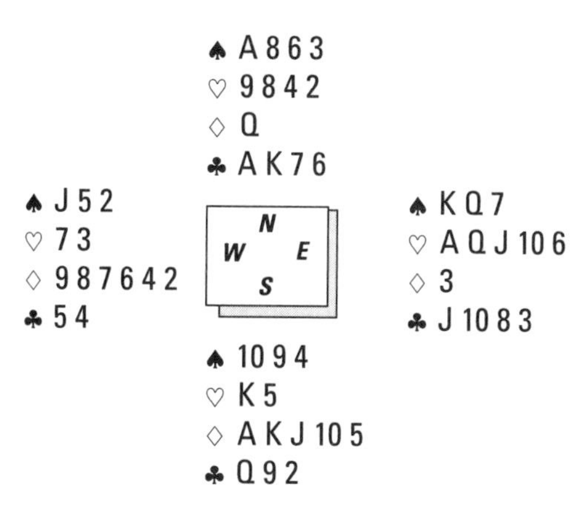

If you fail to redouble, you coudn't blame partner for running to 4♣. Some players contend that South must redouble whenever he has a heart stopper, even with a minimum opener. That may or may not be a good idea, but this hand is certainly worth a redouble, and it must mean that you want to play 3NT redoubled.

This next hand occurred at the 1998 Spring Nationals.

WEST	NORTH	EAST	SOUTH
2♠[1]	2NT[2]	pass	3♣[3]
pass	3♢	dbl	?

1. Weak.
2. 16-18 HCP.
3. Stayman.

♠ 7 ♡ K 8 6 4 ♢ J 10 8 7 6 ♣ A 10 6

You are not sure of making 3♢ here, but you are also not sure of making 3NT. It looks like your best chance for game is to play 3♢ doubled, but if you pass over the double, partner is not likely to pass. The best chance to play in 3♢ is to redouble now.

Similarly, suppose the bidding goes:

WEST	NORTH	EAST	SOUTH
			1♣
4♡	4♠	dbl	?

♠ A Q 10 ♡ 8 7 4 ♢ K Q 6 ♣ Q 7 5 4

Here you should redouble for two reasons:

1) You expect to make it, and the redouble will increase your score;

2) You don't want partner to run.

The whole hand could easily look like this:

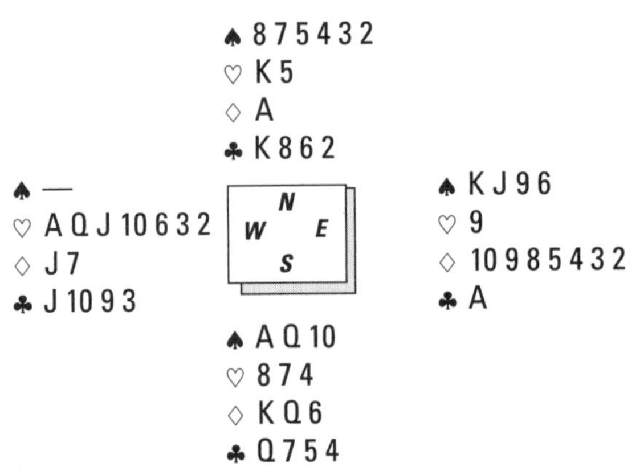

You should realize, with your trump holding and the double, that partner is missing a lot of top spades. If you pass, partner may well run to 5♣. Could you blame him?

So, could your partner possibly interpret your redouble as asking him to run to another suit? No, because you don't know enough about his hand to insist upon a runout. For all you know (unless you have the missing spade honors yourself), he might hold ♠KQJ109653 with nothing on the side, or

♠ K J 10 7 6 4 3 ♡ J 8 ◇ A 7 ♣ 5 4

In the latter case he might easily be set if you have a void in spades, but no better contract is available anyway. So it would be very illogical for you to redouble with

♠ — ♡ A 8 5 4 ◇ J 8 4 2 ♣ A Q 9 6 3

or something similar.

This hand reminds me of a recent 1600-point set I witnessed. The bidding started as follows:

WEST	NORTH	EAST	SOUTH
			1◇
2♣	pass	pass	dbl
pass	pass	?	

♠ J 7 5 3 ♡ J 8 5 4 ◇ Q 6 4 2 ♣ 4

Things looked bad to East since his hand was virtually worthless, but he had no real reason to think he could improve the contract. He redoubled, and West, with

♠ K 8 ♡ A 6 ◇ 9 6 3 ♣ K Q 9 7 5 2

had nowhere to go. Remember, an overcall generally shows a one-suited hand, and it is against the odds to rescue partner without a decent suit of your own. It would be different if the bidding had gone:

WEST	NORTH	EAST	SOUTH
			1♡
dbl	redbl	pass	pass
1♠	dbl	?	

♠ 7 ♡ 9754 ◇ Q963 ♣ J854

This time East should redouble for rescue since, after a takeout double, there is a strong probability of finding a better contract.

This strange sequence is more common than you might think:

WEST	NORTH	EAST	SOUTH
			1NT
dbl	2♣[1]	dbl	pass
pass	redbl	pass	?

1. Natural.

♠ AJ5 ♡ KQ8 ◇ Q654 ♣ A104

What action should you take as South? First, let's analyze the bidding. Does North have a weak hand or a strong hand? With a strong hand (opposite a 15-17 point notrump, 6+ points should be considered strong), partner would either pass West's double or redouble right away. Some players assume the opponents always make the right decisions, so after a double of 1NT, they gear all of their bids toward finding a rescue. That may make sense if you play a weak notrump (although that is debatable too), but not when you play a strong notrump. A direct redouble should say, 'We have the balance of power. Let's play 1NT redoubled, and if the opponents run, I hope one of us will be able to make a penalty double.' But whether you agree with my philosophy or not, no one would bid 2♣ over the double with a long club suit and a good hand (and if North does have a good hand, whatever does East have for his double?). Perhaps partner forgot our system and intended 2♣ as Stayman or perhaps he is being fancy with a 4-4-4-1 shape. But no matter what is going on here, partner cannot want to play 2♣ redoubled, so it is logical for you to bid your cheapest (and in this case your only) four-card suit. As it happens, partner does hold:

♠ Q843 ♡ 9743 ◇ 10932 ♣ 7

Even with no previous discussion, a redouble of 2♣ for play does not make sense, and partner has every reason to trust you to figure it out and remove the redouble.

Here's another case where you can work out what is going on quite easily:

WEST	NORTH	EAST	SOUTH
	1NT[1]	2♠	3NT[2]
dbl	redbl	pass	?

1. 15-17 HCP.
2. Denies a spade stopper.

♠ 5 ♡ K85 ◇ 1063 ♣ AQ9854

Before deciding what action to take, you must determine what partner's redouble means. Is he asking you to run out or telling you not to run out? Since you have denied a spade stopper, partner could not want to play 3NT, undoubled, doubled or redoubled, unless he has a spade stopper. With a balanced hand and no spade stopper, partner would bid 4♣, which you could correct to diamonds if that were your long suit. So he must have at least one spade stopper when he fails to run. Why should he redouble? Surely, to keep you from running, which you might do with a broken suit and a singleton spade. You might be afraid that a single spade stopper was not enough. In fact, partner holds:

♠ Q J 9 7 ♡ A 9 4 ◇ A J 8 ♣ K 10 3

Despite his 'minimum' he holds a double spade stopper, a good fit for your minor suit, whatever it is, and aces. West has probably doubled with ♠Ax or ♠Kx and an outside card. It would be a shame to run out to 4♣ and let his gamble pay off. Actually, you had an easy decision on this hand if you interpreted partner's redouble correctly, but you would need real partnership confidence to pass with:

♠ 5 ♡ K 8 5 ◇ Q 6 3 ♣ A 9 8 7 6 2

Finally, let us consider three sequences that are quite similar to one another — at least, they appear to be similar. You are playing a strong notrump, and the opponents are hopelessly old-fashioned and play the double for penalties.

WEST	NORTH	EAST	SOUTH
			1NT
dbl	redbl		

WEST	NORTH	EAST	SOUTH
			1NT
pass	pass	dbl	pass
pass	redbl		

WEST	NORTH	EAST	SOUTH
			1NT
pass	pass	dbl	redbl

Many players treat all three redoubles as part of a rescue operation. In the first sequence the redouble might show a one-suited hand and ask opener to bid 2♣, while an immediate suit bid would show that suit and the suit just above it. Their theory is that they are in trouble whenever the opponents double 1NT, and they need twenty-nine ways to find a better spot. This seems illogical to me. If North has a long suit and a weak hand, he can bid his suit. If he has only four-card suits, there is no assurance that he can find a better spot and no assurance that East will know what to do if North passes. My recommendation is to play 'system off' after a penalty double (but 'system on' if the double has some other meaning). All bids are natural and redouble means we have the balance of power. If the double is for penalties, North and East should have no more than 8 HCP between them, and often much less. The only likely game after the opponents double 1NT for penalties is 1NT redoubled, and any system that won't allow you to play 1NT redoubled is a loser. At matchpoints you may argue that making any doubled contract will be a good result, so you don't need to redouble. That may or may not be true — perhaps the normal score for most pairs your way is plus 200 or more, and your plus 180 will be well below average. At IMPs the difference between plus 180 and plus 560 or plus 760 (1NT redoubled, making one or two) is 9 to 11 IMPs. But the main reason for redoubling is that partner may be able to double them for penalties when you can't (because partner has length in their suit, and you don't) once he knows you have 6+ HCP.

In the second sequence it may still be wrong to settle for plus 180 when you could make game by redoubling. Furthermore, your chances of taking seven (or eight!) tricks at notrump are increased when the stronger defensive hand is on partner's right, and the opening leader doesn't know what to lead. It is even less logical for North to redouble for rescue. He can bid any long suit (presumably a minor since he passed 1NT) or pass with a balanced hand. The reason some players don't bid naturally over a second seat double is that they want to play 'system on' so that 2♣ is Stayman and 2♢ is a transfer to hearts, and they need gadgets to be able to run to a long minor. I don't think that is the best way to play over an immediate double, but surely it cannot be the best way once responder has passed. In that situation, you don't need to worry about getting to the right major-suit games and slams, and you don't need a way to transfer to a five-card major when you have already failed to do so. So 2♣ and 2♢ should be natural runouts, while a redouble should show a desire to play 1NT redoubled.

In the third sequence, in contrast, the natural meaning of the redouble makes no sense — even if South has his 17-point maximum, his partner could have a Yarborough. The most logical meaning for the redouble is to use it to show that opener has a five-card suit. With 4+ HCP responder can gamble on a pass, with a lot more to gain than to lose. But if he has a very weak, balanced hand, he can bid 2♣, allowing opener to play in his five-card suit.

Now we can state some general principles, which you may have figured out for yourself from the examples.

1) An immediate redouble usually shows extra values and a desire to compete. A redouble in fourth position (when a pass would result in playing a doubled contract) is usually for takeout, on the theory that making a doubled contract will be a good enough result (but note that there are exceptions, especially when the doubled contract is 1NT).

2) The higher the contract, the less likely it is that a redouble is for rescue.

3) A redouble should not be for rescue when partner has shown, or is likely to hold, a one-suited hand.

4) A redouble may have the same meaning as a double would have (if the opponents hadn't doubled) — presumably for takeout.

Redoubles After an Artificial Bid is Doubled

When you are trying for a slam and an opponent doubles a cuebid, a redouble should show a useful control in the suit.

WEST	NORTH	EAST	SOUTH
			1♢
pass	1♠	pass	3♠
pass	4♣	dbl	?

♠ K J 7 5 ♡ 10 7 ♢ A K Q 8 5 ♣ K 7

You are not strong enough to bid a slam yourself, but you don't want partner to worry about club losers — he may hold:

♠ A Q 8 4 2 ♡ K 8 ♢ 9 4 2 ♣ A 9 3

So you should redouble. But if the bidding had gone

WEST	NORTH	EAST	SOUTH
			1♠
pass	4♣[1]	dbl	?

1. Splinter.

you would not redouble with the king of clubs since it would be useless opposite partner's singleton. A redouble here should guarantee the ace.

The following sequence has been mentioned before, but it is worth repeating in this chapter on redoubles.

WEST	NORTH	EAST	SOUTH
	1NT	pass	2♡[1]
dbl	pass	pass	redbl

1. Transfer.

Partner's pass of the double denied three-card spade support, but your redouble simply insists that he bid 2♠. If you then bid 2NT or 3NT you will have guaranteed a heart stopper, while if you bid 2NT or 3NT without redoubling, you deny a heart stopper. If you bid a new suit after redoubling, it is forcing. If you bid a new suit directly, without redoubling, it is weak — an effort to find a better partscore contract than 2♠ since you know partner has only a doubleton spade.

SUMMARY

1. Redoubles can be used to convey a number of messages:

   a) I have a useful control or notrump stopper in the suit which the opponents have doubled for a lead.

   b) I think we are in trouble.

   c) I think we can make this contract.

   d) I have three-card support for your suit.

2. An immediate redouble usually shows extra values and a desire to compete. A redouble in fourth position is usually for takeout.
3. The higher the contract, the less likely it is that a redouble is for rescue.
4. A redouble is not for rescue when partner has shown, or is likely to hold, a one-suited hand.
5. A redouble may have the same meaning as a double would have if the opponents hadn't doubled.

What is your next bid on each of the following hands?

1.

WEST	NORTH	EAST	SOUTH
	1♠	dbl	?

♠ A 7 5 ♡ Q 8 5 ◇ K 8 7 5 ♣ J 5 3

2. *East-West vul., IMPs.*

WEST	NORTH	EAST	SOUTH
			1♠
2♡	2♠	3♡	4♠
pass	pass	dbl	?

♠ A Q J 8 6 ♡ J 10 9 5 ◇ — ♣ A Q J 3

3.

WEST	NORTH	EAST	SOUTH
	4♠	dbl	?

♠ — ♡ A Q 10 7 ◇ A J 7 4 ♣ K Q 6 4 3

4.

WEST	NORTH	EAST	SOUTH
	1♠	pass	2♠
3♡	pass	pass	dbl
redbl	pass	pass	?

♠ A 7 5 ♡ 8 4 ◇ K Q 5 4 ♣ 9 8 7 4

5.

WEST	NORTH	EAST	SOUTH
	1♠	dbl	redbl
2♡	pass	pass	?

♠ K 5 ♡ 8 7 ◇ K Q 7 6 4 ♣ Q 10 8 5

6.

WEST	NORTH	EAST	SOUTH
	1♠	dbl	redbl
3♡	pass	pass	?

♠ K 5 ♡ 8 7 ◇ K Q 7 6 4 ♣ Q 10 8 5

7.

WEST	NORTH	EAST	SOUTH
		1♠	2♡
pass	pass	dbl	?

♠ 7 ♡ A Q J 7 5 ◇ A Q 8 5 ♣ K 10 7

8.

WEST	NORTH	EAST	SOUTH
	2◇[1]	dbl	?

1. Flannery.

♠ A 8 6 ♡ K 3 ◇ Q 9 4 2 ♣ A J 8 3

9. *Both vul., IMPs*

WEST	NORTH	EAST	SOUTH
	1♠	pass	1NT
dbl	pass	pass	?

♠ 10 ♡ Q J 9 6 ◇ A J 7 4 ♣ J 9 7 4

10.

WEST	NORTH	EAST	SOUTH
		4♡	4♠
dbl	pass	pass	?

♠ K 10 7 5 4 ♡ — ◇ A Q 9 5 ♣ Q J 6 2

SOLUTIONS

1. Pass, and plan to bid a minimum number of spades next round. If you were weaker, you would raise spades immediately since it would be too dangerous to bid them later at a higher level. A redouble is too risky. Players like to preempt over a redouble, so East may bid 3♣ or 3♡. If you then bid 3♠ partner will play you for a better hand.

2. Redouble. You don't know for sure that you will make it since it depends upon where partner's values are — he must be short in hearts, but he may have only three spades. Nevertheless, the odds are good, especially since you are not vulnerable. If you make it, you will score plus 880, gaining 5 IMPs against a doubled contract or 10 IMPs against an undoubled game. Since you don't expect to be set more than one trick, your redouble will cost only 3 IMPs if unsuccessful. Nor are you worried that the opponents will run to 5♡ — in fact, you hope they *will* run.

3. Pass. If you redouble and an opponent bids at the five-level, partner might compete to 5♠. You would much rather defend with this hand.

4. Pass. When you doubled, you hoped partner could leave it in, and his pass should show a desire to defend. Besides, what can the 3♡ bidder have to redouble? With nine tricks in his own hand, he would have bid 4♡ the previous round, gambling on finding one trick in his partner's hand. Perhaps the opponents have had a misunderstanding.

5. Bid 2♠. 3◇ would be forcing.

6. Pass. Your redouble did not promise a bid at the three-level. A double (or any other action) is too dangerous.

7. Redouble. You have a good all-round hand, and now is the safest time to show it. Incidentally, with

   ♠ J874 ♡ 2 ◇ K9754 ♣ 983

   partner should bid 3◇ rather than let you play in 2♡ redoubled (if West passes). He should also bid 3◇ if West bids 2♠.

8. Bid 2NT if that asks partner about his distribution despite the double, or 3NT otherwise. Even a pass is risky. Partner might think you had

   ♠ 87 ♡ 3 ◇ J107543 ♣ 10983

   Whatever you do, don't redouble since that should mean that you would like to play 3◇ redoubled, and your diamonds are not good enough. You can redouble to show general strength only when partner's bid is natural, not when it is artificial.

9. Redouble. Are you willing to settle for a pittance when you are entitled to a fortune?

10. West must have good spades to double, so you want to play somewhere else. A redouble would be ambiguous. You could have had a hand where you were tempted to try for slam, but settled for game. Play safe and bid 4NT instead.

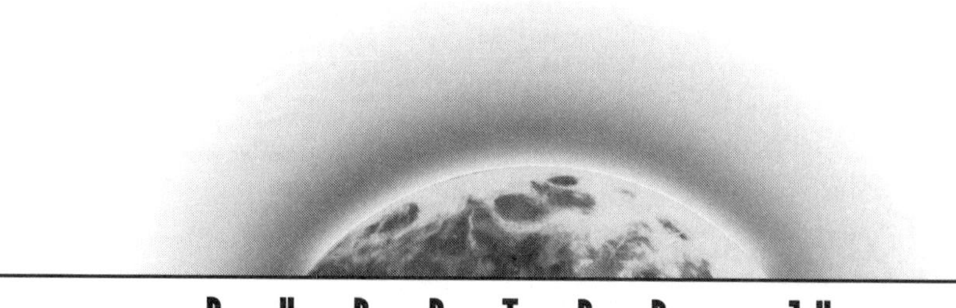

CHAPTER 14

All Fifty-Two Cards

Obviously, it helps you in both the play and defense, to visualize all four hands (all fifty-two cards). It also helps in the bidding to visualize all four hands. Let's consider a very basic example first.

WEST	NORTH	EAST	SOUTH
	1NT[1]	2NT[2]	?

1. 15-17 HCP.
2. Minors.

♠ K Q J 10 5 ♡ Q J 7 ◇ 10 8 6 5 ♣ 8

Perhaps, if you had specifically discussed this sequence, you and partner might have agreed that a double followed by 3♠ would be forcing, an immediate 3♠ bid would be invitational, and a pass followed by 3♠ over whatever they bid would be competitive. But the usual agreement regarding undiscussed sequences is that a new major at the three-level is forcing. Given that, should you bid 3♠?

Despite your nine points and good spades, your diamond holding looks very bad when East has a diamond suit. If you are declarer in 4♠,West is almost certain to lead a singleton diamond, which can't be good for your side. But if partner is declarer, East may not know what to lead. Give partner something like

♠ A 4 3 ♡ A 10 9 6 ◇ K 4 2 ♣ K Q 5

and he is cold for 4♠ from his side (without a diamond ruff and provided the heart finesse works), while a diamond lead through partner's hand would lead to a quick set. If you conveniently play that 4♡ over any opposing bid through 3♣ is Texas, that is what you should bid. Otherwise you should take a pessimistic view and attempt to play 3♠ (by passing now and bidding 3♠ next round).

Here's another example of inferential bidding:

WEST	NORTH	EAST	SOUTH
	1♠	2♠[1]	?

1. Hearts and a minor.

♠ 6 4 ♡ K 10 7 ◇ A Q J 8 5 4 3 ♣ 3

What conclusions can you draw regarding the opponents' holdings, and what would you bid as a result? Obviously East has hearts and clubs, but West doesn't know that. From his point of view, his partner could easily hold hearts and diamonds. It is possible that you are cold for 3NT against any defense, but your chances will be much better if you don't get a club lead. I think you should bid 3NT immediately! If you fool around, East will show which minor he has (if you don't tell West yourself by bidding diamonds). If you bid 3NT immediately, West will probably 'play safe' by leading a heart — the one suit he knows his partner has. If he risks leading a minor, he is as likely to lead your suit as his partner's suit.

Sometimes you can draw useful inferences when only the opponents are bidding:

WEST	NORTH	EAST	SOUTH
	1♡	pass	3♠[1]

1. Splinter.

♠ Q J 10 7 6 ♡ 7 6 4 ◇ 8 ♣ K Q 10 6

You look at the opponents' convention card and see that they are playing Flannery. West is therefore very unlikely to hold more than three spades, while East has a singleton spade or a spade void. So partner has at least four spades and a singleton heart. The Law of Total Tricks tells you that there are eighteen or nineteen total tricks, and you have no reason to think the opponents can't make 4♡ — so you should bid 4♠. If partner has about what you would expect from the bidding

♠ A 8 5 4 ♡ 2 ◇ J 10 7 5 2 ♣ J 5 3

you will be down one in 4♠ since you can't pick up opener's ♠Kxx and still ruff two hearts in dummy. But 4♠ is still a great sacrifice since you had no chance to defeat 4♡.

Here's a very similar hand, which came up recently on OKbridge:

Neither vul., IMPs

WEST	NORTH	EAST	SOUTH
			pass
1♡	pass	3♠[1]	?

1. Splinter.

♠ Q9763 ♡ 64 ◇ AJ10872 ♣ —

Again, East has at most one spade, while West is unlikely to hold more than three spades. If there are any missing honors, they will be favorably located, and you will know how to play the suit (probably by leading the queen). Something like ♠AJ8x in partner's hand would allow you to lose just two heart tricks and probably one diamond. Or partner might have ♠KJxx or ♠K10xx with the king or queen of diamonds. Even if partner doesn't have the perfect cards, 4♠ may be a very cheap sacrifice. So there is something to be said for bidding 4♠. But, as my partner pointed out, there is an even better bid: 4◇! The bidding will not go 'all pass' since East has forced to game. When you pass originally and bid later at a high level, it means you had a two-suiter and partner, if he has listened to the bidding too, will know you have spades. With ♠AJxx and nothing else, he should, and would, bid 4♠. In fact, he would usually bid 4♠ any time he had four spades (and you don't really want to play 4♠ opposite three-card support). But with his actual hand

♠ J842 ♡ 72 ◇ 43 ♣ AK863

he would double 4♡, knowing his cards are in the wrong spot for offense while ideal for defense (he would cash his high clubs and give you a ruff). West is less likely to double a 4◇ bid than he is to double 4♠ if you bid it (since a pass of 4♠ would suggest playing hearts at the five-level).

WEST	NORTH	EAST	SOUTH
			1♡
1♠	pass	pass	?

♠ Q84 ♡ AKQJ65 ◇ J ♣ A93

What call would you make here? First, let's see what we can deduce from the bidding so far. It is quite likely that partner and East each have about six or seven points since if either had the majority of the outstanding high cards, he probably would have bid something. Partner probably does not have three (or more) hearts since he doesn't need many high cards to make a competitive raise. Likewise, East is probably short in spades since he didn't raise. At any heart contract, the first three tricks are likely to be ♠AK and a third spade for a ruff, so it is very unlikely that you can make 4♡. However, at notrump, the ♠Q may be worth both a trick and a stopper. Surely your best chance for game is 3NT, so you should rebid 1NT (purportedly showing 18-19 HCP with a balanced hand). Even if partner has only two or three points, 1NT should be safe since there is no reason to expect a diamond lead (and partner probably has a slow diamond stopper). More important, a 1NT rebid is likely to get a raise from partner when you belong in 3NT. This hand came up on OKbridge, and partner did raise 1NT to 3NT with!

♠ J762 ♡ 43 ◇ KQ1095 ♣ J4

Partner's hand doesn't fit yours very well (you would gladly trade his ◇KQ1095 for the ◇A, or perhaps the ♣K); nevertheless you are almost sure to make 3NT. When you win the spade lead with your queen and lead the ◇J, do you think West will take the ace if he has it? That would be a very unusual play. Suppose East has the ◇A — in that case you will probably make an overtrick! When you overtake the jack with the queen, East will probably hold off, and he will hold off the next trick too when you lead a diamond honor from the dummy. West will show his distribution (an odd or even number of diamonds) on the first round of the suit, but East will think you have three diamonds rather than one. The point is that 3NT is your most likely game, and it will be hard for the opponents to defend. Suppose you had rebid 3♡ instead of 1NT — partner might have raised to 4♡, which has no chance. Even if he bid 3NT, it would be easy for the opponents to defend with your strong hand and long suit in the dummy.

Perhaps I should mention an adverse factor here. One of my favorite partners once said, 'When you make an inferential bid that works, no one seems to notice (except for me and the opponents at the table). When you bid 3NT without a stopper and are set four tricks, vulnerable, everybody hears about it, and it makes it more difficult to get good teammates.' There is some truth in what he said. But I shall bravely carry on, taking what I believe is the percentage action.

My final hand shows you how even with the right inferences, it is not always easy to take the right action in a complex auction.

With both sides vulnerable, the bidding has gone:

WEST	NORTH	EAST	SOUTH
		2♡	2♠
3NT	pass	pass	?

♠ AJ942 ♡ KQ87 ◇ AKQ5 ♣ —

What call do you make? Let's start with the problem of figuring out what West has for his vulnerable 3NT bid. Surely it must be a long, solid club suit (and a spade stopper). I'll admit that his 'solid' suit may not be solid, and partner may have ♣Jxxx, but I'd hate to count on that. If you play that a double asks for an unusual lead (probably a heart on this bidding), a double should at least assure you of a plus score (unless West has eight clubs). But your offensive chances are too good to settle for a small penalty, so I think you should bid 4◇! It is possible that partner would pull your penalty double to 4♠ with

♠ Q863 ♡ J42 ◇ 107643 ♣ 82

but I'm not so sure that he would, if only because I held the latter hand and passed.

SUMMARY

1. Just as it does during play and defense, it helps in the auction to visualize all four hands.
2. Be alert for inferences regarding high-card and suit distribution from partner's and the opponents' bids — and also from what is not bid.
3. Have the courage of your convictions and act on the conclusions that you draw.

What is your next bid with each of the following hands?

1.

WEST	NORTH	EAST	SOUTH
	1♣	1♢	pass
1♠	dbl	4♠	pass
pass	dbl	pass	?

♠ 6 5 3 ♡ 10 7 6 5 2 ♢ 8 7 ♣ Q 6 3

2.

WEST	NORTH	EAST	SOUTH
	pass	pass	1♣
dbl	1♡	1♠	?

♠ K 5 ♡ 7 ♢ 10 8 3 ♣ A K Q J 9 5 4

3.

WEST	NORTH	EAST	SOUTH
2♡	pass	5NT	?

♠ A K 6 4 ♡ 9 7 5 ♢ 6 ♣ Q J 7 6 5

4.

WEST	NORTH	EAST	SOUTH
			1♡
pass	pass	dbl	?

♠ A 6 ♡ A K 9 7 6 5 2 ♢ A 9 ♣ J 4

5.

WEST	NORTH	EAST	SOUTH
	pass	pass	1♣
3♢	3♡	pass	?

♠ A 10 8 ♡ J ♢ 9 8 3 ♣ A K Q 10 6 5

6.

WEST	NORTH	EAST	SOUTH
	pass	pass	1♢
pass	1NT	2♣	?

♠ 8 6 ♡ A K Q 8 5 ♢ A K Q 7 5 2 ♣ —

7. *IMPs*

WEST	NORTH	EAST	SOUTH
	1♡	dbl	2♡
pass	pass	dbl	?

♠ A Q 7 ♡ 9 5 2 ♢ K 8 7 ♣ 9 8 5 2

SOLUTIONS

1. As it happens, it doesn't matter what you bid (within reason), just so long as you don't pass. 4NT (logically asking partner to make a choice between hearts and clubs), 5♣ and 5♡ are all winning actions since you can take eleven tricks in clubs or twelve tricks in hearts (as long as you or partner, whoever is declarer, plays the 4♠ bidder for two singletons) while the opponents can take ten tricks at spades. Partner held a very good hand

   ♠ 7 ♡ AKJ4 ◇ A52 ♣ AKJ42

   but, as you might guess from East's overcalling 1◇ and raising spades to the four-level, he was very distributional.

2. Bid 2NT! I confess that didn't get much moral support from my bidding panel on this hand since all of the panelists but one bid 3♣ (the one bid 3NT). The North hand was

   ♠ 743 ♡ A8654 ◇ K952 ♣ 3

   and North passed 3♣ with near minimum values, no spade stopper, and a misfit for clubs (he didn't know his partner's clubs were solid).

   As South, if you are getting a spade lead, aren't you willing to gamble on partner's holding an ace? And if he doesn't, and you can only run eight tricks, won't that probably be a good sacrifice against 3♠ or 4♠? (The opponents are less likely to bid more spades over 2NT or 3NT than over 3♣.) So I like 3NT better than 3♣. But the bid I like best is 2NT! If you bid 3NT, showing long, solid clubs, you are less likely to get a spade lead than if you bid 2NT, purportedly showing a balanced 18-19 point hand. There is no danger that partner, having passed originally, will bid a slam. Since he didn't open a weak two-bid, he isn't likely to insist upon a heart contract. (For that matter, I play that rebidding hearts shows six, and if opener doesn't raise, I don't have to repeat the story I've already told.)

3. East had no reason to believe you would enter the bidding, so he must be bidding to make, not just to confuse the issue. If he has a genuine grand slam try, he must have a void in spades. That leaves partner with a lot of spades (and a poor hand since he didn't bid).

   At this stage I think you should pass so that you can find out whether West has two top honors (he might overbid or underbid, forcing you to guess what he is doing, if you show an interest in sacrificing). If he bids 7♡, you will bid 7♠. Rather than gamble that partner can establish a trick on the opening lead and win a trick with his stiff heart honor, you will probably bid 6♠ if West fails to bid 7♡ (indicating that partner has a high heart honor). The four hands are as follows:

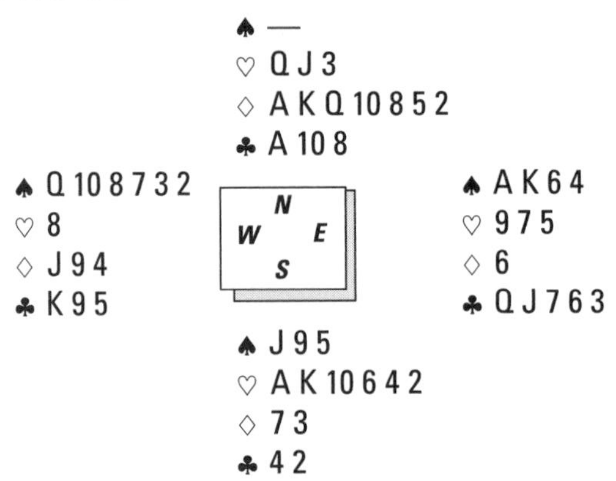

4. Bid 2NT. If you can run your heart suit without loss, you should make 3NT. All partner needs is ♣Qxx or ♣10xxx to guard the club suit. Besides, it is unlikely that either opponent has a five-card club suit, and if it is East, West would have to find the club lead. So there is something to be said in favor of just bidding 3NT. The hand will probably take nine tricks or six tricks (seldom exactly eight). But if you bid 3NT and West has hearts stacked, he will double, and it could be a disaster. If you bid 2NT, partner will realize that you have a long heart suit, otherwise your bidding wouldn't make sense, so if he has the queen of hearts, he should raise to 3NT. With three small hearts and, of course, a very weak hand, he would bid 3♡, and you would stubbornly bid 3NT (which is what happened at the table). But with a singleton heart and a long minor suit, he would bid three of his minor, and you would pass.

5. On this hand sixteen out of twenty international panelists bid 3♠. Partner isn't likely to hold six hearts since he didn't open a weak two-bid, and if he had four spades, along with his hearts, he might have made a negative double. So the risk that partner will raise spades (or pass) is very small. This bid gives partner a chance to bid 3NT with something like

   ♠ 765 ♡ AK842 ◇ K42 ♣ 73.

   This problem is from the June 1999 *International Popular Bridge Monthly*.

6. Bid 6◇! I kibitzed this hand on OKbridge, and that is what South bid. Partner's hand is:

   ♠ 973 ♡ 973 ◇ J108 ♣ KQ104

   The opening lead was a small club, ten, ace, ruff; making seven! The 2♣ bid improves your chances of making a slam considerably, since now partner is more likely to have his values in spades. Partner is also more likely to have 3-3-4-3 distribution (rather than 3-3-3-4 or 3-3-2-5), and if he has:

♠ QJ3 ♡ J93 ◇ 10843 ♣ K87

for example, you are cold for a slam without a spade lead by discarding two of dummy's spades on your hearts. Even when you 'belong' in slam, opposite

♠ KJ3 ♡ J93 ◇ 1083 ♣ Q876

for example, you have extra chances without a spade lead (diamonds may split 2-2). But you will give up the advantage of the 2♣ bid if you show a strong red two-suiter. Instead of an 80% chance of not getting a spade lead, you probably have a 40% chance — even less if you show a red two-suiter and cuebid in clubs in an effort to be scientific.

7. Pass. This hand isn't as spectacular as some in this chapter, but it is a type of situation that frequently arises. It is tempting to redouble to show maximum defense for your heart raise. However, if you do, West will probably pass with three spades and a four-card minor, and East will probably bid 2♠ on his four-card suit. You can't safely double 2♠ at IMPs, and partner won't have the sort of spade holding that will allow him to double, so the opponents will avoid a disaster. But if you pass, West will bid his four-card minor, and, if the bidding is passed back to you, you will be delighted to double. If partner passes West's bid, he will have a somewhat balanced hand since with a sixth heart or a singleton in their suit, he would usually bid 3♡ (relying upon the Law). Incidentally, if the opponents bid 2♠ and partner doesn't bid 3♡, neither should you. When both sides have an eight-card fit, it doesn't usually pay to compete to the three-level — especially when your hand is balanced and your honors are outside your trump suit. You will probably set 2♠, but you can't be confident enough to double.

CHAPTER 15

Optional Treatments

It is impossible to cover every aspect of competitive auctions even in a book as lengthy as this one. I have omitted, for instance, any real discussion of the multitudinous variety of defenses available against notrump openings: Landy, a method called Hamilton on the West coast and Cappelletti most other places, Astro, Woolsey, DONT, Mohan (vs. weak notrump) and Suction, to name but a few. All of them have their good points and bad points, so you might as well choose whatever pleases you. Another topic I shall not cover is how to play against Mid-Chart conventions such as Multi 2♢ and an opening 2♠ or 2NT showing a minor-suit preempt or both minors. The ACBL has prepared recommended defenses against these conventions, which are all quite good, and those who use these methods are supposed to provide you with the defense at the table. But I do have a few more suggestions to make in this final chapter.

Of course, after reading this book, you may well decide to adopt some of my ideas and reject others. However, most of my recommendations up until now are consistent one with another, and form a coherent structure of competitive bidding. As a result, if you reject one of them, you may find that you run into difficulties using some of the others. By contrast, the ideas described in this chapter are independent both of each other and of those in the rest of the book — make your decision on each of them independently.

Auctions After a Double

Suppose the bidding goes:

WEST	NORTH	EAST	SOUTH
		1♢	dbl
pass	1♠	pass	?

What would you do with any of the following hands:

♠ AQ5 ♡ AKJ7 ♢ 86 ♣ AK75

♠ KJ9 ♡ AKQ5 ♢ 876 ♣ AKJ

♠ AK ♡ AQJ9 ♢ 973 ♣ AKJ6

You can't very well bid any number of notrump with no diamond stopper (and if you do belong in notrump, partner, with possibly ♢Kxx or ♢Qxx should be the declarer), and you can't be enthusiastic about raising to three or four spades with less than four-card support. Most players, for lack of anything better to do, would cuebid 2♢, which is what I also recommend. But now the complications start. What should North rebid with:

♠ 8743 ♡ 864 ♢ Q5 ♣ 9872

Should he rebid his suit to show weakness? Should he jump to 3♠ with:

♠ K8742 ♡ 87 ♢ 876 ♣ Q94

Does the cuebidder guarantee another bid? How high is the partnership forced to go? The following treatment is not my original idea, but I recommend it.

The cuebid shows a minimum of a good twenty points and it implies a hand unsuitable for a notrump bid or a strong raise of partner's suit. The partner of the cuebidder makes the cheapest bid (2♡ in this case) to deny 5 HCP or the equivalent (he should not count the jack or unguarded queen of the opponent's suit, but with good distribution he can pretend he has more points). After the cheapest bid, which is completely artificial, the cuebidder must bid again, but neither partner is forced to bid after that. After anything but the cheapest bid, the partnership must get to game. With all of the example hands, after:

WEST	NORTH	EAST	SOUTH
		1♢	dbl
pass	1♠	pass	2♢
pass	2♡	pass	?

South would bid 3♡. Yes, this might easily be too high, but it is better than getting to 4♡ opposite a Yarborough. North can bid again. He would raise to 4♡ with:

♠ 8654 ♡ Q93 ♢ 87 ♣ Q543

or rebid 3♠ with:

♠ 987542 ♡ 75 ♢ Q8 ♣ J54

If the bidding had gone

WEST	NORTH	EAST	SOUTH
		1♣	dbl
pass	1♠	pass	2♣
pass	2♢	pass	2♡
pass	?		

it might even be possible for the partnership to stop at the two-level. North would pass with

♠ J765 ♡ J82 ♢ 9762 ♣ 84

or he would rebid 2♠ with

♠ 108754 ♡ 82 ♢ Q764 ♣ 95

which South would pass.

If the bidding had gone:

WEST	NORTH	EAST	SOUTH
		1♡	dbl
pass	1♠	pass	2♡
pass	?		

North would bid 3♠ with

♠ Q10742 ♡ A8 ♢ 543 ♣ 1087

or he would bid 3♢ with:

♠ Q854 ♡ 754 ♢ K1054 ♣ 92

Obviously, even with this treatment, you will run into some difficulties, but any agreement is better than nothing, and I haven't discovered anything that works better than this.

Two-Way Doubles

Most doubles are somewhat optional, especially at high levels. The ones I have mentioned so far describe a specific type of hand and are primarily either for takeout or for penalties. However, it is possible to play doubles that show either of two types of hand despite the fact that these hands are not in the least like each other. For example, look at these auctions:

WEST	NORTH	EAST	SOUTH
		1♠	pass
2♠	pass	pass	dbl

WEST	NORTH	EAST	SOUTH
		1♠	pass
1NT	pass	2♠	dbl

Both of these doubles are usually played as takeout doubles. For either sequence South might hold:

♠ 7 ♡ KJ83 ◇ Q954 ♣ K873

He was too weak for an immediate takeout double, but good enough to compete when the opponents limited their hands. (It is more dangerous to come into the auction in the second sequence because, if 1NT was forcing, as most people play, West could have extra values, intending to bid again). Suppose, however, that South holds

♠ KJ1084 ♡ J3 ◇ A87 ♣ J106

and the opponents stop in 2♠. They don't know that spades are splitting 5-0, so if they stop at the two-level, partner must have a few high cards. With this hand, South would like to make a penalty double, and I think he should be able to. His partner will assume it is a takeout double unless he has a singleton or void in the opponents' suit, in which case he will assume it is a penalty double. Another sequence would be

WEST	NORTH	EAST	SOUTH
1◇	pass	1♠	pass
2◇	pass	2♠	dbl

where South could have either of the following hands:

♠ 7 ♡ KQ87 ◇ A62 ♣ J9654

♠ KQ986 ♡ Q7 ◇ 95 ♣ A753

Partner can tell which type of hand you have nineteen times out of twenty, and you will gain more on these nineteen hands than you will lose on the one disaster. The disadvantage of playing that way is that you cannot safely make a reopening bid with three small of the opponents' suit — you need zero, one, two, or five. Also, whenever you make a reopening double, although 98% of the time it is for takeout, you could run into trouble with the director or a committee unless you alert each time that the double could be either for takeout or penalties.

Suppose the bidding goes:

WEST	NORTH	EAST	SOUTH
1♡	pass	2♡	pass
4♡	dbl	pass	?

If ever there was a penalty double, this sounds like one. However, you (South) hold

♠ Q9842 ♡ J763 ◇ QJ ♣ 84

and the vulnerability is favorable. Something is wrong. How can partner have a penalty double of hearts? He can't have a stack in hearts. In fact, he probably doesn't have *any* hearts. You look at the backs of partner's cards to be sure he is playing with the same deck as everyone else, and come to this conclusion: he has a void in hearts and a fairly weak 4-0-4-5 or 4-0-5-4 hand, something like

♠ KJ63 ♡ — ◇ K8754 ♣ J1062

Otherwise, how could the bidding make sense? You may not approve of partner's bidding, but it is not your duty to punish him, so you bid 4♠. Partner thought you would be able to tell, by looking at your heart holding, what kind of hand he held. This sort of bidding keeps you alert.

Preempting and Bidding Again

According to traditional rules, when you preempt you describe and limit your hand, and after that partner must make all the decisions. Perhaps that was a good rule in the old days when preempts showed a good suit and followed the Rule of Two and Three; that way the preemptor described his hand within very narrow limits. The present philosophy is to preempt frequently, with hands of varying strength. The preemptor is gambling that, since his hand is far below normal in high cards, the opponents have the balance of strength, and the preempt may make it harder for them to find their right contract. Consequently a non-vulnerable 3♣ opening may vary from a traditional preempt like:

♠ 97 ♡ 7 ◇ J87 ♣ KQJ9432

to

♠ 7 ♡ 10654 ◇ Q7 ♣ KQ10985

or even

♠ J8 ♡ 97 ◇ 73 ♣ Q1098653

Likewise, a weak 3♣ overcall might be made with any of these hands. So you can't say nowadays that the 3♣ bidder has described his hand perfectly with his one bid. I mentioned in Chapter 13 that after a preempt, a takeout double and a redouble by partner, the preemptor was permitted to bid again with a good offensive hand. I think there should be another exception to the rule:

WEST	NORTH	EAST	SOUTH
			3♣
3♡	4♣	4♡	?

What should partner have for his 4♣ bid? Theoretically, he might think the opponents could make exactly 3♡ and you could make exactly 4♣, but that isn't very likely, is it? Since your hand could vary considerably in offensive strength, partner can't judge the hand so accurately, so I think a non-vulnerable raise of a preempt to one under game should suggest the possibility of a sacrifice. With this understanding, partner might bid 4♣ with:

♠ AJ8642 ♡ J7 ◇ 98 ♣ A76

With a slightly better defensive hand he would not bid 4♣ for fear of encouraging you to take a phantom sacrifice, while with a slightly weaker hand he would be afraid that a sacrifice would be too expensive. You would compete to 5♣ with a traditional preempt or with

♠ 875 ♡ — ◇ QJ8 ♣ KJ109743

(a void in the opponents' suit often justifies another bid). With a singleton spade and two small hearts you would pass since you might get a spade ruff on defense. It's obvious to pass 4♡ with

♠ 7 ♡ 10654 ◇ Q7 ♣ KQ10985

but you would also pass if the opponents were bidding spades since, with only a six-card suit and a side queen, you might have too much defensive strength and not enough offensive strength. Needless to say, you would pass with seven clubs to the queen and 2-2-2-7 distribution since the sacrifice would be too expensive. In other words, I think the raise gives you the right to bid again, but you won't often exercise that right.

WEST	NORTH	EAST	SOUTH
			2♠
3♡	3♠	4♡	?

Here's a similar situation. Most of the time you will pass and let partner decide what to do, but with a much better offensive than defensive hand I think you are entitled to bid 4♠ — for example, with either of these hands:

♠ KQ10962 ♡ — ◇ J985 ♣ 854

♠ KQJ742 ♡ 8 ◇ Q1095 ♣ 74

Who knows? You might even make it.

The Forcing Pass

Everyone plays forcing passes in certain sequences, but there is a wide difference of opinion as to when they apply, which is why my suggestions on the subject are in this chapter on optional treatments. When you know your side has the balance of strength, and the opponents are sacrificing, a pass gives partner the option of bidding more or doubling the opponents; the difficult question is when that pass is forcing.

The simplest situation is when either you or partner has made a game-forcing bid.

WEST	NORTH	EAST	SOUTH
			2♣[1]
pass	2♢	2♡	?

1. Strong, artificial.

Since your 2♣ bid is forcing to game (except after a few agreed-upon sequences) you can pass with a good balanced hand or with a three-suiter, short in hearts; partner must either bid or double. My regular partner and I play reverse Lebensohl in this sequence: responder's three-level bid is non-forcing, so as to allow for a Yarborough opposite twenty-two balanced points, and with 4+ HCP he bids 2NT.

A two-over-one response guarantees a rebid in most sequences and is forcing to the 2NT level. So when the bidding goes

WEST	NORTH	EAST	SOUTH
			1♠
pass	2♣	2♡	?

opener can pass, knowing that his partner will do something, perhaps double 2♡.

Likewise, in this auction

WEST	NORTH	EAST	SOUTH
			1♠
pass	2♣	4♡	pass

South's pass is forcing. Note that if East had bid only 3♡, a pass by South would not be forcing. Certainly, 90% of the time responder will take some action, but if he has

♠ 97 ♡ J3 ◇ AJ87 ♣ KQ642

he has no safe bid since he doesn't want to risk doubling the opponents into game. This is similar to:

WEST	NORTH	EAST	SOUTH
	1♡	dbl	redbl
3◇	pass	pass	?

where I don't think the redoubler is obligated to bid at the three-level. Let the poor opponents steal a hand for minus 50 occasionally. A tougher decision is whether this auction

WEST	NORTH	EAST	SOUTH
			1♡
1♠	2♣	4♠	pass

should be forcing since North's bid in competition could be weaker than normal. Since I don't play as many forcing passes as most people, my inclination would be to treat the pass as non-forcing.

Some players adopt rules such as, 'When we bid a vulnerable game and the opponents bid over it, a pass is forcing,' or 'When responder shows a limit raise or better, a pass by either player over a four-level bid is forcing.' They have several more rules pertaining to specific sequences plus general rules for undiscussed sequences, so that they know for sure (if they can remember their complicated rules) whether a pass is forcing. I have to admit there is some advantage in having definite rules, but I am a rebel at heart. Except when the bidding is forced to a certain level, I would rather rely upon common sense, even though my common sense may, on rare occasions, differ from my partner's common sense. Suppose the bidding is:

WEST	NORTH	EAST	SOUTH
		pass	pass
3◇	3♠	5◇	?

♠ K 6 2 ♡ A 9 7 5 4 ◇ 8 7 3 ♣ Q 2

Can partner make 5♠ or should you double 5◇? You can't tell from your hand. This is an ideal hand for a forcing pass, provided a pass is forcing. How often will East expect to make 5◇ when he is a passed hand and his partner has opened a third hand preempt? Almost never. So you can assume that East is taking an advance sacrifice, and partner will also assume that he is taking an advance sacrifice. So a pass by you is forcing, and it is the recommended bid. With

♠ A Q 10 7 5 3 ♡ K 10 6 ◇ — ♣ K J 8 7

partner will bid 5♠, and with

♠ A J 9 8 3 ♡ K 8 3 ◇ J ♣ A J 9 6

he will double. However, if East hadn't passed originally, he could be expecting to make 5◇. You are pretty sure, from your hand, that he is sacrificing, but if you pass, partner won't know. So if the bidding had gone:

WEST	NORTH	EAST	SOUTH
3♢	3♠	5♢	?

♠ K 6 2 ♡ A 9 7 5 4 ♢ 8 7 3 ♣ Q 2

you would have to double to show offensive values, and if you held

♠ 7 ♡ Q 9 5 4 ♢ K Q 10 ♣ J 8 7 5 4

you would have to pass.

Here is a somewhat similar hand:

North-South vul., IMPs

WEST	NORTH	EAST	SOUTH
pass	3♡	pass	4♡
pass	pass	4♠	?

♠ 5 3 ♡ A J 5 ♢ A 10 8 6 5 4 ♣ A 7

Should you pass, bid 5♡ or double? A pass would be your best action if a pass is forcing. Is it? Could East have a good hand and be trapping? It is very unlikely because he didn't know whether you would bid. If he had a good offensive hand, he would almost have to bid 3♠ or 4♠ rather than risk letting your partner play 3♡. No doubt East has a weak, distributional hand, quite likely a two-suiter, and is gambling on finding a cheap sacrifice. Partner is capable of drawing the same inferences from the bidding as you, and since the opponents are sacrificing, he will either bid 5♡ or double if you pass.

However, when the bidding goes

WEST	NORTH	EAST	SOUTH
			1♠
4♡	4♠	5♡	?

no one can be sure whose hand it is. Everybody, except opener, may be bidding on wild distribution. For his 4♠ bid responder may hold either of the following:

♠ K Q 5 3 ♡ A 6 ♢ K 9 6 5 ♣ J 10 4

♠ 10 9 6 5 2 ♡ — ♢ J 10 8 5 4 2 ♣ J 5

As a result, it doesn't matter who is vulnerable and who is not — a pass would not be forcing. With a borderline hand and values mostly outside of spades, say

♠ A 9 8 6 4 ♡ 8 7 ♢ A J 8 ♣ K 9 5

you should tend to double, and with

♠ A Q J 8 4 ♡ 8 7 ♢ K Q 6 3 ♣ Q 8

you should pass. This is a matter of judgment, not convention, and you must accept the fact that you will often guess wrong.

Vasilevsky

I suppose someone named Vasilevsky initiated this convention, and he deserves credit for a good idea. But I don't know him and I heard about this convention from Bill Wickham.

WEST	NORTH	EAST	SOUTH
1♡ or 1♠	pass	1NT	?

You would like to compete with hands widely varying in strength (without misleading partner), and you would like to have some way of showing two-suiters. By switching some bids around, you can do that:

dbl	transfer to clubs
2♣	transfer to diamonds
2◇	transfer to the unbid major
2 of their major	good, distributional takeout 'double'
2 of unbid major	weaker takeout double, guaranteeing four of the major you bid
2NT	distributional takeout for the minors
3♣ and 3◇	natural, but shows 6-4, the four being the unbid major.

Let's see how it works. The bidding goes:

WEST	NORTH	EAST	SOUTH
1♡	pass	1NT	?

a) ♠ Q 10 6 5 4 ♡ A 5 ◇ 9 ♣ K J 10 7 6.

Double, showing clubs. If opener passes and partner bids 2♣, you will bid 2♠ next, showing both suits. Even if opener bids 2◇ or 2♡, you will probably be able to show your spades.

b) ♠ A 6 ♡ J 4 ◇ K 10 9 ♣ A K Q J 6 2

Double, transferring to clubs, then raise to 3♣ to show a strong hand and invite further action by partner.

c) ♠ A J 6 4 2 ♡ J 3 ◇ A K 10 9 4 ♣ 5

You could show diamonds and spades by bidding 2♣, followed by 2♠. With:

♠ A J 5 4 ♡ 7 ◇ A Q J 9 6 5 ♣ Q 7

you would bid 3◇ directly to show six diamonds and four spades.

d) ♠ A J 5 4 ♡ 7 ◇ A K 9 3 ♣ A 8 7 4

Bid 2♡, showing a strong takeout double.

e) ♠ AJ54 ♡ 72 ◇ Q87 ♣ KJ74

♠ 954 ♡ 7 ◇ KJ854 ♣ Q107

With either of these hands, you would bid 2♠, a weak takeout double.

You won't be able to defend 1NT doubled playing this method, but you don't very often have the sort of hand where you want to do that. Having an extra tempo to show a second suit or extra values, and being able to show a strong or a weak 'takeout double', more than compensate for the few lost penalties.

However, when you are a passed hand, Vasilevsky no longer applies. Can you guess why? You will not have a good enough hand to want to take two bids, and therefore you do not need the convention:

WEST	NORTH	EAST	SOUTH
			pass
1♠	pass	1NT	?

And if you hold

♠ 86 ♡ A985 ◇ Q98 ♣ A1042

for example, you might risk a takeout double, but you wouldn't want to bid 2♡ for takeout, forcing partner to the three-level if his suit is a minor. Of course, the convention has the same disadvantage when you are not a passed hand, but then you have its good features to compensate for this one weakness.

The Useful Space Principle

Many times, by replacing one call for another, you can make better use of the bidding room than standard bidding does. Jeff Rubens introduced this concept many years ago, and I have recommended it in two situations so far: transfer responses to overcalls and Vasilevsky. There are many more opportunities to use this idea.

If you had hearts, you would double for penalties. If you wanted to cuebid,

WEST	NORTH	EAST	SOUTH
1♣	dbl	1♡	?

you could bid 2♣. So what should 2♡ mean? Mark Bartusek says it should mean you have a strong enough hand to bid 2♠, but that your spades are only four long — bidding 2♠ would show five.

WEST	NORTH	EAST	SOUTH
1♡	dbl	1NT	?

Likewise, in this sequence you could play that 2♠ shows a five-card suit while 2♡ shows the values for a 2♠ bid with only a four card spade suit.

Roman Jump Overcalls, which show the suit bid and the next unbid suit above it were mentioned in the third chapter. Mark recommends their use — even when there is no room to jump! For example:

WEST	NORTH	EAST	SOUTH
2♠	pass	3♠	?

WEST	NORTH	EAST	SOUTH
		3♠	?

In both sequences he thinks a 4♣ bid should show clubs and hearts; that means if you just have clubs, you must either pass or jump to 5♣. Which is more important, to be able to show a major-minor two-suiter, or to show a marginal club overcall? (I actually think it is very close.)

Another bid he recommends is something he calls 'Hamilton over three of a minor.' I'm not sure whether Fred Hamilton recommended this bid or whether Mark just named it after him because it is similar to the Hamilton convention over notrump (Cappelletti if you're from the East coast). When the opponents open 3♣ or 3♢, all bids at the three-level are natural, while 4♣ shows an unspecified one-suiter (and a good hand since you could have overcalled at the three-level if you needed help from partner to make game). Over 4♣, not knowing what partner's suit is, if you have enough to raise and make a slam try over some suit, you make a bid that bypasses that suit. Here's an example:

WEST	NORTH	EAST	SOUTH
3♣	4♣	pass	?

♠ 8 ♡ K984 ♢ AQ763 ♣ 973

Since partner was too strong to overcall at the three-level, you have a good hand for him if his suit is diamonds or hearts. So rather than bid 4♢, which he might conceivably pass, or 4♡, which he is almost sure to pass if his suit is hearts, you bid 4♠, forcing partner to the five-level and inviting six if he has either red suit. Even if partner's suit is spades, he may bid a slam with something like

♠ AKQJ1075 ♡ QJ5 ♢ KJ4 ♣ —

since his suit is solid, and he now knows you have values in the red suits.

These were just a few examples of exchanging the normal meaning of bids; you can invent many more if you are so inclined. Perhaps you will get enough good results eventually to compensate for the bad results you got at first when one of you forgot what you were playing!

What is your next bid on each of the following hands?

1. *North-South vul., matchpoints*

WEST	NORTH	EAST	SOUTH
			1♠
2♢	2♠	3♠	?

♠ A Q 8 7 4 ♡ A J 8 ♢ 6 ♣ K Q 10 6

2.

WEST	NORTH	EAST	SOUTH
		1♠	pass
1NT	dbl[1]	pass	?

1. Vasilevsky.

♠ 8 7 ♡ A 9 4 ♢ K J 8 4 3 ♣ Q 9 6

3.

WEST	NORTH	EAST	SOUTH
1♠	pass	1NT	pass
2♠	dbl	pass	?

♠ 8 7 ♡ A 9 5 4 ♢ Q 7 4 ♣ J 8 7 6

4.

WEST	NORTH	EAST	SOUTH
			2♠
3♡	3♠	4♡	?

♠ J 10 9 7 6 3 ♡ — ♢ K Q 7 6 ♣ Q 10 6

5.

WEST	NORTH	EAST	SOUTH
			pass
1♡	dbl	1NT	?

♠ A K Q 10 ♡ 9 7 6 5 ♢ Q 9 ♣ 8 4 2

SOLUTIONS

1. Bid 4♢. East's bid shows a good raise in diamonds. Looking at your hand, you don't believe it, but partner may think that East really has his bid. If you just bid 4♠ and one of the opponents bids 5♢, what will partner think? He may pass when he should double, or he may bid 5♠ as a sacrifice when it is the opponents who are sacrificing against you. You should bid 4♢ yourself now. Then, if East bids 5♢ you can make a forcing pass, since you have clearly told partner you have a good hand and the balance of power. If you just bid 4♠, partner may think you have something like

   ♠ AKQ8764 ♡ K7 ♢ 4 ♣ J84

   and if East bids 5♢, you can't make a forcing pass.

2. Bid 3♣. If partner had overcalled 2♣ (naturally) you would raise, so you should 'raise' now.

3. Bid 2NT. There is a possibility that partner is doubling for penalties (and that responder has a void in spades), but it is too dangerous to pass. Bid 2NT and pass if partner bids 3♣; if partner bids 3♢, bid 3♡. You are not looking for the biggest plus score with this hand — any plus score should be all right, and you would probably settle for a small, undoubled minus. Who says I'm not fair? Although I recommend two-way doubles, this is an example of the problems you might encounter if you play them.

4. Pass. A void is not a sufficient excuse, in itself, to bid again. Missing the top trumps and with honors outside your suit, you have too much defense and not enough offense to bid 4♠.

5. Bid 3♠. A 3♡ bid would show a hand worth a jump to 3♠, but with only a four-card suit. That is the bid you would make with:

   ♠ AQ52 ♡ 9765 ♢ Q8 ♣ K94

   With such a strong four-card suit, you can pretend you have five because you would like partner to raise to 4♠ with

   ♠ J63 ♡ J ♢ AK1054 ♣ AJ52

   for example. He would take a conservative view if he thought you had only a four-card spade suit.

Conclusion

If you have an open mind, you will probably want to experiment with some, if not all, of the suggestions contained in this book. In a Swiss Teams event, suppose you pick up:

♠ KQ754 ♡ 6 ◇ QJ95 ♣ K105

You open 1♠ and LHO bids 2♡, which is passed around to you. Remembering my recommendation, you pass instead of making a reopening double. Partner has

♠ 8 ♡ KJ1096 ◇ A104 ♣ AJ62

and you set the opponent three tricks for only plus 300 while your teammates were minus 800. Since you have loaned him this book, your partner knows why you passed, but your teammates and the opponents are incredulous. 'Don't you play negative doubles?' they ask. 'Everybody knows you have to reopen with a double when you're short in the opponents' suit.'

It is discouraging to get a bad result, and the other players' comments cause this hand to stick in your memory. Unless you play a lot of bridge, it may be several months before you get a similar hand, but this time partner holds:

♠ 62 ♡ KJ103 ◇ 8742 ♣ QJ7

Dummy has ♡Qx and declarer has 3-6-2-2 distribution. If you refrain from making a reopening double again, on this hand you will regain the 11 IMPs you lost months ago. Of course, nobody pays much attention — to most players it seems as though your result (minus 110 instead of minus 670) was just a fluke. You failed to make a clear-cut balancing double (in their opinion), and 'it just happened to work out well for you.' The two hands should cancel each other out, but, for psychological reasons, the loss makes a bigger impression on everyone than the 'undeserved' gain. No one counts the hands where you take the 'normal' action and it works out badly. Meanwhile nobody notices your gain on hands like this next one:

♠ AK752 ♡ 97 ◊ QJ6 ♣ Q52

At the other table the bidding goes 1♠ by your hand, 2♡ by LHO, pass, pass, and your hand makes a reopening double. Partner, who has

♠ 103 ♡ KJ54 ◊ K72 ♣ 9753

would rather defend than bid, but he is afraid to pass because the stakes have been raised, and if the opponents make 2♡ doubled, it will give them an undeserved game. So he bids 2♠, which is down two. But if you (opener) have the courage of your convictions, you pass instead of reopening, for a one-trick set. This gains you anywhere from 4 to 7 IMPs, depending upon who is vulnerable, but it isn't the sort of spectacular result (good or bad) that attracts attention.

At matchpoints you open 1◊, and LHO holds

♠ AQ94 ♡ 7 ◊ K8 ♣ AKQ752

Instead of overcalling 1♠, nine players out of ten would bid 2♣, figuring someone will keep the bidding open so that they can bid spades next round. At most tables opener does keep the bidding open — by doubling after two passes with

♠ J105 ♡ KJ8 ◊ AQJ43 ♣ 83

and whenever he does so, the overcaller redoubles and then bids spades, getting to game opposite:

♠ K762 ♡ Q43 ◊ 9762 ♣ J4

But you can see no future in reopening unless partner can pass the double, so you let your opponents play 2♣.

Obviously I have chosen hands to support my ideas but I've tried to be fair in presenting both the good and bad points of my recommended methods. The real point of this discussion is that it is hard to evaluate a new approach to bidding over a short period of time. No one blames you for a bad result from 'doing the normal thing', but when you depart from 'standard' practice, your bad results will make more of an impression on everyone than your good results. So you shouldn't go back to your old ways just because of one or two bad results. I admit that my advocacy of four-card major overcalls when you have a longer suit, my refusal to make reopening doubles on poor defensive hands, and my tendency to leave in negative doubles at the three-or four-level with balanced hands are not (yet!) popular, even among experts. But most of what I have recommended is standard expert practice. So give it a try!